Social Jurisprudence in the Changing of Social Norms:

Emerging Research and Opportunities

Karla L. Drenner
Purdue University Global, USA

A volume in the Advances in Public Policy and Administration (APPA) Book Series

IGI Global
DISSEMINATOR OF KNOWLEDGE

Published in the United States of America by
IGI Global
Information Science Reference (an imprint of IGI Global)
701 E. Chocolate Avenue
Hershey PA, USA 17033
Tel: 717-533-8845
Fax: 717-533-8661
E-mail: cust@igi-global.com
Web site: http://www.igi-global.com

Library of Congress Cataloging-in-Publication Data

Names: Drenner, Karla, author.
Title: Social jurisprudence in the changing of social norms : emerging research and opportunities / by Karla L. Drenner.
Description: Hershey, PA : Information Science Reference, [2019]
Identifiers: LCCN 2018038727| ISBN 9781522579618 (hardcover) | ISBN 9781522579625 (ebook)
Subjects: LCSH: Sociological jurisprudence--United States. | Freedom of religion--United States. | Sex discrimination--Law and legislation--United States.
Classification: LCC KF380 .D74 2019 | DDC 340/.1150973--dc23 LC record available at https://lccn.loc.gov/2018038727

This book is published in the IGI Global book series Advances in Public Policy and Administration (APPA) (ISSN: 2475-6644; eISSN: 2475-6652)

British Cataloguing in Publication Data
A Cataloguing in Publication record for this book is available from the British Library.

Advances in Public Policy and Administration (APPA) Book Series

ISSN:2475-6644
EISSN:2475-6652

Editor-in-Chief: G. David Garson, North Carolina State University, USA

MISSION

Proper management of the public sphere is necessary in order to maintain order in modern society. Research developments in the field of public policy and administration can assist in uncovering the latest tools, practices, and methodologies for governing societies around the world.

The **Advances in Public Policy and Administration (APPA) Book Series** aims to publish scholarly publications focused on topics pertaining to the governance of the public domain. APPA's focus on timely topics relating to government, public funding, politics, public safety, policy, and law enforcement is particularly relevant to academicians, government officials, and upper-level students seeking the most up-to-date research in their field.

COVERAGE

- Government
- Law Enforcement
- Political Economy
- Politics
- Public Administration
- Public Funding
- Public Policy
- Resource Allocation
- Urban Planning

IGI Global is currently accepting manuscripts for publication within this series. To submit a proposal for a volume in this series, please contact our Acquisition Editors at Acquisitions@igi-global.com or visit: http://www.igi-global.com/publish/.

The Advances in Public Policy and Administration (APPA) Book Series (ISSN 2475-6644) is published by IGI Global, 701 E. Chocolate Avenue, Hershey, PA 17033-1240, USA, www.igi-global.com. This series is composed of titles available for purchase individually; each title is edited to be contextually exclusive from any other title within the series. For pricing and ordering information please visit http://www.igi-global.com/book-series/advances-public-policy-administration/97862. Postmaster: Send all address changes to above address.

Titles in this Series

For a list of additional titles in this series, please visit:
https://www.igi-global.com/book-series/advances-public-policy-administration/97862

Advanced Methodologies and Technologies in Government and Society
Mehdi Khosrow-Pour, D.B.A. (Information Resources Management Association, USA)
Information Science Reference • ©2019 • 726pp • H/C (ISBN: 9781522576617) • US $275.00

Handbook of Research on Promoting Peace Through Practice, Academia, and the Arts
Mohamed Walid Lutfy (London School of Economics, UK) and Cris Toffolo (Northeastern Illinois University, USA)
Information Science Reference • ©2019 • 553pp • H/C (ISBN: 9781522530015) • US $275.00

Handbook of Research on Military Expenditure on Economic and Political Resources
Ramesh Chandra Das (Katwa College, India)
Information Science Reference • ©2018 • 564pp • H/C (ISBN: 9781522547785) • US $325.00

Technology and the New Generation of Active Citizens Emerging Research and Opportunities
Paolo Beneventi (Independent Researcher, Italy)
Information Science Reference • ©2018 • 173pp • H/C (ISBN: 9781522537700) • US $135.00

Examining the Private Sector's Role in Wealth Creation and Poverty Reduction
Scott A. Hipsher (Webster University, Thailand)
Information Science Reference • ©2018 • 325pp • H/C (ISBN: 9781522531173) • US $185.00

Handbook of Research on Examining Global Peacemaking in the Digital Age
Bruce L. Cook (Chicago ORT Technical Institute, USA)
Information Science Reference • ©2018 • 435pp • H/C (ISBN: 9781522530329) • US $295.00

Positioning Markets and Governments in Public Management
Helisse Levine (Long Island University, USA) and Karina Moreno (Long Island University, USA)
Information Science Reference • ©2018 • 294pp • H/C (ISBN: 9781522541776) • US $215.00

For an entire list of titles in this series, please visit:
https://www.igi-global.com/book-series/advances-public-policy-administration/97862

IGI Global
DISSEMINATOR OF KNOWLEDGE

701 East Chocolate Avenue, Hershey, PA 17033, USA
Tel: 717-533-8845 x100 • Fax: 717-533-8661
E-Mail: cust@igi-global.com • www.igi-global.com

Table of Contents

Section 4
The Future of LGBT Rights

Preface

The past 20 years have seen significant victories for LGBT civil rights in both courthouses and legislatures alike. Many say that these victories culminated in 2015 in *Obergefell v. Hodges*, in which the United States Supreme Court held that same-sex couples share in the fundamental right to marry. The first same-sex marriage case was *Baker v. Nelson* (1972), which involved two Minnesota men who applied for and were denied a marriage license. They appealed to the Minnesota Supreme Court and made three arguments as to why a marriage license should be granted.

First, Minnesota had no explicit ban on same-sex marriage, and therefore they should be allowed to marry. Second, they used *Griswold v. Connecticut* (1965) as an analogy, the case that had overturned a law prohibiting the use of birth control by married couples on the basis an individual's right to privacy. Last, they argued that the case of *Loving v. Virginia* (1967), which extended the right to marry people of different races, applied analogously to them. The Minnesota Supreme Court did not support their arguments, and the U.S. Supreme Court refused to grant them a hearing for "want of a substantial federal question" (Pierceson, 2013). The issue of same-sex marriage disappeared from the scenes for several decades, but changes were afoot during these years that while rejected in *Baker*, were made more persuasive the next time around.

When a 1993 Hawaii Supreme Court decision declared marriage restricted to heterosexuals discriminatory, the debate about the reasonableness of same-sex marriage moved to the national stage. An immediate public reaction to the court ruling in years that followed were statutes and constitutional amendments enacted in state after state that defined marriage as between one man and one woman.

REVOLUTIONS AS SOCIAL CHANGE

These reactions began a widespread revolution that drastically modified the entire social order including beliefs, values, and attitudes (Yoder, 1926) of some people and places across the United States. Because of their impact on the political, economic, and social structures of a society, revolutions affect social order, morals, and values that were previously internalized by each and every group member (Heslop, 2016).

Revolutions are far from being only a dramatic political change or the desperate attempt of a subgroup to better its relative position in the group's hierarchy: the ripple effect of genuine revolutions spreads to all group members, thereby inducing a change in culture. With these changes, which are driven by a range of legal statuses and relationships—familial, economic, juridical—it is perhaps unsurprising that people expect the law to perform the cultural work required to invoke change.

At least for some, the source of law's cultural power is its assumed ability to produce cultural equality through pronouncements of legal equality. However, this belief appears naïve, given the instances in which formal legal equality has not translated into cultural equality for subordinated groups, but the prevalence of such a belief in the face of contradictory evidence attests to the central place of law in the cultural imaginations of social actors. These individuals looked to the law to perform an essentially cultural task, communicating to the broader society that gay and lesbian couples are "normal," "the same," and "just like you"—deserving of recognition and respect for the commitment they have made.

This book discusses the ways as well in which Western definitions of marriage evolved from an opposite-sex merger to secure wealth and property to coupling based on romantic love and emotional attachment. The changing nature of heterosexual marriage gave primacy to the arguments of gay rights advocates that the emotional and romantic relationships of same-sex partners fell within current-day definitions of the role of marriage in U.S. society. The 1970s ushered in a gender revolution that reworked the relationship between men and women. Birth control became legal, and women began to work outside the home.

The goal of providing a place to raise children had been replaced with the desire for love and companionship. When these needs were not met, spouses were availed a no-fault divorce (Cherlin, 2009). Marriage had changed.

ORGANIZATION OF THE BOOK

The book is organized into four sections containing six chapters. A brief description of each of the chapters follows:

The Introduction provides an overview of the psychosocial dynamics of sweeping social change and the role of courts in delaying or ushering in societal change. It includes a brief history of laws criminalizing homosexuality as well as the court cases that overturned these laws and eventually led to same-sex marriage.

Moghaddam (2018) elaborates a framework for applying the concept of political plasticity to political behavior, suggesting that changes in collectives and networks occur not just in individual units or in isolation. The application of this framework to the issue of gay rights and same-sex marriage suggests that macro-level changes such as a Supreme Court decision does not necessarily bring about change at micro levels. When a revolutionary court case is decided, the larger society's norms stay the same. Social relationships hold their actions and cognitions in place.

Despite the embeddedness of the institution of legal marriage, people in same-sex relationships also wanted the symbolic benefits that legal marriage conferred. At a minimum, these symbolic benefits consisted of a grudging recognition from straight society that committed same-sex relationships exist.

Chapter 1 begins with a brief history of law and the role of social science in courtroom battles, further reviewing the use of social science in marriage equality cases. One of the more striking features in marriage equality litigation was the prominent role of social science in addressing issues germane to the legal arguments on both sides. The chapter concludes by discussing how social science may have influenced litigation and whether such influence was appropriate.

An underlying assumption in this chapter and throughout this book is the fact that courts, as active and frequent makers of public policy, make a great deal of difference in American life. Theories of law wax and wane and have shifting emphases subject to developments at the time and place of their formulation. This includes broad influences such as a period of social turmoil or rapid social change as well as more immediate influences within the intellectual settings in which legal theories are developed—academic specialization, institutional support, and current scholarly norms or fads.

Chapter 2 examines culture shifts relating to LGBT rights from the perspective of a 1997 article written by Thomas Stoddard titled "Bleeding Heart: Reflections on Using the Law to Make Social Change" ("Bleeding Heart"). This chapter uses his framework for social change and examines how rule shifting and cultural shifts interact with the legalization of same-sex marriage. The discussion in this chapter applied Stoddard's (1997) social change model to the issue of same-sex marriage. These interactions were examined through judicial decisions, public opinion, and media.

The social change that had seemed improbable decades earlier for the LGBT community is now law of the land. With *Obergefell*, the public meaning of being gay was officially transformed from that of outlaws and outcasts to a legitimate category of U.S. citizen.

Between 2003 and 2013 American society changed. In courts and legislative hearings as well as in the larger society, the public discourse around gays and lesbians was transformed. If we conceptualize change as a matter of changing hearts and minds, then social change in this instance would be categorized as how someone now talks about a person who is gay. Previously, courts, legislative hearings, and a larger society treated homosexuality as a matter of conduct, a "lifestyle" choice criticized for its immorality. Talking about sexual orientation as a matter of conduct has not disappeared entirely, but this discourse has lost ground. By 2013 treating sexual orientation as a matter of conduct had become morally problematic. Those who used this type of discourse were increasingly perceived as bigots. Public talk about gay marriage became talk about a person, an American citizen entitled to rights granted to other citizens.

For many, the legalization of marriage for same-sex couples was a desirable social change, a journey towards greater equality. Public engagement is a critical component to change, and this chapter incorporated it as a fifth factor to explain the rapidity of the cultural shift that occurred in various parts of the country since Stoddard's article regarding lesbian, gay, bisexual and transgendered (LGBT) rights.

But with any change there are consequences. The chapter concludes with a discussion as to how change in many instances creates conflict that results in backlash. Consider how the backlash claims of progressives and conservatives diverged as the debate over marriage evolved. Over time, progressives shifted from whether a court should intervene on behalf of minority rights to claims about when and how they should intervene.

This brings us to the issues of public accommodations and the intersection of discrimination and place, which are the subjects of Chapters 3 and 4.

Chapter 3 examines U.S. religious liberty principles in historical context. The 1960s to present day are reviewed, providing an analysis of religious liberty cases and the ongoing role courts play in this debate coupled with the legalization of same-sex marriage. In response to same-sex marriage rulings, there have been businesses refusing to extend their services to same-sex couples, local ordinances protecting sexual minorities against discrimination, and a now-rescinded Obama administration federal interpretation concerning school bathrooms for transgender students (U.S. Department of Justice, 2016).

States have considered—and some have enacted—new versions of state religious freedom laws intended to protect such businesses. The governor of North Carolina, who signed such a law in March 2016, intended to nullify provisions in a Charlotte ordinance expanding protections for gays and lesbians (Harrison, 2016). A few days later, the governor of Georgia vetoed a similar measure that would have insulated businesses refusing service to same-sex couples on religious grounds (Telegraph Herald, 2016).

In their article, Nejaime and Siegel (2015) characterized the RFRA claim in *Burwell v. Hobby Lobby Stores* (2014) as a "complicity-based conscience claim." They point out the complicity-based conscience claim, as typified by *Hobby Lobby*'s RFRA claim, has the "potential to inflict harms on specific third parties." This is the crux of concern about state RFRA claims and how they will be used to inflict harm by discriminating against third parties, specifically members of the LGBT community.

Against this backdrop, *Hobby Lobby* seems like a natural extension of the health care refusal laws, granting the same type of protections to a broader group of individuals. These protections have moved from medical facilities and providers to the boardroom and employers.

The next frontier is the business owner claiming conscience-based objections to serving LGBT persons. An extension of these conscience-based claims to providing services to LGBT couples and families threatens a slippery slope. There could be no end to religious claimants' objections to providing goods and services to the LGBT community, as is required by public accommodation laws and professional ethical standards based on complicity in or facilitation of morally objectionable conduct by third parties. Echoing the aftermath of *Roe*, the losing side on the same-sex marriage issue has and will continue to lobby state legislatures to pass robust RFRA laws as well as laws banning local nondiscrimination ordinances that extend protections to members of the LGBT community.

Having lost in the court, same-sex marriage opponents have garnered legislative support to impose their religious view of morally correct behavior on others. The next chapter of religious indignation claims will give license to discriminate. Although not framed as religious liberty versus freedom from discrimination, Justice Ginsburg parroted the concerns she raised in her *Hobby Lobby* dissent that in accommodating free exercise claims, courts should consider the harm caused to third persons who do not share the RFRA claimant's religious beliefs. Extending this principle to scenarios in which individuals and businesses refuse services to LGBT persons and families based on religious freedom, those discriminated against will certainly suffer harm.

Inference upon inference must be made to link the two. Originally RFRA was intended to reinstate free exercise analysis prior to *Employment Division v. Smith* (1990). It was not intended to be the basis on which private persons and companies could discriminate in public life by elevating their private religious beliefs above the rights of persons to be treated equally.

Even before the court published its *Obergefell* decision, opponents of same-sex marriage, who feared an unfavorable decision, marshaled their energies toward legislative rather than court support. Attempting to stem the tide of support for LGBT-expanding civil rights, the anti-same-sex marriage movement galvanized efforts to win legislative victories on the state level that would neutralize, or even block, this growing pro-LGBT rights trend. Those discriminating against LGBT individuals relabeled themselves as the "discriminated." Invoking religious freedom, citizens lobbied their state legislators to pass robust mini-RFRA laws and laws intended to nullify local nondiscrimination ordinances protecting the LGBT community.

Like the success of anti-abortion supporters who lobbied state and federal legislators to limit the effects of *Roe v. Wade* (1973) by passing health refusal laws, the opponents to same-sex marriage have found a way to undermine *Obergefell* and stymie local LGBT antidiscrimination efforts through their legislative successes. With the rise of robust mini-RFRAs and other laws protecting religious freedom at the expense of civil rights, the country is at a crossroads.

Indeed, robust state RFRA laws and state laws that intend to preempt local, LGBT-inclusive, nondiscrimination ordinances threaten to create a system that in the aggregate legally sanctions discrimination in the name of religious freedom. Emboldened by *Hobby Lobby*, public entities can now demand exemptions from public accommodation laws by refusing to provide services and goods to members of the LGBT community with conscience-based objections to same-sex marriage.

Groups of religious entities have pursued legislative exemptions from generally applicable laws on the theory that religious liberty demands freedom from the law. They have used the First Amendment as a presumptive constitutional right to avoid the law pursuant to federal and state free exercise of religion guarantees. They also have employed due process, ex post facto, and separation of power theories to argue that the law should not apply to them because they are religious. These wars of religious power have greatly intensified since the legalization of same-sex marriage.

Chapter 4 illustrates the way in which the tensions between religion and LGBT rights have and will continue to play out inside the courtroom. A review of recent cases of discrimination due to the legalization of same-sex marriage are analyzed in the context of the arguments regarding freedom of speech and freedom of religion. The focus of this chapter is the change in our values and beliefs associated with the notion that all people, regardless of his or her sexual orientation, have the right to be free from discrimination, and how our courts are reconciling this notion with our fundamental First Amendment rights.

In 1964, for the first time since the end of Reconstruction, Congress enacted a law banning race discrimination in public accommodations, Title II of the Civil Rights Act of 1964. It is difficult today to understand why this law, which forbade hotels, restaurants, gas stations, and places of entertainment to discriminate based on race, color, or national origin, gave rise to such heated opposition and the longest filibuster in the history of the U.S. Senate.

Advocates for the rights of sexual minorities quite reasonably want the same rights—on the same terms—as everyone else. Unquestionably, that wish runs counter to many persons' sincerely held religious or moral beliefs. Either side can—and often does—take an absolutist approach (Feldblum, 2006). Sexual minorities often want to compel all people to recognize and deal with them as equals in all matters, including matters with religious overtones (Feldblum, 2006). People who object for sincere religious reasons (or possibly less sincere and less religious reasons) often want to not only refuse to accommodate sexual minorities but prevent others from doing so.

Cogent arguments can be made on each side of this divide. Sexual minorities may justifiably argue that private prejudices can never be the basis for public policy (Palmore v. Sidoti, 1984). They may assert that public officials are sworn to uphold the law and, if they feel they cannot do so, their duty is to resign. They may argue that private individuals or entities, for-profit or otherwise, that enter the stream of commerce must make their services available to all individuals on an equal basis. Further, should it become acceptable for public officials or private entities providing public accommodations to discriminate based on sexuality, this will readily lead to other forms of divisive discrimination. For instance, could a baker refuse to bake a cake, or a florist refuse to provide flowers for a marriage involving an interracial couple, an interfaith couple, a Jewish or Muslim or Greek couple, a second marriage, a marriage in which the parties are "living in sin," a marriage that has already produced a child, a marriage where the bride is pregnant, a marriage where one of the parties is not a virgin, etc.?

Recognizing that prejudice will not end overnight, with or without a Supreme Court decision, is it not better to enforce nondiscrimination with the hope that, over time, prejudice will dissipate? Probably relatively few Americans today really believe stores should be allowed to refuse service based on race or religion, or that black Americans should have to sit in the back of the bus, as was the law in many places until our country took a firm stand on these matters a half century ago in *Brown v. Board. of Education*, 1954.

On the other side, persons of certain religious beliefs may assert that they should not be compelled to commit acts that force them to commit what they believe to be sin, nor be complicit in sin, and that the Free Exercise Clause was specifically designed to prevent such a result. They may assert that at least if sexual minorities have other options readily available to them to achieve their desired ends, those with religious objections should be allowed to adhere to their sincere beliefs. They may assert that they should be protected against compelled speech they find objectionable (*Glickman v. Wileman Bros. & Elliott, Inc.*, 1997).

They might ask, if they can be forced to bake a cake for a same-sex marriage, could a bakery owned by a same-sex couple be compelled to bake a cake with an anti-gay message ? They may assert that compelling individuals to act against their sincere beliefs, or risk a heavy fine, or go out of business, will only heighten antagonisms not diffuse them.

This chapter illustrates that tolerance and compromise in the beliefs held by Americans is an important "glue" to our nation. As such, when values and beliefs of that society change and grow, so too do the laws that govern its citizens. Our country has experienced this changing and growing throughout its history, especially with regards to equality for its citizens, from slavery to the civil rights movement, to gender equality and, more recently, sexual orientation and transgender issues. However, what happens when the idea of equality clashes with an individual's fundamental rights? That is when these changing values and beliefs hurl our justice system into a balancing act within the gray area of the law.

Chapter 5 applies Stoddard's (1997) model of social change to the same-sex policy debate suggesting geography matters in American politics today above all (Green & Silk, 2004). There are ideological differences associated with red and blue maps. Socially shared, intensely felt values are a fundamental part of our lives in the United States.

The differences between states and within states are profound, and while that has long been true, it is much more consequential to LGBT individuals since the legalization of same-sex marriage. In Stoddard's (1997) view, legislative change is preferred to litigation due to the greater likelihood that it will result in a culture shift. Currently, various places across the United States have undergone a cultural transformation, and other areas are currently in a period of cultural lag, still struggling to adapt to new conditions.

However, in a globalized world, many social identities, from those associated with small face-to-face communities to those of nations, often have a spatial referent such that, as group members move from one place to another, they may not only experience a change in physical place but a change in their social environment. Individuals' understanding of what such changes mean for their identity may be an important aspect of place attachment. Put simply, people may feel attached to a place not only because of the meanings associated with the location itself but also because of their ability to "be themselves" when there.

The wider implications illustrate the significance of social identity concerns regarding how people deliberate upon spatial behavior such as the crossing of an identity-relevant (in this case, national) boundary. Furthermore, it illustrates the complexity of place attachment. How one orients to place seems shaped in part by the spatial distribution of people and identities and one's understanding of what this means in practice for the ability to live out our various identities. Everywhere, constructions of place are both politically charged and psychologically relevant, for as Edward Said (1993) said:

Just as none of us is outside or beyond geography, none of us is completely free from the struggle over geography. That struggle is complex and interesting because it is not only about soldiers and cannons but also about ideas, about forms, about images and imaginings.

Chapter 6 summarizes the role of the US Supreme Court in national policy making. In the United States there exists a nationally shared set of beliefs, values, and customs, or cultural universals. However, these shared attributes vary according to place and political affiliation. Extending the right to marry same-sex couples through judicial means precipitated a backlash in which religious groups and individuals turned to legislative solutions to contest the court's decision and their obligation to recognize marriage equality. As the final arbiter of law in the United States, the nine unelected justices of the US Supreme Court play a significant role in policymaking, and their attitudes and decisions regarding policy are tied to the political selection of justices. In the future, decision-making from the court to further extend the rights of LGBT citizens may be directly tied to the increasingly partisan selection process for justices. In filing dissents, judges emulate legislators by entering statements into the record to explain their policy commitments. Policy disputes have become as highly personal among judges as they are among legislators.

Responsiveness to organized interests when choosing its docket and citing amici briefs is an indicator of social and political forces at play. Judicial decisions are a function of what judges prefer and what they think they ought to do and are constrained by what they perceive as feasible. In other words, institutional context structures and shapes individual behavior. Only one thing is certain: the struggles for and against gay rights in the United States will continue far into the indefinite future.

Evidence suggests that policymaking by the Supreme Court reflects the ideological preferences of the justices, and that such attitudes are formed even before justices are appointed to the court. What's more, most justices are highly consistent is casting ideologically oriented votes in the cases that come before them from term to term (Segal & Spaethe, 1993). If in fact this is true, then Supreme Court policymaking is largely a reflection of the justices' values, rather than a closely circumscribed rendering of constitutional and statutory language. This, then, is the inherent contradiction between our ideals of judicial objectivity and the realities of the policymaking practices of unelected life-term justices.

CONCLUSION

In conclusion, *Obergefell* is not a panacea for the LGBT community, however. Approximately 28 states do not have an antidiscrimination statute that includes sexual orientation within its protected classes; in these states, an LGBT person may get married on Sunday but then be denied goods or services in a public accommodation on Monday based on his or her sexual orientation or gender identity.

In doing so, the courts should distinguish between offense and religious belief. When denial of services is based on offense (even if grounded in religious doctrine), enforcing public accommodation laws is not at odds with religious freedom.

The push for religious-exemption bills is “Plan B” for social conservatives after their “Plan A” failed when the U.S. Supreme Court ruled in 2015 that same-sex marriage should be legal nationwide. Concluding that if they have to live in a world with LGBT equality, they want to carve out a refuge for themselves. While *Obergefell* certainly marked a watershed moment for LGBT Americans and their allies, anti-LGBT sentiment continues to run deep and strong in the United States. For example, since *Obergefell*, a wave of explicitly anti-LGBT laws has been proposed or passed in several states—these laws include “bathroom bills” that target transgender people and bills that expressly allow for-profit businesses to discriminate against LGBT people based on religious beliefs.

Moreover, in the approximately 20 states, as well as the District of Columbia, that *do* have antidiscrimination statutes that prohibit discrimination against LGBT people in public accommodations, marriage equality has strengthened the backlash against LGBT equality. This backlash is occurring when for-profit businesses, such as photographers, bakers, and florists, assert that they should be exempt from complying with these antidiscrimination laws based on the business owners’ religious beliefs about LGBT people and same-sex marriage. These arguments have already been made in Colorado, New Mexico, New Jersey, and Oregon, and are likely to arise in more states in the wake of *Obergefell* and the Supreme Court’s decision in *Hobby Lobby*.

Thus, the next battle in the legal and culture wars for LGBT civil rights will be fought over the answer to the question: When a for-profit business seeks a religious exemption from a state antidiscrimination law, which should prevail—the principle of religious liberty or the principle of antidiscrimination?

Karla L. Drenner
Purdue University Global, USA

REFERENCES

Baker v. Nelson, 291 Minn. 310, 191 N.W.2d 185 (1971).

Brown v. Board of Education of Topeka, 347 U.S. 483 (1954).

Burwell v. Hobby Lobby Stores, Inc., 134 S. Ct. 2751, 2762,2785 (2014).

Employment Division v. Smith, 494 U.S. 872 (1990).

Feldblum, C. R. (2006). Moral conflict and liberty: Gay rights and religion. *Brooklyn Law Review*, *72*, 61–123.

Glickman v. Wileman Bros. & Elliott, Inc., 512 U.S. 457, 470-72 (1997).

Griswold v. Connecticut, 381 U.S. 479 (1965).

Harrison, S. (2016, March 23). N. C. gov Pat McCrory signs into law bill restricting LGBT protections. *Charlotte Observer*. Retrieved from http://www.charlotteobserver.com/news/local/arti cle67845317.html

Heslop, D. D. (2016). Political system. In *Encyclopedia Britannica*. Retrieved from https://www.britannica.com/topic/political-system

Loving v. Virginia, 388 U.S. 1 (1967).

Moghaddam, F. M. (2018). *Multiculturalism and intergroup relations: Psychological implications for democracy in global context*. Washington, DC: American Psychological Association Press.

Nejaime, D., & Siegel, R. B. (2015). Conscience claims in religion and politics. *The Yale Law Journal*, *124*, 2510–2524.

Obergefell v. Hodges, 135 S. Ct. 2584 (2015).

Palmore v. Sidoti, 466 U.S. 429, 433 (1984).

Pierceson, J. (2013). *Same-sex marriage in the United States: The road to the Supreme Court*. Lanham, MD: Rowan & Littlefield.

Roe v. Wade, 410 U.S. 113 (1973).

Said, E. (1993). *Culture and imperialism*. Knopf.

Segal, J. A., & Spaeth, H. J. (1993). *The Supreme Court and the attitudinal model*. New York, NY: Cambridge University Press.

Stoddard, T. (1997). Bleeding heart: Reflections on using the law to make social change. *New York University Law Review*, *72*(5), 967–991.

Telegraph Herald. (2016, March 28). *Georgia governor vetoes religious exemption bill.* Retrieved from http://www.thonline.com/news/national_world/article_ce5d679a-f4fa-1 Ie5-ac9f-07236633ff48.html/

U.S. Department of Justice. (2016, May 13). *Dear colleague letter on transgender students*. Retrieved from https://www2.ed.gov/about/offices/list/ocr/letters/colleague-201605-title-ix-transgender.pdf

Yoder, D. (1926). Current definitions of revolution. *American Journal of Sociology, 32*(3), 443–441. doi:10.1086/214128

Acknowledgment

I would like to sincerely acknowledge and recognize all the people involved in helping me see this project through to completion. Specifically, my appreciation to the publisher for welcoming my idea and giving me the opportunity to explore and present the subject matter I am passionate about. I would like to express my sincere appreciation for IGI Global's support throughout the publication process of this research insights book. The reviewers provided important feedback and, without their support, this book would not have become a reality.

I want to thank my editor Stacey Jones and, most importantly, my family.

Introduction

INTRODUCTION

In the past several decades, questions have arisen as to whether and how society should recognize committed relationships between two people of the same sex. Supporters of legal recognition have typically framed their arguments in terms of fairness and equality. Opponents have invoked religious teachings and tradition to support their positions (Price, Nir, & Cappella, 2005).

To understand the national debate surrounding marriage equality, the issue must be understood in its broader historical context (Cherlin, 2004; Coontz, 2005). For most of Western history, marriage was an institution for securing wealth, property rights, and power. Only in the 19th century did marriage come to be defined as an institution based mainly on romantic love. In the mid-20th century, the dominant model of marriage in the United States centered on emotional intimacy (husbands and wives were lovers, friends, and companions to each other), with clear gender roles (a male breadwinner-father and a female homemaker-mother). By the 1960s, however, cultural shifts threw this "Ozzie and Harriet" model into upheaval. Increasing labor force participation by women, and the rise of a feminist movement, led to challenges to longstanding roles, including those at the core of traditional marriage. Improved birth control and a revolution in sexual mores facilitated the separation of sexual behavior from reproduction, along with societal acceptance of nonmarital sex. In the face of these changes, many people increasingly came to understand and evaluate marriage according to more individualistic criteria, with marital satisfaction increasingly defined in terms of self-fulfillment and self-expression rather than by the performance of culturally prescribed spousal roles (Cherlin, 2004; Coontz, 2005).

Around the same time, gay and lesbian (and, later, bisexual) people began to publicly affirm their sexual orientation, forming visible communities and working to end discrimination based on sexuality (D'Emilio, 1983). As early as the 1970s, significant numbers of LGBT citizens began to recognize in their intimate relationships a manifestation of the characteristics that had increasingly come to be viewed as central to marriage (Nardi, 1997).

In the 1990s, sexual-minority individuals asserted that their unions met contemporary criteria for civil marriage and argued with growing insistence that the institution's social and legal benefits should be extended to them (Chauncey, 2004; Lewin, 1998). Meanwhile, political and religious conservatives called for the restoration of marriage as an institution for defining the boundaries of acceptable sexuality, child rearing, and gender roles. Many of those same conservatives had consistently fought the gay community's efforts to eliminate inequalities between heterosexuals and sexual minorities in other areas such as employment and housing, and the marriage question provided yet another arena for battle (Chauncey, 2004; Herman, 1997). While most of the public opposes many forms of discrimination based on sexual orientation (Yang, 1997), the fight against marriage equality proved to be a winning issue for conservatives in most of the electoral and legislative arenas in which it had been contested.

That was the case until June 26, 2015, when the US Supreme Court issued its 5–4 decision in *Obergefell v. Hodges* (2015) extending to same-sex couples nationwide the right to marry. Although public opinion on the same-sex marriage (SSM) issue shifted quickly and dramatically in recent years (Hull, 2016), the legal path to marriage equality was a long one, traversing many courts and legislatures over the course of nearly half a century.

The purpose of this book is to examine the intersection of religion, equality, and the law as it relates to gay rights and marriage equality cases. These clashes have played out in communities, legislatures, and courtrooms across America. This chapter begins with a brief discussion of the history of courtroom battles.

THE COURTS

Revolution or Evolution?

Revolution, in the political or cultural sense, is a metaphor for change. Revolution is not one thing. The uses of the word vary widely—some are superficial and some are profound. In the political sense, revolution contrasts with other modes of change. Evolution is a process of gradual change; that is, only some features of a system or practice change, though if given enough time, these may be considered profound changes. The idea of political revolution depends on the possibility of social change. For this idea to make sense, there must be aspects of the social order that will be replaced with something different.

In a political or cultural revolution, change to the system is abrupt. At least in principle, a revolution involves total change of attributes of the system relative to their importance. This kind of revolution is the topic of this book. Conditions, people, and place are all important aspects of change.

Political theorists and historians have been at the forefront of investigating revolution. In his *The Crowd: A Study of the Popular Mind* (1896) and later *The Psychology of Revolution* (1912), psychological theorist Gustave Le Bon formulated a theory that put collective mentalities and leader-crowd dynamics at revolution's core. This was followed by Ellwood (1905) and others, who saw revolution in terms of group habits and adaptability to new conditions. A second wave of theorists emerged in the 1960s who explained revolution through the lens of "relative deprivation." Davies (1962) argued that revolutions are not sparked by people living in poverty and comparing themselves to those living in luxury but are rather the result of frustrated expectations. When their situation declined, prospective revolutionaries were left with an "intolerable gap" between what they want and what they get. This is the point at which revolution occurs, not before. However, a major shortcoming of this model is that it fails to explain how revolution works under different social-political conditions and leads to different revolutionary outcomes. More recently, social psychologists have contributed to a better understanding of intergroup conflict through research on system justification theory, social identity theory, equity theory, and various offshoots of psychodynamic theory (Moghaddam, 2008). One major research challenge is to better understand how people attempt to bring about change and the psychology of the change process.

Central to both science and revolution is change in the ways of being and feelings about change. The latter particularly sets limits to change. In assessing the psychology of change, a useful distinction has been made between three levels of systems (Moghaddam, 2013).

A First-Order System

A first-order system is one in which both formal laws and the informal normative system justify group-based injustices. This was the case for same-sex marriage. Philosophical, religious, and other rhetorical devices were used to legitimize the differential power roles of social groups.

In the mid-1800s, most states had sodomy laws—what acts and persons these laws were understood to regulate differed from how the laws came to be interpreted in the 20th century. Many of the early laws did not use the term "sodomy," but often referred to "crime against nature" without specifying which acts were included in this category. The law of Illinois, established in 1858, named it the "infamous crime against nature, wither man or beast"; and Rhode Island (1857) "the detestable and abominable crime against nature either with mankind or any beast." Georgia's 1867 law offered somewhat more detail: sodomy was "the carnal knowledge and connection against the order of nature by man with man or in the same unnatural manner with woman" (Eskridge & Levy, 2003). What acts have been included as prohibited under sodomy laws have changed with time. In 1878 fellatio was not a crime, but by 1921 almost all states considered it one.

Sodomy laws in the 19th century had multiple purposes, such as to ensure public decency. Eskridge (2008) states that the most important purpose of these laws was to protect the vulnerable from assault—those who could be preyed upon and coerced. At the time, there were many jurisdictions in which a man could not be convicted of sodomy if the potential testimony was from a willing partner (Eskridge & Levy, 2003). Between 1820 and 1920, states began to make more specific sodomy laws and to vigorously enforce them. In 1915 California included cunninlingus and fellatio in its law and categorized sodomy as a felony. Moreover, people committing "moral turpitude" crimes, largely sexual acts performed by homosexuals and prostitutes, were required to be sterilized. In 1939 in California alone, there were close to 900 sterilizations (Eskridge, 2008). Such forced sterilization of "sexual perverts" or mentally disabled persons did not come to an end until the US Supreme Court case *Skinner v. Oklahoma* in 1942 (Gertsmann, 2008). In 1948 before Earl Warren, considered a liberal figure, joined the Supreme Court, he was governor of California. During that time in California, a person who was convicted of a second offense of sodomy received an automatic life sentence (Eskridge, 2008).

Until the late 1800s, sexuality was what a person did not who a person was. Michel Foucault (1973) identifies 1870 as the time when talk about a kind of person began. It was at this juncture the term *homosexual* was coined.

Initially a medical term, soon after its creation ordinary people began to use the word *homosexual* to understand the self and seek societal tolerance (Goldstein, 1997). Throughout the early 20th century, blackmail and threats to gay people were common. Whether enforced or not, sodomy laws "situated homosexuals outside the normal protection of the law" (Eskridge, 2008). According to Mohr (1997), these laws functioned as a "systematic way that society as a whole [told] gays they are scum."

Following World War II, discrimination against gays ramped up. Federal jobs were denied to anyone who had been arrested for a homosexual act. In addition, states were revising their indecency laws. Whereas a person was previously likely to be arrested for sodomy only if an act was performed in a public or semi-public space, 21 states had rewritten their laws by 1960 to make same-sex activity of any kind a crime.

In the 1950s, "homosexuality" was added to the American Psychiatric Association's *Diagnostic and Statistical Manual* (DSM). The manual defined homosexuality as a sociopathic personality disorder, which it remained in the manual until 1987. In 1969 things began to change. The New York police raided Stonewall Inn, a gay bar in Greenwich Village. The raid turned into a riot, which elicited major media support. By the second anniversary of Stonewall, gay men and women decided it was time for a change.

A Second-Order System

In a second-order system there is reformed formal law, but the informal normative system continues to justify group-based injustices. An example of this would be when some laws against members of the gay community are changed, but discrimination against members of the LGBT community continues and is upheld by the informal normative system.

Beginning in the 1970s and increasing in frequency in the 1980s and 1990s, gay rights groups began to bring grievances to state and federal courts, sometimes succeeding and other times failing (Pinello, 2003). The right being contested made a difference. Gary Mucciaroni in *Same Sex, Different Politics: Success and Failures in the Struggles over Gay Rights* (2008) identified three of six gay rights issues that had resulted in relatively high levels of political success: the legalization of homosexual conduct, the prohibition of hate crimes, and civil rights laws related to employment and housing. On the other three issues, social change was much slower. Slow or no change took place on issues concerning marriage and civil unions, adoption, and the rights of gays to serve in the military.

Between the 1980s and 2003, there were three important gay rights cases heard by the US Supreme Court. In the first, *Bowers v. Hardwick* (1986), a Georgian named Michael Hardwick threw an open beer in the trash can outside the bar where he worked in 1982. He was issued a citation for public drinking. When he did not appear in court for the citation, a warrant was issued for his arrest. When a police officer came to his door, he saw Hardwick engaged in oral sex with another man. Hardwick was arrested and charged with sodomy, a crime punishable by one to 20 years in prison[1].

The case made its way to the Supreme Court, where by a 5–4 vote, the court found that the right to privacy, which is implicated in the Due Process Clause of the Fourteenth Amendment, did not confer "a fundamental right upon homosexuals to engage in sodomy" (*Bowers v. Hardwick*, 1986). The decision was taken as a significant statement to the gay community that there would be no expansion in how the court understood privacy rights as it pertained to gay people and sodomy laws[2]. In 1987, according to the National Opinion Research Center, 82 percent of the American public considered homosexual relations to be "always" or "almost always" wrong.

The second gay rights case was *Romer v. Evans* (1996). Three cities in Colorado, Aspen, Boulder, and Denver had passed ordinances prohibiting sexual orientation discrimination. Then, in 1992 a ballot initiative[3] to change the constitution called "Amendment 2"[4] was launched, a conceptual child of Florida anti-gay activist Anita Bryant's "Save the Children" campaign. Colorado for Family Values (CFV), the sponsoring organization, collected more than 60,000 signatures from registered voters in the state (O'Rourke & Dellinger, 1997). The CFV campaign portrayed homosexuality as a behavior disconnected from relational or identity consideration (Colorado for Family Values, 1992); emphasized the central role of sex with explicit descriptions of sexual behavior (Family Research Institute, 1992); and linked homosexuality to pedophilia (Colorado for Family Values, 1992). It is within this context that Amendment 2 passed, with 53.4 percent of voters endorsing the initiative (Colorado State Legislative Council, n.d.). The initiative process generated considerable hostility as well as public stigmatization for members of the LGBT community (Donovan & Bowler, 1997).

The state of Colorado, of which Roy Romer was governor at the time, argued that it should have the right to signal the moral inferiority of homosexuality. Gays, the state argued, did not deserve the same protections as women and blacks. The amendment was challenged as a violation of the Constitution's Equal Protection Clause (Richards, 2009). By a 6–3 vote, the Supreme Court struck down the Colorado law, declaring it to be unconstitutional, motivated by animus toward gays, and having "no rational basis." In a scathing dissent, Justice Antonin Scalia cited *Bowers v. Hardwick* (1986), arguing that "Coloradans are entitled to be hostile towards homosexual conduct" (Romer v. Evans, 1996) and making the unlikely assertion at the time that this decision was the first step toward legalizing same-sex marriage.

The last case was the decision in *Lawrence v. Texas* (2003). A police officer in Houston, Texas, went to John Lawrence's home on what was a false report of a weapons disturbance. The officer saw him having sex with another man, and he was charged with sodomy. In a 6–3 opinion, the Texas law was ruled unconstitutional, and five of the six justices also voted to overturn *Bowers* (1986). With this decision, persons engaged in consenting sexual acts with an adult partner of the same sex would no longer be committing a crime.

A Third-Order System

A third-order system is one in which both the formal law and the informal normative system support group-based justice. Such concordance can be found in many of the major metropolitan areas across the US for members of the gay community. This is an ideal that many participants in revolutions strive for, but it difficult for such a system to come out of the confrontational ethos of demolishing the old that is usual in revolutions. This revolution is evidenced in the urban-rural divide, in which people have a place-based identity that is intertwined with a perception of deprivation. Research has examined why location matters, and how a person being from a certain type of place matters for political understanding.

There are four main ways in which place has been studied with respect to political behavior.

First, previous work has looked for composition effects, or the way other social categories affect behavior (Agnew, 1987; Freudenburg, 1991; Keith & Pile, 1993). For example, scholars have paid attention to the relationship between place, level of political and cultural diversity, and political behavior and attitudes (Gainsborough, 2001; Oliver, 2001; Putnam, 2007).

Second, scholars have expected different demographic compositions across geographic areas to result in differences in social structure and culture (Knoke & Henry, 1977; Wirth, 1938), and thus in socialization (Agnew, 1987; Lipset, 1981).

For example, Campbell, Converse, Miller & Stokes (1960) argued that farming occupations exposed people to less political information and mobilization than was the case with industrial labor jobs in urban areas, resulting in rural-urban differences. Third, scholars have conceptualized rural-urban differences as labels for underlying class conflict (Black & Black, 1987; Key, 1949). Finally, another argument has been that the rural-urban divide is a conflict that arises from competition over material resources (Bowen, Haynes, & Rosentraub, 2006).

It continues to be a matter of debate whether urban-rural distinctions matter for political behavior. Decades ago, scholars presumed that differences between urban and rural life underlay much of the structure of society (Tonnies, 1957) and readily recognized rural-urban divides in political behavior (Key, 1949; Lipset, 1981).

But this presumption gave way to arguments that globalization, the advance of mass media, and reapportionment of US Congressional districts were leading to the disappearance of a rural-urban cleavage (Knoke & Henry, 1977). In this way of thinking, rural communities are not considered a distinct type, just less urban than cities (Parker, 2004). Some scholars have attempted to remind political scientists that the urban versus rural distinction is undeniably important for politics (Gimpel & Karnes, 2006; Gimpel & Schuknecht, 2003). Even though the United States is increasingly urban, most of the area represented in US legislative bodies is rural, as 80% of US land is rural.

An important dimension of this rural-urban divide is the way in which the identification of rural is imbued with claims that rural people have distinctive values and lifestyles in contrast to people who live in metro areas. Cramer's (2016) research shows how rural identity includes lifestyle claims interwoven with inequality, based on the perception that members of an "out" group represented a threat to their community, their values, and their livelihood. This divide is evident for members of the gay community.

Political Plasticity

Moghaddam (2018) elaborates a framework for applying the concept of political plasticity to political behavior, suggesting that changes in collectives and networks occur not just in individual units or in isolation. This was recognized by Hebb (1949) with the central role of cell assemblies and the possibilities for the continuous shaping and re-shaping of neural networks. Rather than trying to understand the single cells in isolation, he postulated the workings of a collection of cells. This led to a picture of neural networks as continuously changing cells that "fire together, wire together." Contemporary research endorses the idea that networks and context are important as well as established in a discussion of "plasticity" at the micro level (Green & Bavelier, 2010; Voss, Vivar, Kramer & Van Praag, 2013).

The application of several of these rules to the issue of gay rights and same-sex marriage suggests that macro-level changes such as a Supreme Court decision does not necessarily bring about change at micro levels. When a revolutionary court case is decided, the larger society's norms stay the same. Social relationships hold their actions and cognitions in place.

The first same-sex marriage case was *Baker v. Nelson* (1972), which involved two Minnesota men who applied for and were denied a marriage license. They appealed to the Minnesota Supreme Court and made three arguments as to why a marriage license should be granted. First, Minnesota had no explicit ban on same-sex marriage, and therefore they should be allowed to marry. Second, they used *Griswold v. Connecticut* (1965) as an analogy, the case that had overturned a law prohibiting the use of birth control by married couples on the basis an individual's right to privacy. Last, they argued that the case of *Loving v. Virginia* (1967), which extended the right to marry to people of different races, applied analogously to them. The Minnesota Supreme Court did not support their arguments, and the US Supreme Court refused to grant them a hearing for "want of a substantial federal question" (Pierceson, 2013).

Political plasticity is regulated by embeddedness—the connection between the individual and others within themselves. The assumption is that a person's original source of "self" arises through social interactions. Thus, the depth of embeddedness is dependent on resiliency and connectivity. The resiliency of a connection depends on how strong a connection is between an individual and others. The quantity of connectivity concerns how many connections there are between an individual and others. Despite the embeddedness of the institution of legal marriage, people in same-sex relationships also wanted the symbolic benefits that legal marriage conferred. At a minimum, these symbolic benefits consisted of a grudging recognition from straight society that committed same-sex relationships exist. However, most people who speak of the symbolic benefits of legal same-sex marriage frame them more positively.

These individuals looked to the law to perform an essentially cultural task, communicating to the broader society that gay and lesbian couples are "normal," "the same," and "just like you"—deserving of recognition and respect for the commitment they have made.

FUTURE RESEARCH DIRECTIONS

An underlying assumption in this chapter and throughout this book is the idea that courts being active and frequent makers of public policy makes a great deal of difference in American life. With the legalization of same-sex marriage, the tensions that exist between the faith and gay communities will continue to play out in courts and legislatures across the country, requiring additional research.

CONCLUSION

The issue of same-sex marriage disappeared from the national scene for several decades. While rejected in Baker (1972), changes were afoot during these years that would make claims about same-sex marriage more persuasive the next time around. The 1970s ushered in a gender revolution that reworked the relationship between men and women. Birth control had become legal and women began to work outside the home. The goal of providing a place to raise children had been replaced with the desire for love and companionship. When these needs were not met, spouses were availed a no-fault divorce (Cherlin, 2009). Marriage had changed.

When a 1993 Hawaii Supreme Court decision declared marriage restricted to heterosexuals discriminatory, the debate about the reasonableness of same-sex marriage moved to the national stage. An immediate public reaction to the court ruling in the years that followed were statutes and constitutional amendments enacted in state after state that defined marriage as between one man and one woman. However, the changes brought about by most revolutions are within-system not between-system.

In a society in which identities are so deeply saturated by a range of legal statuses and relationships—familial, economic, juridical—it is perhaps unsurprising that people expect the law to perform the cultural work required to invoke change. At least for some, the source of law's cultural power is its assumed ability to produce cultural equality through pronouncements of legal equality. However, this belief appears naïve, given the instances in which formal legal equality has not translated into cultural equality for subordinated groups, but the prevalence of such a belief in the face of contradictory evidence attests to the central place of law in the cultural imaginations of social actors.

REFERENCES

American Psychiatric Association. (1980). *Diagnostic and statistical manual* (3rd ed.). Washington, DC: APA.

Baker v. Nelson, 409 U.S. 810 (1972).

Black, E., & Black, M. (1987). *Politics and society in the South*. Cambridge, MA: Harvard University Press.

Bowen, W. M., Haynes, M. E., & Rosentraub, M. S. (2006). Cities, tax revenues, and a state's fiscal future: The value of major urban centers. *Public Budgeting & Finance*, *26*(1), 47–65. doi:10.1111/j.1540-5850.2006.00838.x

Bowers v. Hardwick, 478 U.S. 186 (1986)

Chauncey, G. (2004). *Why marriage? The history shaping today's debate over gay equality*. New York, NY: Basic Books.

Cherlin, A. J. (2004). The deinstitutionalization of American marriage. *Journal of Marriage and the Family*, *66*(4), 848–861. doi:10.1111/j.0022-2445.2004.00058.x

Cherlin, A. J. (2009). *The marriage go-round: The state of marriage and the family in America today*. New York, NY: Alfred A. Knopf.

Colorado for Family Values. (1992). *Equal rights–not special rights!* Colorado Springs, CO: Campaign Tabloid.

Colorado State Legislative Council. (n.d.). *Ballot History*. Retrieved from http://www.leg.state.co.us/lcs/ballothistory.nsf/835d2ada8de735e787256ffe0074333d/f92307749e2caea387256ffd006a4986?OpenDocument

Coontz, S. (2005). *Marriage, a history: From obedience to intimacy or how love conquered marriage*. New York, NY: Viking.

Cramer, K. J. (2016). *The politics of resentment*. Chicago, IL: The University of Chicago Press. doi:10.7208/chicago/9780226349251.001.0001

D'Emilio, J. (1983). *Sexual politics, sexual communities: The making of a homosexual minority in the United States 1940–1970*. Chicago, IL: University of Chicago Press.

Davies, J. (1962). Toward a theory of revelation. *American Sociological Review*, *27*(1), 5–18. doi:10.2307/2089714

Donovan, T., & Bowler, S. (1997). Direct democracy and minority rights: Opinions on anti-gay and lesbian ballot initiatives. In S. L. Witt & S. McCorkle (Eds.), *Anti-gay Rights: Assessing Voter Initiatives* (pp. 107–125). Westport, CT: Praeger.

Ellwood, C. A. (1905). A psychological theory of revolution. *American Journal of Sociology*, *11*(1), 49–59. doi:10.1086/211375

Eskridge, W. (2008). *Dishonorable passions*. New York, NY: Viking.

Eskridge, W. N., & Levy, R. E. (2003). *Texas v. Lawrence*. Brief of the Cato Institute. Retrieved from http://object.cato.org/sites/cato.org/files/pubs/pdf/lawrencevtexas.pdf

Family Research Institute. (1992). *Medical consequences of what homosexuals do*. Washington, DC: Brochure.

Foucault, M. (1973). *The order of things: An archeology of the human sciences*. New York, NY: Vintage.

Franck, M. J. (2013, January 4). Same-sex marriage and social change: Exceeding the speed of thought. *Public Discourse*.

Freudenburg, W. R. (1991). Rural-urban differences in environmental concern: A closer look. *Sociological Inquiry*, *61*(2), 167–198. doi:10.1111/j.1475-682X.1991.tb00274.x

Gainsborough, J. F. (2001). *Fenced off: The suburbanization of American politics*. Washington, DC: Georgetown University Press.

Gertsmann, E. (2008). *Same-sex marriage and the Constitution* (2nd ed.). Cambridge, UK: Cambridge University Press.

Gimpel, J. G., & Karnes, K. A. (2006). The rural side of the rural-urban gap. *PS, Political Science & Politics*, *39*(3), 467–472. doi:10.1017/S1049096506060859

Gimpel, J. G., & Schuknecht, J. E. (2003). *Patchwork nation: Sectionalism and political change in American politics*. Ann Arbor, MI: University of Michigan Press. doi:10.3998/mpub.17820

Goldstein, A. B. (1997). History, homosexuality, and political values: Searching for the hidden determinants of Bowers v. Hardwick. In L. Gruen & G. Panichas (Eds.), *Sex, morality, and the law* (pp. 32–43). New York, NY: Routledge.

Green, C. S., & Bavelier, D. (2010). Exercising your brain: A review of human brain plasticity and training-induced learning. *Psychology and Aging*, *23*(4), 692–701. doi:10.1037/a0014345 PMID:19140641

Griswold v. Connecticut, 381 U.S. 479 (1965).

Hebb, D. O. (1949). *The organization of behavior: A neuropsychological theory*. New York, NY: John Wiley & Sons.

Herman, D. (1997). *The antigay agenda: Orthodox vison and the Christian right*. Chicago, IL: University of Chicago Press. doi:10.7208/chicago/9780226327693.001.0001

Hull, K. E. (2016). The evolution of same-sex marriage politics in the U.S. In N. L. Fischer & S. Seidman (Eds.), *Introducing the new sexuality studies* (3rd ed.). London: Routledge.

Keith, M., & Pile, S. (1993). Introduction part 1: The politics of place. In M. Keith & S. Pile (Eds.), *Place and the politics of identity* (pp. 1–21). London: Routledge.

Key, V. O. (1949). *Southern politics in state and nation*. New York, NY: A. A. Knopf.

Knoke, D., & Henry, C. (1977). Political structure of rural America. *The Annals of the American Academy of Political and Social Science*, *429*(1), 51–62. doi:10.1177/000271627742900106

Lawrence v. Texas, 539 U.S. 558 (2003).

Le Bon, G. (1912). *The psychology of revolution*. London: Fisher Unwin.

Le Bon, G. (2002). *The crowd: A study of the popular mind*. New York, NY: Dover. (Original work published 1895)

Lewin, E. (1998). *Recognizing ourselves: Ceremonies of lesbian and gay commitment*. New York, NY: Columbia University Press.

Lipset, S. M. (1981). *Political man: The social bases of politics*. Baltimore, MD: Johns Hopkins University Press.

Loving v. Virginia, 388 U.S. 1 (1967).

Moghaddam, F. M. (2008). *Multiculturalism and intergroup relations: Psychological implications for democracy in global context*. Washington, DC: American Psychological Association Press. doi:10.1037/11682-000

Moghaddam, F. M. (2013). *The psychology of dictatorship*. Washington, DC: American Psychological Association Press. doi:10.1037/14138-000

Mohr, R. D. (1997). Gay basics. In L. Gruen & G. Panichas (Eds.), *Sex, morality, and the law* (pp. 52–63). New York, NY: Routledge.

Mucciaroni, G. (2008). *Same sex, different politics: Success and failures in the struggles over gay rights*. Chicago, IL: University of Chicago Press. doi:10.7208/chicago/9780226544106.001.0001

Nardi, P. M. (1997). Friends, lovers, and families: The impact of AIDS on gay and lesbian relationships. In M. P. Levine, P. M. Nardi, & J. H. Gagnon (Eds.), *In changing times: Gay men and lesbians encounter HIV/AIDS* (pp. 55–82). Chicago, IL: University of Chicago Press.

O'Rourke, S. P., & Dellinger, K. L. (1997). Romer v. Evans: The Centerpiece of the American gay-rights debate. In S. L. Witt & S. McCorkle (Eds.), *Anti-gay rights: Assessing voter initiatives* (pp. 133–139). Westport, CT: Praeger.

Obergefell v. Hodges, 135 S. Ct. 2584 (2015).

Oliver, J. E. (2001). *Democracy in suburbia*. Princeton, NJ: Princeton University Press.

Parker, S. (2004). *Urban theory and the urban experience: Encountering the city*. New York, NY: Routledge.

Pierceson, J. (2013). *Same-sex marriage in the United States: The road to the Supreme Court*. Lanham, MD: Rowan & Littlefield.

Pinello, D. R. (2003). *Gay rights and American law*. New York, NY: Cambridge University Press.

Price, V., Nir, L., & Capella, J. (2005). Framing public discussion of gay civil unions. *Public Opinion Quarterly*, *69*(2), 179–212. doi:10.1093/poq/nfi014

Putnam, R. D. (2007). E pluribus unum: Diversity and community in the twenty-first century. The 2006 Johan Skytte Prize Lecture. *Scandinavian Political Studies*, *30*(2), 137–174. doi:10.1111/j.1467-9477.2007.00176.x

Richards, D. A. (2009). *The sodomy cases: Bowers v. Hardwick and Lawrence v. Texas*. Lawrence, KS: University of Kansas.

Romer v. Evans, 517 U.S. 620 (1996).

Skinner v. Oklahoma ex rel. Williamson, 316 U.S. 535 (1942).

Tonnies, F. (1957). *Community and society* [gemeinschaft und gesellschaft] (C. P. Loomis, Trans.). East Lansing, MI: Michigan State University Press.

Voss, M. W., Vivar, C., Kramer, A. F., & Van Praag, H. (2013). Bridging animal and human models of exercise-induced brain plasticity. *Trends in Cognitive Neurosciences*, *17*(10), 525–544. doi:10.1016/j.tics.2013.08.001 PMID:24029446

Wirth, L. (1938). Urbanism as a way of life. *American Journal of Sociology*, *44*(1), 3–24. doi:10.1086/217913

Yang, A. S. (1997). Trends: Attitudes toward homosexuality. *Public Opinion Quarterly*, *61*(3), 477–507. doi:10.1086/297810

KEY TERMS AND DEFINITIONS

Ballot Initiative: This process allows citizens a means by which a petition signed by a certain minimum number of registered voters can bring about a public vote on a proposed statute.

Plasticity: The ability of something to be shaped or molded.

Privacy Rights: The right to privacy alluded to in the Fourth Amendment to the US Constitution, which some have referred to as "the right to be left alone."

Rural: A geographic area outside a city or town.

Urban: A geographic area that relates to a city or town.

ENDNOTES

1 At the time the law also forbade out-of-wedlock sex and required intercourse to be performed in the missionary position.

2 Straight men at the time began to invoke the sodomy law to deny child support payments to women who were lesbian.

3 Twenty-four states have an initiative process. The initiative enables citizens to bypass their state legislature by placing proposed statutes and, in some states, constitutional amendments on the ballot.

4 The Colorado No Protected Status for Sexual Orientation Amendment also known as Amendment 2.

Section 1

Social Jurisprudence and the Creation of Revolutions

Chapter 1
Social Jurisprudence

ABSTRACT

This chapter provides a brief history of law and the role of social science in courtroom battles, further reviewing the use of social science in marriage equality cases. One of the more striking features in marriage equality litigation was the prominent role of social science in addressing issues germane to the legal arguments on both sides. The chapter concludes by discussing how social science may have influenced litigation and whether such influence was appropriate.

INTRODUCTION

This chapter begins with a short discussion of the history of law and the role of social science in courtroom battles as well as a review of the general literature on social science in the courts and the nascent social science literature on marriage equality cases. This review focuses on the role of social science in the courtroom battles over same-sex marriage and provides a descriptive review of social science in several key marriage equality cases: three state and federal trials and three U.S. Supreme Court cases decided from 2013 to 2015.

One of the more striking features of same-sex litigation in the United States was the prominent role of social science in addressing factual issues germane to the legal arguments on both sides. The chapter concludes by discussing how social science may have influenced litigation and whether such influence was appropriate.

DOI: 10.4018/978-1-5225-7961-8.ch001

JURISPRUDENCE

Courts

To understand the concept of jurisprudence, you must begin with an understanding of what courts do. The simplest answer is that courts hear lawsuits. They decide cases in which individuals, organizations, or government officials argue about their rights, obligations, and responsibilities under the law. A lawsuit is a type of dispute. Thus, what courts do is to try to decide between or among those who have some sort of disagreement, and in doing so the court produces a decision. Unless overruled by a higher court, this decision is binding on the parties to the dispute.

The authoritative character of these judicial decisions results because judges make policy. Policymaking involves choosing among alternative courses of action, in which the choice binds the behavior of those subject to the policymaker's action (Segal & Spaeth, 1993). These decisions allocate resources among the parties to a lawsuit, but at the Supreme Court level, these decisions affect persons other than the litigants. These decisions are supported by opinions that apprise others of the reasoning and the fate that may befall them if they engage in similar actions.

Because judges' decisions adjudicate the legality of contested matters, by necessity judges make both policy and law. Only those who believe in fairy tales think otherwise. Even so, Americans find it unsettling at times to admit that judges make policy except, of course, when there is disagreement about a decision. However, the essence of the fairy tale is that the judges and their decisions are objective, impartial, and dispassionate.

Actions or decisions of courts do not fully terminate the social problems brought before them, because the conflicts that come before a court are rarely simple (Yngvesson & Hennessey, 1975). To initiate a court case requires a substantial investment of time and money, an investment that ensures that people whose disputes are decided have an intense commitment to their cause that will not easily dissipate once the decision has been rendered. These decisions represent the legal termination of a dispute but not the end of the underlying cause of the problem.

Disagreement is the case with many of the Supreme Court rulings. It is not a stretch to draw a straight line from the most recent marriage equality decision, in which the Supreme Court decided marriage is a fundamental right (*Obergefell v. Hodges,* 2015), to the election results of 2016, which left Republicans in control of most of the nation's governorships and state legislatures.

History of Law and Changing Legal Thought

The concept of jurisprudence regularly appears in scholarly literature notwithstanding the fact that a precise definition is elusive. In general, jurisprudence is a philosophy of law that describes how the legal process works. When contemporary legal theorists engage the question "What is law?" their analyses typically are framed in terms of a contest between legal positivism and natural law—in that order—followed by legal realism and then a host of contemporary schools of thought (Hayman, 2002; Murphy & Coleman, 1990).

This chronological ordering is thematic: natural law theory began in classical times (Murphy & Coleman, 1990); legal positivism arose in the 19th century to challenge natural law (Pound, 1921); legal realism arose in the 1920s and 1930s to debunk formalist views of law (Hayman, 2002); and the Hart-Fuller debate of the late 1950s marked the reenergizing of legal positivism (Murphy & Coleman, 1990, pp. 36–39. In the 1970s, Dworkin challenged Hart's dominance and examined law from an economic perspective (Kelly, 1992) and critical legal studies of the radical left attacked mainstream legal liberalism (Murphy & Coleman, 1990 pp. 51–55).

There is a hodge-podge of descendants and variations on these schools, with natural law and legal positivism—depending on the scholars—enjoying prominence above all others. The differences between these schools of thought are explained in the sections that follow. Contrary to this division, it is not my contention that every existing legal theory can be squeezed into one of these jurisprudential approaches. Nor do I claim that this is the only way to categorize theories about law.

Natural Law

Early in our nation's history, law students were taught that judicial decisions were derived from rules of law that sprang from first principles (Berman & Greiner, 1980). There were "natural law" theorists such as Blackstone, who described in his *Commentaries* how judges must look up and ponder the heavens to discover the first principles that would guide them to render just decisions (Blackstone, Tucker & Christian, 1803). This methodology was deeply grounded in Judeo-Christian principles (Kretzman, 1995). In jurisprudence, natural law can refer to several doctrines. The first is that just laws are immanent in nature; that is, they can be "discovered" or "found" but not created by such things as a bill of rights. Second, the meaning of law is such that its content cannot be determined except about moral principles. Kelsen (1941) described natural law theory as deriving its doctrine from the assumption that what is just can be determined by human reason or the will of God.

Much of the legal opposition to lesbian, gay, bisexual, and transgender (LGBT) rights and to same-sex marriage has been expressed through natural law–type arguments. As Catholic ethicist and Princeton Professor Robert P. George (2003) insisted, writing in the *Wall Street Journal*, there is a natural law justification for fighting same-sex marriage on the basis of the self-evident "nature of marriage as a one flesh union of sexually complementary spouses" and a corresponding self-evident entitlement of mixed-sex marriages to receive "benefits, privileges, rights or immunities" because the spouses are of the opposite sex.

Legal Positivism

The natural law theory came into disfavor with the advent of the 18th century "scientific revolution," and legal positivism, another school of jurisprudence, came into vogue (Fineberg & Hyman, 1995). Legal positivists rejected the notion that judicial decisions were components of immutable first principles.

As legal thinkers such as Jeremy Bentham and John Austin developed the theory, empiricism set the theoretical foundations for such developments to occur. H. L. A. Hart, who in 1958 found common usages of "positivism" as applied to law to include the contention that "a legal system is a closed, logical system in which correct decisions can be deduced from predetermined legal rules without reference to social considerations." This rejection of value considerations in judicial thinking resulted in decisions that sometimes lacked the indicia of fairness. Judicial decisions were read by practitioners with an eye to simply plucking out useful phrases and arguing deductively from them. This led to criticism of legal positivism as slot machine justice, or "mechanical jurisprudence" (Pound, 1908).

Legal Realism

The school of legal realism, a 19th-century outgrowth of 18th-century French socialist philosophy, modified the legal positivist position by recognizing that a value choice is implicit in all decision-making (Altman, 1995). Legal realism disapproved of the "heartless" justice dispensed under legal positivism.

Montesquieu's *The Spirit of the Laws,* published in 1748, sets the tone for these ideas, as contained in this passage:

Laws must relate to the nature and the principle of the government that is established or that one wants to establish, whether those laws form it as do political laws, or maintain it, as do civil laws.

They should be related to the physical aspect of the country; to the climate, be it freezing, torrid, or temperate; to the properties of the terrain, its location and extent; to the way of life of the peoples, be they plowmen, hunters, or herdsmen; they should relate to the degree of liberty that the constitution can sustain, to the religion of the inhabitants, their inclinations, their wealth, their number, their commerce, their mores and their manners; finally, the laws are related to one another, to their origin, to the purpose of the legislator, and to the order of things on which they are established. They must be considered from all these points of view. (Berlin, 2013)

Montesquieu set forth a descriptive account of law as a social institution that fits its environment, and one that should match the legal system if a society is to function well. Law is shaped by society and in turn shaping society. Law is holistic, reflecting and the product of the polity, religion, trade, manners, moral views, customs, temperature, geography, and everything else about and within a society (Tamanaha, 2015). Emile Durkheim (1960) wrote that Montesquieu "saw quite clearly that all these elements form a whole and that if taken separately, without reference to the others, they cannot be understood, as he highlights 'the interrelatedness of social phenomena.'"

Berlin (2013) describes the law as best apprehended via scientific methods, gathering a large body of information on historical and current societies, engaging in close observation of facts, applying inductive and deductive reasoning, observing connections and patterns, constructing ideal types, and formulating general propositions about social-legal arrangements. Durkheim (1960) credits Montesquieu as the theorist who "first laid down the fundamental principles of social science," and "instituted a new field of study" serving as an alternative to both positivism and naturalism.

Realists focused on the law in action. The law is what judges and lawyers do as they practice law. In other words, the decision of the judge becomes the law. These changes in legal philosophy reflected a loss of confidence in natural law theories and an increasing tendency to view law as a means of establishing social policy. A clear sign of this change was the publication of Karl Llewellyn's *A Realistic Jurisprudence – The Next Step* (1930), which suggested a decisive break with the past had occurred. Llewellyn's views were influenced by Holmes (1881) and by the beliefs of Brandis (1907) and Pound (1912), each a theorist instrumental in changing the national consensus about the nature of law. Their criticisms undermined the mechanical method of classical jurisprudence and changed the notion that law, in part, should be concerned with making public policy. This dramatic shift, and its implications, continue to arouse debate. Each jurist laid the foundation for the use of social science materials in resolving legal problems.

The differences between naturalists and positivists are both analytically and normatively important. Both systems consider the law to be a human construct. But where legal positivism would say that an unjust law is nevertheless a law, a natural law jurisprudent would posit there is something legally deficient about an unjust norm. Unlike the American legal realists, positivists believe that, in many instances and in some courts, the law provides reasonably determinate guidance to its subjects and to judges.

This section of the chapter traces the evolvement of legal thought and notes the differences between each jurisprudential approach. The next section traces the application of social science–related information in courts.

SOCIAL SCIENCE IN THE COURTS

For the social sciences, the 1950s were in fact a period of unprecedented ascendance in both popular acceptance (Riesman, 1954) and as a form of governmental knowledge (Simon, 1999). The social here refers to the domain of relations, norms, and institutions that have indeed been the focus of social sciences since the late 19th century (Rose, 1999).

The origins of social science in law can be found in the jurisprudential revolution that took place in the latter part of the 19th and 20th centuries. Until this time, American law had been dominated by the belief that there was a single, correct legal solution that could be applied to each case through the application of the rules of logic to a set of self-evident principles (Monahan & Walker, 1994). This view of jurisprudence was understood to be rational, deductive, and mechanistic. Judges sought to follow these immutable principles to render a decision in a case. Dissatisfaction and decision-making changes in legal philosophy transformed from an exclusively deductive process to one that incorporated inductive elements. The law came to be viewed more as a means of establishing social policy and less as the rational analysis of doctrine. This new type of jurisprudence came to be called legal realism.

Historical reviews of social science in the courts reach back to the turn of the 20th century and cite the influence of legal giants such as Holmes, Pound, and Brandeis (Larsen, 2014; Monahan & Walker, 2014, pp. 1–13). Commentators point to the famous footnote 11 in the majority opinion in *Brown v. Board of Education of Topeka* (1954) citing psychological studies on the negative effects of school segregation on children as one of the milestones in social science influence in Supreme Court jurisprudence (Moran, 2010; Rublin, 2011).

U.S. courts, especially the Supreme Court during the first third of the 20th century, often seemed to be the branch of government most inclined to ignore or even deny the importance of the social—a factor that surely contributed to the perception of the courts as solidly conservative and pro-business in that era (*Lochner v. New York*, 1905). The jurisprudence supporting judicial hostility toward acknowledging social relations, norms, and institutions came under increasing assault from a broad array of academic legal writing under the banner of legal realism (Hull, Pound & Llewellyn, 1997).

While individual justices since Holmes and Brandeis had voiced this criticism and invoked the social in various ways in their opinions (occasionally for the majority), the majority that emerged during the New Deal fight never articulated a doctrinal expression of the social to accompany their overturning of formalist precedents (*United States v. Caroline Products*, 1938).

Despite admitted tensions, U.S. courts have turned to social science, albeit in inconsistent and episodic ways. There are numerous ways in which social science knowledge can affect legal developments. Expert witnesses testify at trials about relevant social science studies; social scientists contribute to amicus briefs to inform courts of the current state of knowledge in their fields; social science also enters the legal door through legislative hearings, and so forth.

Legal historians typically point to the Brandeis brief as a watershed event in the introduction of social science to legal decision making in the United States (Rosen, 1972). This famous brief, more than 100 pages in length, was filed by Louis Brandeis in the 1908 case of *Muller v. Oregon*. It drew upon the social science of the day, which purported to document inherent differences between men and women. Although the science Brandeis cited therein was later largely discredited, the brief itself has been hailed as a legal innovation that began a long-standing effort to marry law and the social sciences.

Beginning with *Brown*, the Warren Court[1] included in many of its important decisions broad invitations to the bar and bench to incorporate knowledge about social relations, norms, and institutions (collectively, "the social") into the analysis of constitutional rights (*Miranda v. Arizona*, 1966). The 1930s movement had bolstered the role of social science in legal cases, with an emphasis on incorporating empirical information into legal decision making. Almost 50 years later, many social scientists would take issue with the studies used in *Brown* and the inferences drawn from them (Jackson, 2000). Although broad consensus remains about the overall harms caused by segregation, critics such as Gregor (1963) pointed out methodological flaws of the studies, saying there is an institutional and political component not only to how social science is generated and how it is received by courts, but also to how it is subsequently critiqued.

Exemplified in *Brown* are the major tensions over the question of the legitimacy of social science, particularly when viewed over time. As in the case of natural science, social science once deemed acceptable will later be rejected, as methods and understandings change. Using a realist critique, one could easily argue for overturning much prior precedent based on current social science norms. By contrast, a historicist approach would insist that we understand decisions considering the knowledge available at the time they were formed. Just as law evolves in accordance with changed information from other sources, from time to time it would also have to revisit issues by considering the changed social science understandings underpinning legal decisions (to the degree that decisions are based upon such data). There are numerous examples of an ongoing dialogue through which the courts slowly take in changed understandings from social science—shifting from the naturalist-based view in *Bowers v. Hardwick* (1986) to the social and environmentally based vision of *Obergefell*.

Social Fact, Social Authority, and Social Frameworks

In general, social science enjoys a unique perspective from which to describe how the law intersects with individual behavior and social structure. Some argue that to promote specific values, law should consider social reality instead of social myth. Judicial decisions are not isolated from social reality, and judges do not rely solely on the syllogisms of black letter law but allow their own social reality to color their opinions.

In a classic law review article, Kenneth Davis (1942) articulated a distinction between adjudicative and legislative facts in legal cases. Adjudicative facts are specific to the case and the involved parties, whereas legislative facts address broader questions of law or policy that transcend the individual case and inform legal decision makers when they make law. Scholars discussing the role of social science in courts routinely employ this distinction, and much of the social science introduced in courts falls into the realm of legislative facts relevant to the constitutional question addressed in the case (Monahan & Walker 2014, p. 175).

Professors Monohan and Walker (1988, 1991) further refined the adjudicative/legislative fact dichotomy and advocated renaming adjudicative facts[2] *social facts*[3]. They advocated replacing the term *legislative fact* with *social authority* and argued that "social science research, when used to create a legal rule, is more analogous to 'law' than to 'fact,' and hence should be treated much as courts treat legal precedent" (Monahan &Walker, 1986, p. 478) or a state legislature as part of testimony delivered at a legislative or administrative hearing (Wursten & Sales, 1992). Social authority compares replicated research results produced under rigorous conditions to legal precedent supported by the holdings of appellate courts across jurisdictions. Both replicated research and legal precedent are not specific to the facts of a case but instead are intended to describe or prescribe principles that would pertain to whole classes of human behavior and should be presented to courts in the form of briefs.

In renaming adjudicative facts as *social facts* this would create a third category called *social frameworks* (Walker & Monahan, 1987). Like social authority, social frameworks are not based on the fact pattern of a specific case, but like social fact, social frameworks are used to provide background information about social life that is relevant to determining case-specific facts.

Empirical research on social science in courts includes works that review and assess the impact of social science to areas of law. There are studies that evaluate the impact of amicus briefs on opinion content and case outcomes as well as examinations of the experiences of social scientists, attorneys, judges, and law clerks in presenting or evaluating social science evidence. Evaluation of the direct impact of social science on opinion content or case outcomes faces two significant obstacles.

First, judges may cite social science evidence in their rulings, even when this evidence had little or no impact on how they decided the case (Moran, 2010; Zick, 2003). Second, the absence of direct citation to social science evidence presented in briefs or expert testimony should not assume to signal its lack of influence. Judges may factor social science information into their analysis without specifically citing it. Further, social science evidence may have an indirect influence through other channels, such as influencing the reasoning of cases cited as precedent or shifts in public opinion that weigh on jurists' views of a case.

Studies that assess the impact of social science in different areas of legal decision making have produced mixed results. Some studies suggest social science may be influential (Acker, 1990; Fiske & Borgida, 2008; Vidmar & Schuller, 1989), but a Nelson, Barry & Nielsen (2008) and Lempert (2013) review of social science in employment discrimination cases concludes that judges tend to grant little credence to social science, in large measure because their worldview and legal training is inconsistent with the behavioral realist perspective that is the norm in social scientific research. The social sciences have not gained authority within law, even regarding issues on which scholars have produced an enormous body of published, refereed research.

Numerous studies have analyzed the impacts of amicus briefs, which often convey social science evidence not introduced at trial. The number of amicus filings has exploded in recent years (Franze & Anderson, 2015; Kearney & Merrill, 2000), and their content sometimes impacts the crafting of judicial opinions (Collins, Corley & Hammer, 2015). Briefs from certain high-profile interest groups, states, and the U.S. solicitor general appear to be most influential (Box-Steffensmeier, Christenson & Hitt, 2013; Caldeira &Wright, 1988; Kearney & Merrill, 2000). However, it remains unclear whether social science evidence delivered in amicus briefs has much impact.

> *Even with a dramatic increase in amicus participation, there is no decisive support for the argument that briefs filed by social scientists shape the judicial decision-making process . . . Until further study is done, the impact of social science evidence—at least when introduced in amicus briefs—will remain an open question. (Moran, 2010, p. 535)*

A study of law students and judges found subjects rated social science evidence more favorably when it matched their existing views, and their written comments often reflected a distrust of social science and expert witnesses (Redding & Reppucci,1999). By contrast, in a survey of 70 former

Supreme Court clerks more than half said briefs with social science content merited special consideration and were especially helpful when they added new facts or gave insight into the practical consequences of court decisions (Lynch, 2004).

Others have theorized factors that might determine when social science affects legal outcomes as well as its impacts on legal legitimacy (Stryker, 1994). Rublin (2011) speculates that social science evidence may have greater impact when scientific consensus is high, when an issue is in play across many jurisdictions, and when public opinion on an issue has begun to coalesce. Goldberg (2006) theorizes that social science research has the most influence when it "can destabilize traditional views of social groups" by exposing the inaccuracy of perceived facts and the effects of bias on perceptions.

Going beyond the question of whether social science has significant influence, scholars also address the question of whether it *should* have influence. The differences among distinct schools of thought in various disciplines are dramatic, with a diversity in theories and accepted methods for demonstrating "truths." These divisions attract attention. One example is the divide between biologically oriented psychological models and more psychodynamic models. The differences between these two groups led to an institutional splintering in the US, in which some laboratory researchers formed their own group, the American Psychological Society (APS) in contradistinction to the larger American Psychological Association (APA), which has traditionally served as an umbrella organization for psychologists of all kinds. Although members of both groups conduct studies accepted as scientific by their relevant communities, and regularly pass peer review in approved journals, there have been attempts to characterize the APS as somehow more scientific—attempts which in themselves have a sociology and politics that merit analysis (Dezalay & Garth, 2002). These sociological divisions within the academy and professions are a struggle over legitimacy that complicates the debate over the application of social science theories. The next section explores some of the social science that has been used in the litigation of same-sex marriage cases.

Social Science Studies Used in Same-Sex Marriage Litigation

A sizable interdisciplinary literature has emerged over the last two decades on the role of litigation in LGBT movements (Andersen, 2006; Kane &

Elliott, 2014; Mezey, 2007; Pierceson, 2005) and specifically in the fight for same-sex marriage recognition (Cummings & NeJaime, 2009–2010; Hume, 2013; Keck, 2009; Klarman, 2013; Mezey, 2009; NeJaime, 2011; Pierceson, 2013; Rosenberg, 2008), but the literature on the role of social science in such litigation is much more compact. An early study examined social science citations in cases through 1987 in four areas of gay rights, not including marriage or partnership recognition (Falk, 1994). The study found high rates of citation to social science and attributed this pattern to the controversial nature of gay rights issues and the high volume of social science evidence proffered by litigants, advocacy groups, and professional organizations in legal briefs. Recent work specifically examines social science evidence relevant to marriage litigation.

Yoshino (2015) provides a description of the first federal court trial on same-sex marriage, the case that eventually made its way to the U.S. Supreme Court as *Hollingsworth v. Perry* (2013). His book details the role of expert witnesses from the disciplines of history and social science in addressing several key questions in the *Perry* trial and concludes the legislative facts established reverberated beyond the specific case in several ways. The trial findings were cited by several other courts that struck down same-sex marriage bans and served to "discredit fringe scholars and viewpoints with finality and authority" (Yoshino, 2015, p. 271).

Powell, Quadlin & Pizmony-Levy (2015) use data from the 2010 Constructing the Family Survey to assess several other issues raised in same-sex marriage court cases. The survey data show a high correlation between negative views of homosexuality and opposition to same-sex marriage, contrary to assertions in the courtroom that disapproval is not driven by animus. Two-thirds of the survey respondents pointed to religious or moral disapproval of homosexuality as reasons for opposing same-sex marriage.

Another study compared different forms of expertise in battles over gay family rights, including marriage, in France and the United States (Stambolis-Ruhstorfer, 2015). It notes that elite experts—academics and professional organizations—who have weighed in on marriage cases through amicus briefs or expert testimony in trials have disproportionately favored legal recognition of same-sex marriage.

Stambolis-Ruhstorfer (2015) concludes that the institutional logic of American courts molds knowledge presentation by academic experts. The adversarial system of justice and existing rules about expert evidence means witnesses must establish their credibility, stick to the issues they are qualified to address, and withstand harsh questioning by opposing counsel in depositions and cross-examinations. Reflecting on personal experience as an expert witness in Canadian same-sex marriage cases, Stacey (2004) likewise concludes that social science experts cede control over question framing and standards of scientific credibility to legal actors in the courtroom context.

To gain further insight into the role of social science in same-sex litigation Hull (2017) reviewed selected case materials from six key court cases including three state same-sex marriage trials in Hawaii, *Baehr v. Miike*, (1996); California, *Perry v. Schwarzenegger* (2010); and Michigan, *DeBoer v. Snyder* (2014) and the three U.S. Supreme Court cases *Hollingsworth v. Perry* (2013), *U.S. v. Windsor* (2013), and *Obergefell v. Hodges* (2015).

Trial transcripts; written opinions; parties' briefs; amicus briefs filed by social scientists and historians; transcripts of oral arguments; and court opinions were reviewed. Hull (2017) was not to conduct an empirical analysis but to provide an overview regarding social science experts and evidence used in marriage equality litigation as illustrated in Tables 1 and 2. These trials produced a substantial body of social science evidence delivered by a range of expert witnesses. This evidence was subject to the rigors of the adversarial process, and these findings figured prominently in the judicial opinions in each of the cases.

The U.S. Supreme Court cases selected for examination considered their significance and the evidence put forward in lower state and federal courts that appeared in parties' briefs, amicus briefs, and oral arguments. Hull's (2017) review was limited to amicus briefs from social science and history experts (Table 2) filed in these same-sex marriage cases. Franze & Anderson (2015) found that a very high volume of amicus briefs was filed in the Supreme Court marriage cases, and some of those briefs from parties other than social scientists and historians also referenced social scientific evidence.

These experts from psychology, economics, sociology, political science, anthropology, and related fields such as history and psychiatry presented a broad range of social scientific evidence, which was introduced in same-sex marriage court cases. Almost all the social science evidence addressed legislative facts—general information about the social world—rather than case-specific questions. By and large, social science's largest contributions were on the issues of parenting impacts as well as responsible procreation and deinstitutionalization arguments, but social scientific input was also present on other questions including the social purpose of marriage, the harms of marriage bans, and the criteria for evaluating whether sexual orientation classifications merit heightened scrutiny (Hull, 2015).

Table 1. Expert witnesses in same-sex marriage trials

Case	Pro-Same-Sex Marriage Experts	Anti-Same-Sex Marriage Experts
Baehr v. Miike (1996)	Pepper Schwartz (sociology)	Kyle D. Pruett (psychiatry)
	Charlotte Patterson (psychology)	David Eggebeen (sociology)
	David Brodzinsky (psychology)	Richard Williams (psychology)
	Robert Bidwell (pediatrics)	Thomas S. Merrill (private practice clinical psychology)
Perry v. Schwarzenegger (2010)	Nancy Cott (history)	Kenneth Miller (political science)
	George Chauncey (history)	David Blankenhorn (family studies)
	Letitia Anne Peplau (psychology)	
	Edmund Egan (economics)	
	Ilan Meyer (social epidemiology)	
	Michael Lamb (psychology)	
	Lee Badgett (economics)	
	Gary Segura (political science)	
	Gregory M. Herek (psychology)	
DeBoer v. Snyder (2014)	David Brodzinsky (psychology)	Mark Regnerus (sociology)
	Michael Rosenfeld (sociology)	Loren Marks (family studies)
	Vivek Sankaran (law)	Joseph Price (economics)
	Gary Gates (demography)	Douglas Allen (economics)
	Nancy Cott (history)	

(Hull, 2017)

Each side's use of social science evidence in the legal contests over same-sex marriage engaged in a series of credibility contests. On issue after issue, judges were required to assess the weight and credibility of each side's evidence. The trial court opinions in *Baehr*, *Perry,* and *DeBoer* encapsulate this assessment process. The judges in each of these rulings explicitly state which witnesses and evidence they found credible and how such evidence linked to their legal conclusions.

It is impossible to say with certainty whether social science played a decisive role—whether it influenced legal outcomes in the litigation. It is difficult to gauge indirect influences such as impacts on legal decisions that serve as precedent in later court cases as well.

Whether it did, should social science have played a decisive role in marriage equality litigation? Certainly, the cases could have been decided based on legal principles alone, without reference to social science evidence. Indeed, significant prior Supreme Court jurisprudence on marriage (including

Table 2. Amicus briefs from social science and history experts filed in U.S. Supreme Court same-sex marriage cases

Case	Pro-Same-Sex Marriage Briefs	Anti-Same-Sex Marriage Briefs
Hollingsworth v. Perry (2013)	American Psychological Association, et al.	Scholars of history and related disciplines
	American Anthropological Association, et al.	Professor Daniel N. Robinson, PhD
	Political science professors	Social science professors
	Organization of American Historians and American Studies Association	Leon R. Kass, Harvey C. Mansfield, and the Institute for Marriage and Public Policy
	Gary J. Gates	
	American Sociological Association	
U.S. v. Windsor (2013)	Political science professors	Social science professors
	American Sociological Association	
	Organization of American Historians, et al.	
	Gary J. Gates	
	Historians, American Historical Association, et al.	
	American Psychological Association, et al.	
Obergefell v. Hodges (2015)	Organization of American Historians	Professor Daniel N. Robinson, PhD
	American Sociological Association	Scholars of history and related disciplines
	American Psychological Association, et al.	100 scholars of marriage
	Gary J. Gates	American College of Pediatricians, et al
	American Public Health Association and Whitman-Walker Health	Ruth Institute and Jennifer Roback Morse, PhD
	Historians of marriage and American Historical Association	Organizations and scholars of gender-diverse parenting
		47 scholars
		Dr. Judith Reisman and Liberty Center for Child Protection
		Scholars of fertility and marriage
		Scholars on the welfare of women, children, and underprivileged populations

(Hull, 2015)

dismantling interracial marriage bans and protecting the legal status of nonmarital offspring) disregarded social science evidence in favor of broad legal principles of equal treatment and nondiscrimination (Ball, 2014, pp.126–27).

By incorporating social science into its justification for marriage equality, the courts may have set a dangerous precedent by making groups' "access to constitutional rights contingent on tests not imposed on other groups, such as the ability to produce child outcomes equivalent to the gold standard of intact biological parent families" (Ball, 2014; Meadow, 2013).

Reliance on social science also runs the risk that future evidence will point toward a different outcome, or that existing scientific consensus will be clouded by future research findings (Nagin, et al. 2012).

Finally, to the extent courts relied on the social science evidence presented in amicus briefs rather than at trial, such evidence lacked the built-in quality control provided by the adversarial process. The symbolic impact of the law educates citizens and guides their behavior toward the normative values of the community. It is said most individuals follow the law not because of the deterrent power of punishment but rather because of the pronounced influence of the symbolic guidelines that the law makes in our everyday lives (Melton, 1990).

FUTURE RESEARCH DIRECTIONS

There are pervasive tensions between social science and law. The two fields have vastly different epistemologies, rules, and social purposes. On the one hand, social science stands poised to provide useful and trenchant critiques of legal systems and assumptions. Social science is also a promising source of information and critical questioning when the law attempts to interpret and understand aspects of society that social scientists are trained to analyze.

On the first issue, social science as a source of critique, Sarat and Silbey (1988) issued a well-taken warning: if social science is truly to provide trenchant criticism, it must stand outside the frames provided by law and policy discourses. There is a "pull" to these frames, and it is tempting to simply offer small amendments, or ways of tinkering with existing systems, rather than stand outside frameworks and question them. At the same time, the risk of standing totally outside of existing frameworks is that the critique will not be heard. Discourse from a completely different frame can be very difficult—if not impossible—to absorb (Mertz, 2000).

The second role of social science is to provide information and analysis relevant to the social "facts" with which courts must deal and noting the pervasiveness of ongoing tensions. First is the political issue as to what degree courts in a democratic state should delegate the construction of social facts and the assessment thereof to experts. Social science asks questions for different reasons than law, and so it is not completely obvious that law should subject itself too completely to social science. Nevertheless, dialogue between the two seems not only desirable but inevitable as agents of the law engage in at times flawed but nonetheless active efforts to translate the knowledge of social science into legal discourse. In the process, tensions also emerge over the definition of valid science, the arbitration of disputes among bona fide social scientists, and the status of hybrid discourses created when law appropriates areas of social science.

Therefore, the complex relationship between the law and social science urges caution when attempting to translate between the two. Discourse surrounding professional cultures is crucial. Lawyers are trained in advocacy and adversarial contest—the terms are painted in black and white and the point of discursive exchange is to win. Social scientists revel in hedging and probability, cushioning their claims to truth in layers of methodological and epistemological caution and nuance. It is not enough to teach lawyers the content of a social science translation, rather the norms of social science discourse must also be conveyed as part of any effective translation.

Efforts to build a new legal realism, one that would put today's social science to effective use in legal settings, must begin by taking this aspect of translation much more seriously. As the anthropologist Renato Rosaldo (1994) observed, in the "contact zones" where different disciplines meet, "social relations are often unequal, and people may speak different languages or the same language with different inflections, meanings, or purposes." At times, those wielding power, such as courts, will not be willing to bend sufficiently to make the effort to understand other paradigms without pressure from outside the legal system, as with the LGBT movement surrounding marriage (Hull, 2017). In their study of the use of social science data in U.S. Supreme Court opinions, Erickson and Simon (1998) note that "data are used in the courtroom in a manner consistent with the standards of the legal community, not the social sciences community." It is hoped that future progress in this dialogue will involve more of a compromise, enabling the legal system to bring to fuller fruition the promise of social science as a source of critique and information.

CONCLUSION

An underlying assumption in this chapter and throughout this book is the fact that courts, as active and frequent makers of public policy, make a great deal of difference in American life. Theories of law wax and wane and have shifting emphases subject to developments at the time and place of their formulation. This includes broad influences such as a period of social turmoil or rapid social change as well as more immediate influences within the intellectual settings in which legal theories are developed—academic specialization, institutional support, and current scholarly norms or fads.

It is critical that a jurist—or citizen—believes that legal rules are valid, even when they feel they are immoral, that law should be just, and some moral norms are objectively right, and that they believe the law is a social institution applied to achieve ends. Most likely, this combination of beliefs is a common framework in jurisprudence. Only when these beliefs are framed at higher levels of abstraction, and counterposed as opposing theoretical positions with defining elements, do incompatibilities arise.

REFERENCES

Acker, J. R. (1990). Social science in Supreme Court criminal cases and briefs: The actual and potential contribution of social scientists as amici curiae. *Law and Human Behavior*, *14*(1), 25–42. doi:10.1007/BF01055787

Andersen, E. A. (2006). *Out of the closets and into the courts: Legal opportunity structure and gay rights litigation*. Ann Arbor, MI: University Michigan Press.

Baehr v. Miike, 1996 WL 694235 (1996)

Ball, C. A. (2014). *Same-sex marriage and children: A tale of history*. New York, NY: Oxford University Press. doi:10.1093/acprof:oso/9780199977871.001.0001

Berlin, I. (2013). *Against the current: Essays in the history of ideas* (2nd ed.). Princeton, NJ: Princeton University Press. doi:10.1515/9781400843237

Berman, H. J., & Greiner, W. R. (1980). *The nature and function of the law* (4th ed.). St. Paul, MN: Foundation Press.

Blackstone, W., Tucker, S. G., & Christian, E. (1803). *Blackstone's commentaries: With notes of reference to the Constitution and laws of the federal government of the United States and of the commonwealth of Virginia in five volumes: with an appendix to each volume containing short tracts upon such subjects as appeared necessary to form a connected view of the laws of Virginia*. Philadelphia, PA: W. Y. Birch and A. Small.

Bowers v. Hardwick, 478 U.S. 186 (1986).

Box-Steffensmeier, J. M., Christenson, D. P., & Hitt, M. P. (2013). Quality over quantity: Amici influence and judicial decision making. *The American Political Science Review*, *107*(3), 446–460. doi:10.1017/S000305541300021X

Brandis, L. D. (1907). *The Brandis brief.* University of Louisville. Retrieved from https://louisville.edu/law/library/special-collections/the-louis-d.-brandeis-collection/the-brandeis-brief-in-its-entirety

Brown v. Board of Education of Topeka, 347 U.S. 483 (1954).

Caldeira, G. A., & Wright, J. R. (1988). Organized interests and agenda setting in the U.S. Supreme Court. *The American Political Science Review*, *82*(4), 1109–1127. doi:10.2307/1961752

Collins, P. M. Jr, Corley, P. C., & Hamner, J. (2015). The influence of amicus curiae briefs on U.S. Supreme Court opinion content. *Law & Society Review*, *49*(4), 917–944. doi:10.1111/lasr.12166

Cummings, S. L. & NeJaime, D. (2009–2010). Lawyering for marriage equality. *UCLA Law Review. University of California, Los Angeles. School of Law*, *57*, 1235–1331.

Davis, K. C. (1942). An approach to problems of evidence in the administrative process. *Harvard Law Review*, *55*(3), 364–425. doi:10.2307/1335092

DeBoer v. Snyder, 973 F. Supp. 2d 757 (2014).

Dezalay, Y., & Garth, B. (2002). *The internationalization of palace wars: Lawyers, economists, and the contest to transform Latin America*. Chicago, IL: University of Chicago Press. doi:10.7208/chicago/9780226144276.001.0001

Durkheim, E. (1960). *Montesquieu and Rousseau: Forerunners of sociology*. Ann Arbor, MI: University of Michigan Press. doi:10.3998/mpub.9689969

Erickson, R., & Simon, R. (1998). *The use of social science data in Supreme Court decisions*. Urbana, IL: University of Illinois Press.

Falk, P. J. (1994). The prevalence of social science in gay rights cases: The synergistic influences of historical context, justificatory citation, and dissemination efforts. *Wayne Law Review*, *41*, 1–69.

Feinberg, J., & Hyman, G. (1995). *Philosophy of law* (5th ed.). Belmont, CA: Wadsworth Publishing Company.

Fiske, S. T., & Borgida, E. (2008). Providing expert knowledge in an adversarial context: Social cognitive science in employment discrimination cases. *Annual Review of Law and Social Science*, *4*(1), 123–148. doi:10.1146/annurev.lawsocsci.4.110707.172350

Franze, A. J., & Anderson, R. R. (2015). Record-breaking term for amicus curiae in Supreme Court reflects new norm. *National Law Journal*. Retrieved from https://files.arnoldporter.com/recordbreakingtermforamicuscuriaeinsupremecourtreflectnewnorm.pdf

George, R. P. (2003, November 28). One man and one woman. *Wall Street Journal*, p. A8.

Goldberg, S. B. (2006). Constitutional tipping points: Civil rights, social change, and fact-based adjudication. *Columbia Law Review*, *106*(8), 1955–2022.

Gregor, A. I. (1963). The law, social science, and school segregation: An assessment. *Western Reserve Law Review*, *14*, 621–636.

Hart, H. L. A. (1958). Positivism and the separation of law and morals. *Harvard Law Review*, *71*(4), 601–602. doi:10.2307/1338225

Hayman, R. L., Levit, N., Delgado, R., & Stefancie, J. (Eds.). (2002). *Jurisprudence: Classical and contemporary from natural law to postmodernism* (2nd ed.). St. Paul, MN: West Group.

Hollingsworth v. Perry, 133 S. Ct. 2652 (2013).

Holmes, O. W. (1881). *The common law*. Boston, MA: Little, Brown and Company.

Hull, K. E. (2017). The role of social science expertise in same-sex marriage litigation. *Annual Review and Social Science*, *13*(1), 471–491. doi:10.1146/annurev-lawsocsci-110615-084729

Hull, N. E. H., Pound, R., & Llewellyn, K. (1997). *Searching for an American jurisprudence*. Chicago: University of Chicago Press.

Hume, R. J. (2013). *Courthouse democracy and minority rights: Same-sex marriage in the states*. New York, NY: Oxford University Press.

Jackson, J. P. (2004). The scientific attack on Brown v. Board of Education, 1954-1964. *The American Psychologist*, *59*(6), 530–537. doi:10.1037/0003-066X.59.6.530 PMID:15367088

Kane, M. D., & Elliott, T. A. (2014). Turning to the courts: A quantitative analysis of the gay and lesbian movement's use of legal mobilization. *Sociological Focus*, *47*(4), 219–237. doi:10.1080/00380237.2014.939901

Kearney, J. D., & Merrill, T. W. (2000). The influence of amicus curiae briefs on the Supreme Court. *University of Pennsylvania Law Review*, *148*(3), 743–855. doi:10.2307/3312826

Keck, T. M. (2009). Beyond backlash: Assessing the impact of judicial decisions on LGBT rights. *Law & Society Review*, *43*(1), 151–186. doi:10.1111/j.1540-5893.2009.00370.x

Kelly, J. M. (1992). *A short history of western legal theory*. New York, NY: Oxford University Press.

Kelsen, H. (1941). The pure theory of law and analytical jurisprudence. *Harvard Law Review*, *55*(1), 44–70. doi:10.2307/1334739

Klarman, M. J. (2013). *From the closet to the altar: Courts, backlash, and the struggle for same-sex marriage*. New York, NY: Oxford University Press.

Kretzman, N. (1995). Lex iniust a non-est lex: Laws on trial in Aquinas' court of conscience. In J. Fienberg & H. Gross (Eds.), *Philosophy of Law* (5th ed.; pp. 7–13). Wadsworth.

Larsen, A. O. (2014). The trouble with amicus facts. *Virginia Law Review*, *100*(8), 1757–1818.

Lempert, R. (2013). Growing up in law and society: The pulls of policy and methods. *Annual Review of Law and Social Science*, *9*(1), 1–32. doi:10.1146/annurev-lawsocsci-102612-134032

Llewellyn, K. (1930). A realistic jurisprudence: The next step. *Columbia Law Review*, *30*(4), 431–465. doi:10.2307/1114548

Lochner v. New York, 198 U.S. 45 (1905).

Lynch, K. J. (2004). Best friends? Supreme Court law clerks on effective amicus curiae briefs. *The Journal of Law & Politics*, *20*(1), 33–75.

Meadow, T. (2013). Queer numbers: social science as cultural heterosexism. *Social (In) Queery Blog*. Retrieved from http://socialinqueery.com/2013/08/14/queer-numbers-social-science-as-cultural-heterosexism

Melton, G. (1990). Law, science, and humanity: The normative foundation of social science in law. *Law and Human Behavior*, *14*(4), 315–332. doi:10.1007/BF01068159

Mertz, E. (2000). Teaching lawyers the language of law: Legal and anthropological translations. *The John Marshall Law Review*, *34*, 91–117.

Mezey, S. G. (2007). *Queers in court: Gay rights law and public policy*. Lanham, MD: Rowman & Littlefield.

Mezey, S. G. (2009). *Gay families and the courts: The quest for equal rights*. Lanham, MD: Rowman & Littlefield.

Miranda v. Arizona, 384 U.S. 436 (1966).

Monahan, J., & Walker, L. (1986). Social authority: Obtaining, evaluating, and establishing social science in law. *University of Pennsylvania Law Review*, *134*(3), 477–517. doi:10.2307/3312111

Monahan, J., & Walker, L. (1988). Social-science research in law: A new paradigm. *The American Psychologist*, *43*(6), 465–472. doi:10.1037/0003-066X.43.6.465

Monahan, J., & Walker, L. (1991). Judicial use of social-science research. *Law and Human Behavior*, *15*(6), 571–584. doi:10.1007/BF01065853

Monahan, J., & Walker, L. (1994). *Social science in law: Cases and materials* (3rd ed.). St. Paul, MN: Foundation Press.

Monahan, J., & Walker, L. (2014). *Social science in law: Cases and materials* (8th ed.). St. Paul, MN: Foundation Press.

Montesquieu. (1748). *The spirit of the law* (A. M. Cohler, ed. & trans.). New York, NY: Cambridge University Press.

Moran, R. F. (2010). What counts as knowledge? A reflection on race, social science, and the law. *Law & Society Review*, *44*(3–4), 515–552. doi:10.1111/j.1540-5893.2010.00415.x

Muller v. Oregon, 208 U.S. 412 (1908).

Murphy, J. G., & Coleman, J. L. (1990). *Philosophy of law: An introduction to jurisprudence*. San Francisco, CA: Westview Press.

Nagin, D. S., & Pepper, J. U. (Eds.). (2012). Committee deterrence death penalty . Washington, DC: National Academy Press.

NeJaime, D. (2011). Winning through losing. *Iowa Law Review*, *96*, 941–1012.

Nelson, R. L., Berrey, E. C., & Nielsen, L. B. (2008). Divergent paths: Conflicting conceptions of employment discrimination in law and the social sciences. *Annual Review of Law and Social Science*, *4*(1), 103–122. doi:10.1146/annurev.lawsocsci.1.041604.115934

Obergefell v. Hodges, 135 S. Ct. 2584 (2015).

Perry v. Schwarzenegger, 704 F. Supp. 2d 921 (2010).

Pierceson, J. (2005). *Courts, liberalism, and rights: Gay law and politics in the United States and Canada*. Philadelphia, PA: Temple University Press.

Pierceson, J. (2013). *Same-sex marriage in the United States: The road to the Supreme Court*. Lanham, MD: Rowman & Littlefield.

Pound, R. (1908). Mechanical jurisprudence. *Columbia Law Review*, *8*(8), 609–610. doi:10.2307/1108954

Pound, R. (1912). The scope and purpose of sociological jurisprudence. *Harvard Law Review*, *25*(6), 489. doi:10.2307/1324775

Pound, R. (1921). Book review. *Harvard Law Review*, *35*, 774. doi:10.2307/1328923

Powell, B., Quadlin, N. Y., & Pizmony-Levy, O. (2015). Public opinion, the courts, and same-sex marriage: Four lessons learned. *Society Current*, *2*(1), 3–12. doi:10.1177/2329496514562964

Redding, R., & Reppucci, N. (1999). Effects of lawyers' socio-political attitudes on their judgments of social science in legal decision making. *Law and Human Behavior*, *23*(1), 31–54. doi:10.1023/A:1022322706533

Riesman, D. (1954 September 27). The lonely crowd. *TIME*. Retrieved from https://nationalhumanitiescenter.org/ows/seminars/tcentury/CharacterSociety.pdf

Rosaldo, R. (1994). Whose cultural studies? *American Anthropologist, 3*(3), 524–529. doi:10.1525/aa.1994.96.3.02a00040

Rose, N. (1999). *Powers of freedom: Reframing political thought*. Cambridge University Press. doi:10.1017/CBO9780511488856

Rosen, P. (1972). *The Supreme Court and social science*. Urbana, IL: University of Illinois Press.

Rosenberg, G. N. (2008). *The hollow hope: Can courts bring about social change* (2nd ed.). Chicago, IL: University Chicago Press. doi:10.7208/chicago/9780226726687.001.0001

Rublin, A. (2011). The role of social science in judicial decision making: How gay rights advocates can learn from integration and capital punishment case law. *Duke Journal of Gender Law & Policy, 19*, 179–222.

Sarat, A., & Silbey, S. (1988). The pull of the policy audience. *Law & Policy, 10*(2-3), 97–166. doi:10.1111/j.1467-9930.1988.tb00007.x

Segal, J. A., & Spaeth, H. J. (1993). *The Supreme Court and the attitudinal model*. New York, NY: Cambridge University Press.

Simon, J. (1999). Law after society. *Law & Social Inquiry, 24*(1), 143–194. doi:10.1111/j.1747-4469.1999.tb00795.x

Stacey, J. (2004). Marital suitors court social science spinsters: The unwittingly conservative effects of public sociology. *Social Problems, 51*(1), 131–145. doi:10.1525p.2004.51.1.131

Stambolis-Ruhstorfer, M. (2015). *The culture of knowledge: constructing "expertise" in legal debates on marriage and kinship for same-sex couples in France and the United States* (Doctoral dissertation). Retrieved from UCLA Electronic Theses and Dissertations: https://escholarship.org/content/qt2qs11675/qt2qs11675.pdf

Stryker, R. (1994). Rules, resources, and legitimacy processes: Some implications for social conflict, order, and change. *American Journal of Sociology, 99*(4), 847–910. doi:10.1086/230366

Tamanaha, B. Z. (2015). The third pillar of jurisprudence: Social legal theory. *William and Mary Law Review, 56*(6), 2235–2277.

U. S. v. Carolene Products, 304 U.S. 144, 153 n.4 (1938).

U.S. v. Windsor, 133 S. Ct. 2675 (2013).

Vidmar, N., & Schuller, R. (1989). Juries and expert evidence: Social framework testimony. *Law and Contemporary Problems*, *52*(4), 133–176. doi:10.2307/1191909

Walker, L., & Monahan, J. (1987). Social frameworks: A new use of social science in law. *Virginia Law Review*, *73*(3), 559–598. doi:10.2307/1072923

Wursten, A., & Sales, B. (1992). Use of psychologists and psychological research in legislative decision making on public interests matters. In D. K. Kagehiro & W. S. Laufer (Eds.), *Handbook of psychological law* (pp. 119–140). New York, NY: Springer-Verlag. doi:10.1007/978-1-4757-4038-7_7

Yngvesson, B., & Hennessey, P. (1975). Small claims, complex disputes. *Law and Society*, *9*(2), 219–274. doi:10.2307/3052976

Yoshino, K. (2015). *Speak Now: Marriage equality on trial: The story of Hollingsworth v. Perry*. New York, NY: Crown.

Zick, T. (2003). Constitutional empiricism: Quasi-neutral principles and constitutional truths. *North Carolina Law Review*, *82*, 115–221.

KEY TERMS AND DEFINITIONS

Adjudicative Fact: Facts that pertain to a case and use traditional rules of evidence.

Jurisprudence: Philosophy of law; how the legal process should proceed, or the science of the law.

Precedent: Adherence to what has been decided. Decisions are linked, and the law develops a quality of connectedness, which creates an appearance of stability. These are frequently cited on both sides of a case.

Social Authority: Social science research relevant to creating a rule of law as a source of authority rather than a fact; compares replicated research to legal precedent. Not specific to the facts of the case but intended to describe general principles that pertain to behavior.

Social Fact: Research results collected as factual evidence in a case. Not generalizable beyond the specific case and does not create new rules of law. Presented at the trial through expert testimony material to the case. The data collection method may set a precedent.

Social Framework: This is off-the-rack research used to help the trier of fact reach a conclusion on a point of law. The research may be a product that was originally conducted to answer a more basic social science question.

Social Jurisprudence: This philosophical approach to law stresses the actual social effects of legal institutions, doctrines, and practices.

ENDNOTES

1 Earl Warren was appointed by Republican President Dwight Eisenhower as the chief justice of the United States Supreme Court and served from 1953–1969.

2 These facts only apply to the parties before the court and are not used for some larger purpose, such as to argue that a law should be changed.

3 Social fact refers to research that was collected as factual evidence in a case. The results of the study do not generalize beyond the fact patterns of the case.

Section 2
Court Rulings and the Capacity for Change

Chapter 2
Framework for Social Change

ABSTRACT

Culture shifts relating to LGBT rights were originally addressed in a 1997 article written by Thomas Stoddard titled "Bleeding Heart: Reflections on Using the Law to Make Social Change." This chapter uses his framework for social change and examines how rule shifting and cultural shifts interact with the legalization of same-sex marriage.

INTRODUCTION

Culture refers to integrated patterns of human behavior that include the language, thoughts, actions, customs, beliefs, and institutions of racial, ethnic, social, or religious groups. Culture is the totality of learned, socially transmitted customs, knowledge, and behavior (Schaefer, 2006). The United States exists in a common culture that reflects the country's basic values, beliefs, and customs, also known as cultural universals. These practices may be universal but vary geographically, resulting in differing political, economic, and social conditions. These value variations have created regional concepts of what is culturally considered good, desirable, and proper, or bad, undesirable and improper. These variations suggest that life patterns differ regionally, creating a political culture reflective of these divides. Values influence our behaviors and serve as criteria for evaluating the actions of others. The values, norms, and sanctions of a culture are directly related and may change, but most remain relatively stable. When a change occurs, the entire fabric of norms and sanctions in a culture are impacted.

DOI: 10.4018/978-1-5225-7961-8.ch002

These turning points can produce cultural shifts and crisis. In "Bleeding Heart: Reflections on Using the Law to Make Social Change" ("Bleeding Heart"), a 1997 article by Thomas Stoddard, he offers a framework for social change—four factors necessary for a culture shift to occur. Using his model, this chapter examines elected officials' responses to the legalization of same-sex marriage. Hunter (1997) and Sobel (2015) added a fifth dimension of social change—public engagement, which explains the speed at which cultural transformation occurs (Guinier & Torres, 2012; Balkin & Siegel, 2006).

Same-sex marriage emerged as a contentious cultural and legal issue in the context of rapid changes in marriage and family structures in late 20th-century America. In the state of Vermont, same-sex couples successfully sued for the right to all the benefits and protections of legal marriage under state law. In a 1999 ruling, the Vermont Supreme Court found that the state was obliged to provide marriage benefits to same-sex couples under the Common Benefits Clause of the Vermont State Constitution (*Baker v. State*, 1999). The court gave the state legislature the option of rewriting state marriage law to include same-sex couples or setting up a parallel legal vehicle to provide the rights and benefits of marriage to these couples. The legislature chose the latter option and set up a variation where gay couples were granted the legal benefits of marriage through civil unions, stopping short of calling it marriage. Then, in 2003, the Massachusetts Supreme Court ruled that under the state's constitution, gay couples had the right to marry (*Goodridge v. Department of Public Health*, 2003) and began recognizing same-sex unions within six months of that decision. These breaches of formal norms rippled throughout the United States, where marriage between people of the same sex had been prohibited. Local government officials in several other jurisdictions around the country briefly issued marriage licenses to same-sex couples, until they were stopped by state courts or officials.

Using Stoddard's (1997) model for social change, this chapter provides an overview of the factors that influence social change. These interactions are examined through judicial decisions, public opinion, and media. The chapter concludes with a discussion on how, in many instances, change creates backlash that in turn encourages greater engagement by the advocates who play a role in continued cultural transformation.

THE FRAMEWORK FOR SOCIAL CHANGE

Social change is a significant alteration over time in behavior patterns and culture including norms and values (Moore, 1967). Frequently, efforts to promote change are met with resistance, especially during periods of rapid change brought on by scientific innovation or the outcomes of judicial decisions. This process of change occurs when circumstances require the sudden violation of long-standing cultural norms that can upset segments of the population. These changes are like earthquakes. They appear and unexpectedly rupture the fabric of society, leading to turmoil in the social order and in human states of mind.

While public support for gay marriage had risen dramatically in the wake of the U.S. Supreme Court decision in *Obergefell v. Hodges* (2015) legalizing same-sex marriage, many Americans remained passionately opposed, especially when viewed through the prisms of age, region, religion, and political party [1] (Pew Research Center, 2015).

Legislators and communities across the country responded with outrage, fearing life would never be the same. The decision overturned traditional doctrine embedded in American culture for centuries[2]. This doctrine carried different articulations and emphases over time: homosexuality as an abomination, marriage as the union between a man and a woman, and a concern for states' rights are but three. But when reduced to essentials, these articulations resulted in a basic belief that being gay was immoral. *Obergefell* constituted a formal, national rebuke of this notion and its full effects are still being played out in legislative bodies across the United States. Citizens fiercely opposed to same-sex marriage continue the fight, and Supreme Court Justice Samuel Alito amplified these concerns in his dissent:

To prevent five unelected Justices from imposing their personal vision of liberty upon the American people, the Court has held that "liberty" under the Due Process Clause should be understood to protect only those rights that are "'deeply rooted in this Nation's history and tradition.'" And it is beyond dispute that the right to same-sex marriage is not among those rights. In this country, no State permitted same-sex marriage until the Massachusetts Supreme Judicial Court held that limiting marriage to opposite-sex couples violated the State Constitution. Nor is the right to same-sex marriage deeply rooted in the traditions of other nations. No country allowed same-sex couples to marry until the Netherlands did so in 2000. What those arguing in favor of a constitutional right to same-sex marriage seek, therefore, is not the protection of a deeply rooted right but the recognition of a very new right, and they seek this innovation not from a legislative body elected by the people, but from unelected judges. Faced with such a request, judges have cause for both caution and humility. For today's majority, it does not matter that the right to same-sex marriage lacks deep roots or even that it is contrary to long-established tradition. The Justices in the majority claim the authority to confer constitutional protection upon that right simply because they believe that it is fundamental. (Obergefell v. Hodges, 2015)

Stoddard's (1997) formulation for social change distinguished between rulemaking and culture shifting. Attempts to reform the law may succeed as a formal matter but have only modest effects in the larger cultural context. In other words, social change and legal change do not always go hand-in-hand. Distinguishing between the two depends on "five general goals" of lawmaking and consists of the following:

(1) To create new rights and remedies for victims; (2) To alter the conduct of the government; (3) To alter the conduct of citizens and private entities; (4) To express a new moral ideal or standard; and (5) To change cultural attitudes and patterns. (Stoddard, 1997, pp. 972–973)

The goals expressed in items one through three are the traditional role of the law in expressing the formal rulemaking function for a society. The law sets, alters, and enforces those rules. These three factors alter the rules and, in their capacity, allow the law to produce a rule shift.

The Supreme Court decisions in *Brown v. Board of Education* (1954), *Baker v. Carr* (1968), and *Roe v. Wade* (1973), each of which transcended mere rulemaking and sought to improve the advancement of rights for those who had been badly mistreated by law and culture either individually or collectively, promoted a set of values some believed should be rights. This is the capacity of a law to produce a shift in culture (Stoddard, 1997). These are the lawmaking elements of goals four and five (Stoddard, 1997). If all four of the factors are not met, only a rule shift has occurred.

Profound Change

Using the elements of change listed below, including the addition of public engagement, this section examines how rule shifting and culture shifting interact through judicial decisions, public opinion, and the media.

(1) A change that is very broad or profound; (2) Public awareness of that change; (3) General sense of the legitimacy (or validity) of the change; and (4) Overall, continuous enforcement of the change. (Stoddard, 1997)

Each of these elements offers examples of their dynamic and interactive nature on the social and political processes, whereby particular relationships are established, reproduced, or transformed. The first factor requires profound change to occur, and marriage equality is one of the most infamous reforms of the 20th and 21st centuries. When the 1993 Hawaii Supreme Court decision declared marriage restricted to heterosexuals as discriminatory, a debate about the reasonableness of same-sex marriage moved to center stage. Although an immediate reaction to the court's ruling occurred in Hawaii (*Baehr v. Lewin,* 1993) and resulted in passing a law in the Hawaii legislature by 1998, which changed the definition of marriage to one man and one woman, the issue of same-sex marriage and what would happen if any state legalized it triggered a national debate.

This ruling became part of a larger public discussion of "marriage" and "family" that initiated the same-sex marriage movement.

The Full Faith and Credit Clause of the U.S. Constitution (Article IV, Section 1) requires states to recognize each other's legal proceedings. Because states feared they would be called upon to recognize same-sex marriages performed in other states, Congress responded to this concern by passing the Defense of Marriage Act of 1996 (DOMA). The act included three short clauses: the first gave title to the bill. The second specified that the power to define marriage was reserved for the states, and no state could be forced to accept another state's definition, and the third stipulated that, for federal benefits, marriage was to be defined as a union between one man and one woman (Public Law 104-199, 1996).

Public Awareness

The second factor required in a culture shift is public awareness. Citizens must be aware of the issue for it to have cultural resonance. In the years that followed the enactment of DOMA, many states passed their own DOMA-like statutes or constitutional amendments.

As of 2003, no state allowed same-sex marriage, and four had passed marriage amendments defining marriage as between one man and one woman. By 2013, 36 states had passed laws or constitutional amendments banning same-sex marriage, 14 states and the District of Columbia allowed it, and six others had legalized civil unions (Warbelow & Diaz, 2016). From 1996, when DOMA was passed by Congress and signed into law, to consideration of its repeal by the U.S. Senate and Supreme Court more than 15 years later, something changed in American society. In questioning the attorney representing Edith Windsor in the 2013 DOMA case, Chief Justice John Roberts asserted there had been a "sea change" since 1996, and he asked the attorney to account for the change. Of interest is the fact that neither the attorneys nor the other justices challenged his notion that a change had occurred.

Public Acceptance

Though public opinion on LGBT issues has shifted drastically, the third factor requires public acceptance. Despite the legalization of same-sex marriage, there are many people and areas of the country that remain highly resistant to this change.

In Texas, some officials chose to overwhelmingly disregard the marriage law by refusing to preside over same-sex weddings, no matter what the federal law (Smith, 2017). While the rule for marriage changed, the culture did not shift in many areas of the country. Many felt the law lacked legitimacy because it was not legalized through the federal legislative process but by a few states and then the judiciary. Supreme Court Justice Antonin Scalia contributes to this perspective by stating in his dissent:

. . . that the Court's decision effectively robs the people of "the freedom to govern themselves" noting that a rigorous debate on same-sex marriage had been taking place and that, by deciding the issue nationwide the democratic process had been unduly halted. (Obergefell v. Hodges, 2015)

In May 1996, a subcommittee of the Judiciary Committee of the U.S. House of Representatives held a hearing to consider H.R. 3396, the Defense of Marriage Act (DOMA). The committee took oral and written testimony and questioned the witnesses. Several weeks after the hearing the committee met and voted to endorse H.R. 3396 and sent it the whole House for consideration. Along with the bill, there was a 45-page report describing the need for the legislation, what happened in the hearing, the committee's votes, details of the kind of financial impact that could be expected by passing the bill, two opinions from the Attorney General's office that the bill was "constitutionally sustainable," and a statement from those dissenting (Committee on Judiciary Report No. 104-664, 1996).

The report contained four government interests identified as being advanced by H.R. 3396:

1. Defending and nurturing the institution of traditional heterosexual marriage.
2. Defending traditional notions of morality.
3. Protecting state sovereignty and democratic self-governance.
4. Preserving scarce government resources.

The second hearing on DOMA was the U.S. Senate Judiciary Committee in July 2011. The hearing, S.598—The Respect for Marriage Act: Assessing the Impact of DOMA on American Families, proposed striking down the act. (Tracy, 2016).

This hearing differed from the first in two important ways. The first hearing restricted testifiers to state-level legislators, organizational spokespersons, and legal experts. However, the 2011 hearing included three gay citizens who could speak about the impact of DOMA on their lives. What's more, witness opinion tilted further away from those favoring DOMA to including more testifying against it. In each hearing, the percentage of testifiers favoring the proposed bill was larger than those against it. In the 1996 hearing, 57% of testifiers favored the passage of DOMA, with 43% against it. In the 2011 hearing for the Respect for Marriage Act (to overturn DOMA), 36% favored retaining DOMA, and 64% favored its overturn (Tracy, 2016).

The Judiciary Committee voted to advance the bill to the Senate. In the end, the bill did not move forward to the full Senate because of concern it did not have enough support to stop debate and call for a vote. By December 2012, the U.S. Supreme Court had agreed to hear the case regarding DOMA's constitutionality. When the bill went to the Supreme Court for consideration,

212 members of Congress filed an amicus supporting the position that Section 3 of DOMA was unconstitutional (Tracy, 2016).

Consideration of DOMA, officially *U.S. v. Windsor* (2013) went to the U.S. Supreme Court as one of two same-sex marriage cases scheduled for oral arguments on consecutive days in 2013. The second case, *Hollingsworth v. Perry* (2013), referred to as the Proposition 8 case, concerned two issues:

1. Whether the petitioners, private California citizens rather than the state, had the standing to sue; and
2. Whether the Equal Protection Clause of the Fourteenth Amendment prohibited California from defining marriage, as Proposition 8 had, as one man and one woman.

The DOMA case, decided by a 5-4 vote of the court, held that each U.S. state has the power to define marriage and found DOMA "goes against legislative and historical precedent by undermining that authority" by denying legally married same-sex couples the federal rights of marriage." The court further held that "the purpose and effect of DOMA is to impose a 'disadvantage, a separate status, and so a stigma on same-sex couple in violation of the Fifth Amendment's guarantee of equal protection" (*U.S. v. Windsor*, 2013).

On June 26, 2013, the Supreme Court announced its two decisions. In the Proposition 8 case, the court declared that private California citizens did not have the right to appeal a case in the U.S. Supreme Court. This kind of action could be taken only by the state. The decision did not engage in the question of whether prohibiting same-sex marriage was unconstitutional and resulted in upholding the lower court ruling that declared Proposition 8 illegal. Gays and lesbians began to marry again (*Hollingsworth v. Perry,* 2013).

What was legal and what is moral is tightly bound. The binding has loosened considerably, but the two remain tethered in 21st-century America (Pew Forum, 2014).

Enforcement

The last of Stoddard's (1997) factors necessary for social change is enforcement. If rules are not enforced, members of the public will simply disregard them. Even though enforcement mechanisms for same-sex marriage are in place that would make the change genuine and universal, in 2015, legislators in Oklahoma and South Carolina introduced measures that required the firing of or a pay cut for government officials and employees recognizing the marriages of same-sex couples (Protect Thy Neighbor, 2016).

The court's decision brought a new brand of anti-same-sex marriage activism. Kentucky town clerk Kim Davis became the face of this movement (Blinder & Perez-Pena, 2015) when, rather than follow the order to issue marriage licenses to same-sex couples, she opted to spend five days in jail for contempt of court. At a press conference following her release, Davis was hailed as a hero. Flanked by her attorney and two Presidential candidates, former Arkansas Governor Mike Huckabee and Texas Senator Ted Cruz, Davis thanked the crowd for supporting her and promised to fight for religious freedom (Blinder & Perez-Pena, 2015).

Davis was not the only government official defying the *Obergefell* decision through civil disobedience. Others echoed her battle cry for religious freedom, as when Texas Attorney General Ken Paxton declared that "no court, no law, no rule, and no words will change the simple truth that marriage is the union of one man and one woman" (McLaughlin, 2015). He encouraged government officials to refuse to issue marriage licenses to same-sex couples and, although officials might be sued, the attorney general promised that his office would assist those religious objectors (McLaughlin, 2015).

Louisiana Republican Governor Bobby Jindal, who was a candidate for the 2016 presidential ticket, stated that the biblical definition of marriage comes from God and that "no earthly court can alter that" (Dann & Rafferty, 2016). He expressed concern that the court's decision was the beginning of an "assault against the religious freedom rights of Christians who disagree with this decision" (Dann & Rafferty, 2016).

Public Engagement

The fifth dimension of social change added by Hunter (1997) and expanded by Sobel (2015) requires that public engagement leading to cultural change requires more than passive support. They suggest there needs to be significant public engagement "beyond a small group of litigators or lobbyists" for a rule shift to create a culture change, as both legislation and litigation have the potential to mobilize and empower those seeking assistance or engagement in equality as a social result. If the constituency is not engaged, then legislative-made laws will not result in culture change. At the time of the *Obergefell* (2015) decision, only 12 states had passed legislation to legalize same-sex marriages compared to those eight states mandated by judicial decision (Wilson, 2014).

Torres and Guinier (2012) began writing about the relationship between social movements and legal change, using Stoddard's (1997) article to support the premise that there needs to be a correlative cultural shift to turn rule shifting into lawmaking. From this premise, they developed the concept of demosprudence, or the jurisprudence of social movements, wherein "social movement activism is as much a source of law as are statutes and judicial decisions" (Torres & Guinier, 2012). This social movement is a collectivity of multiple actors, of both organizations and individuals, which informally work to promote or resist social change in congruence with the movement's collective beliefs and values (Perez, 2003). In the issue of same-sex marriage, demosprudence builds on the concept of collaboration between elites such as judges, legislators, or lawyers and ordinary people (non-elites) to effect change (Guinier, 2009). This participation of non-elites in the democratic process is necessary for genuine culture shift to occur (Torres, 2006, 2007). Guinier (2009) adds that this participation provides courts with a new source of democratic authority if it engages "the people" in lawmaking. Both envision demosprudence as achieving its goal by engaging individuals "to consider, critique, and even take action in response to decisions with which they disagree" (Rosenberg, 2009).

Post and Siegel's (2007) work on democratic constitutionalism is based on the idea that the Constitution's legitimacy depends on its ability to inspire Americans to recognize it as their Constitution and to mobilize citizens in enforcing, guiding, and legitimizing judicial decision making. It recognizes the essential role of the judiciary to interpret the Constitution, inspiring public engagement by individuals who feel a judicial decision does not represent their views. Beginning in the 1970s and with increasing frequency in the 1980s and 1990s, gay rights organizations began to bring grievances to state and federal courts, sometimes succeeding and sometimes failing. Daniel Pinello (2003) found the greater the ethnic, gender, and age diversity of the bench, the more likely a court made a favorable decision regarding gays and lesbians. In addition, those state courts that heard the largest number of gay rights cases made the largest number of favorable decisions. During the civil rights era of the 1960s and 1970s, it was generally thought social change would be facilitated by fighting cases in federal courts rather than in 50 different state courts. The strategy was altered as the makeup of those courts became more conservative.

Once courts intervene in favor of a social movement, Balkin (2005) stresses their responsiveness to broader cultural and political changes, arguing that "when social movement contestation succeeds in delegitimating a practice sufficiently, it also usually succeeds in getting courts to ratify that conclusion through their interpretations of the Constitution" (p. 70). As in the case of same-sex marriage litigation, where advocates chose states in which elites supported LGBT rights, public opinion trended toward favorable relationship recognition, and the state constitution was difficult to amend (Bonauto, 2005). It is no accident that LGBT rights advocates first asserted claims to marriage equality in state courts. As the federal judiciary became more conservative and hostile, and seeing the Supreme Court as an especially dangerous venue, they sought more hospitable courts (NeJaime, 2012). Of course, they did not bring claims in all states. They selected venues not only with potentially supportive judges and doctrine but also favorable conditions outside the courts (NeJaime, 2012).

Furthermore, according to Balkin and Siegel (2006), movements are important because they dare to disturb the legal order by continuously inferring law and civil society's institutions with differing constitutional meanings. The connection between the law and social movements makes legal change legitimate, effective, and enforceable. Individuals often make claims on the Constitution by organizing into social movements that construct, develop, and disseminate constitutional visions. These social movements are vital participants in our protestant constitutional culture (Balkin, 2005, p. 71). If successful, movements influence public opinion in their favor, changing the culture with which constitutional law interacts. At the same time, movements convince political parties to support their views, and those parties may in turn appoint judges with similar outlooks (Balkin, 2005).

Decisions of state supreme courts extending marriage rights to gays and lesbians accounted for same-sex marriage's "ascent from nowhere to near the top of the national political agenda" (Pierceson, 2013). But litigation regarding these marriage cases was not occurring alone. Gay rights groups were working simultaneously to change society on many other fronts—in news coverage and media portrayals, through changing workplace policies, and by encouraging individual gays and lesbians to speak up. State courts were being fueled by the actions of the larger society and were in turn promoting further change.

The new constitutional meaning becomes authoritative not because a court decided so independently but because social movements have persuaded political forces, opinion leaders, the public, and judges that a new position is reasonable and, in fact, correct. In this way, constitutional change is a bottom-up process in which courts are not leading but instead responding to external changes (Balkin, 2007 p. 246). While courts ultimately respond to new constitutional meanings asserted by social movement actors, they also shape those meanings going forward and influence the direction of political contestation. Justice Anthony Kennedy authored the majority opinion in *Obergefell*, tracing the history of marriage that highlighted the engagement efforts of the LGBT community with the court acknowledging those struggles:

From their beginning to their most recent page, the annals of human history reveal the transcendent importance of marriage. The lifelong union of a man and a woman always has promised nobility and dignity to all persons, without regard to their station in life. Marriage is sacred to those who live by their religions and offers unique fulfillment to those who find meaning in the secular realm. Its dynamic allows two people to find a life that could not be found alone, for a marriage becomes greater than just the two persons. Rising from the most basic human needs, marriage is essential to our most profound hopes and aspirations. The centrality of marriage to the human condition makes it unsurprising that the institution has existed for millennia and across civilizations. Since the dawn of history, marriage has transformed strangers into relatives, binding families and societies together. Confucius taught that marriage lies at the foundation of government.

There are untold references to the beauty of marriage in religious and philosophical texts spanning time, cultures, and faiths, as well as in art and literature in all their forms. It is fair and necessary to say these references were based on the understanding that marriage is a union between two persons of the opposite sex. That history is the beginning of these cases.

The respondents say it should be the end as well. To them, it would demean a timeless institution if the concept and lawful status of marriage were extended to two persons of the same sex. Marriage, in their view, is by its nature a gender-differentiated union of man and woman. This view long has been held—and continues to be held—in good faith by reasonable and sincere people here and throughout the world. The petitioners acknowledge this history but contend that these cases cannot end there. Were their intent to demean the revered idea and reality of marriage, the petitioners' claims would be of a different order. But that is neither their purpose nor their submission. To the contrary, it is the enduring importance of marriage that underlies the petitioners' contentions. This, they say, is their whole point. Far from seeking to devalue marriage, the petitioners seek it for themselves because of their respect—and need—for its privileges and responsibilities.

And their immutable nature dictates that same-sex marriage is their only real path to this profound commitment. The ancient origins of marriage confirm its centrality, but it has not stood in isolation from developments in law and society. The history of marriage is one of both continuity and change. That institution—even as confined to opposite-sex relations—has evolved over time. For example, marriage was once viewed as an arrangement by the couple's parents based on political, religious, and financial concerns; but by the time of the Nation's founding it was understood to be a voluntary contract between a man and a woman. As the role and status of women changed, the institution further evolved. Under the centuries-old doctrine of coverture, a married man and woman were treated by the State as a single, male-dominated legal entity.

As women gained legal, political, and property rights, and as society began to understand that women have their own equal dignity, the law of coverture was abandoned. These and other developments in the institution of marriage over the past centuries were not mere superficial changes. Rather, they worked deep transformations in its structure, affecting aspects of marriage long viewed by many as essential.

These new insights have strengthened, not weakened, the institution of marriage. Indeed, changed understandings of marriage are characteristic of a Nation where new dimensions of freedom become apparent to new generations, often through perspectives that begin in pleas or protests and then are considered in the political sphere and the judicial process. This dynamic can be seen in the Nation's experiences with the rights of gays and lesbians.

Until the mid-20th century, same-sex intimacy long had been condemned as immoral by the state itself in most Western nations, a belief often embodied in the criminal law. For this reason, among others, many persons did not deem homosexuals to have dignity in their own distinct identity. A truthful declaration by same-sex couples of what was in their hearts had to remain unspoken. Even when a greater awareness of the humanity and integrity of homosexual persons came in the period after World War II, the argument that gays and lesbians had a just claim to dignity conflicted with both law and widespread social conventions. Same-sex intimacy remained a crime in many States.

Gays and lesbians were prohibited from most government employment, barred from military service, excluded under immigration laws, targeted by police, and burdened in their rights to associate. For much of the 20th century, moreover, homosexuality was treated as an illness. When the American Psychiatric Association published the first Diagnostic and Statistical Manual of Mental Disorders in 1952, homosexuality was classified as a mental disorder, a position adhered to until 1973. Only in more recent years have psychiatrists and others recognized that sexual orientation is both a normal expression of human sexuality and immutable.

In the late 20th century, following substantial cultural and political developments, same-sex couples began to lead more open and public lives and to establish families. This development was followed by a quite extensive discussion of the issue in both governmental and private sectors and by a shift in public attitudes toward greater tolerance. As a result, questions about the rights of gays and lesbians soon reached the courts, where the issue could be discussed in the formal discourse of the law.

This Court first considered the legal status of homosexuals in Bowers v. Hardwick, (1986). There it upheld the constitutionality of a Georgia law deemed to criminalize certain homosexual acts. Ten years later, in Romer v. Evans, (1996), the Court invalidated an amendment to Colorado's Constitution that sought to foreclose any branch or political subdivision of the State from protecting persons against discrimination based on sexual orientation. Then, in 2003, the Court over ruled Bowers, holding that laws making same-sex intimacy a crime "demean the lives of homosexual persons." Lawrence v. Texas.

Against this background, the legal question of same-sex marriage arose. In 1993, the Hawaii Supreme Court held Hawaii's law restricting marriage to opposite-sex couples constituted a classification based on sex and was therefore subject to strict scrutiny under the Hawaii Constitution. Baehr v. Lewin. Although this decision did not mandate that same-sex marriage be allowed, some States were concerned by its implications and reaffirmed in their laws that marriage is defined as a union between opposite-sex partners.

So too in 1996, Congress passed the Defense of Marriage Act (DOMA), 110 Stat. 2419, defining marriage for all federal law purposes as "only a legal union between one man and one woman as husband and wife." 1 U. S. C. §7. The new and widespread discussion of the subject led other States to a different conclusion. In 2003, the Supreme Judicial Court of Massachusetts held the State's Constitution guaranteed same-sex couples the right to marry. After that ruling, some additional States granted marriage rights to same sex couples, either through judicial or legislative processes.

Two Terms ago, in United States v. Windsor, (2013), this Court invalidated DOMA to the extent it barred the Federal Government from treating same-sex marriages as valid even when they were lawful in the State where they were licensed. DOMA, the Court held, impermissibly disparaged those same-sex couples "who wanted to affirm their commitment to one another before their children, their family, their friends, and their community."

Numerous cases about same-sex marriage have reached the United States Courts of Appeals in recent years. In accordance with the judicial duty to base their decisions on principled reasons and neutral discussions, without scornful or disparaging commentary, courts have written a substantial body of law considering all sides of these issues. That case law helps to explain and formulate the underlying principles this Court now must consider. (Obergefell v. Hodges, 2015)

Important decisions become part of the narrative that social-movement actors, among others, use to explain legitimate social change, repudiate past injustices, and justify calls for further development. Social movements may seize on canonical cases to articulate demands in the present day. Part of our constitutional narrative requires disclaiming how certain decisions were never true to the spirit of the Constitution and attests to the vital role that courts—and their rulings—play in the process of social change.

When "Bleeding Heart" was written, few people participated in organized or individual political mobilization with regard to LGBT issues (Vaid, 1996). However, LGBT organizations experienced organizational growth beginning in the early 1990s (D'Emilio, 2002). Most LGBT-related organizing in the 1980s and into the 1990s was linked to HIV/AIDs advocacy, and there were fledgling mobilization efforts from state organizations (Clendineu & Nagourney, 1999). Therefore, it is not surprising that Stoddard (1997) did not include public engagement as a key component in social change. Community activism related to attempts to attain LGBT rights through local, state, and federal legislation, and the fight against anti-LGBT ballot initiatives in conjunction with varied litigation efforts, has led to the rule shifts achieved thus far. These would not have occurred as quickly—or with the same level of culture shifting—without the active engagement of the public or the efforts of social movements.

This section incorporated a vision of public engagement as a critical component to the social change that has occurred in throughout country since Stoddard's article, with some areas embracing change more readily than others.

BACKLASH TO CHANGE

Long before the court announced its decision in *Obergefell*, opponents of same-sex marriage galvanized political support and successfully lobbied legislators to minimize or block the aftershock of an anticipated decision favoring same-sex marriage rights. These legislative responses took various forms. At the state level, state religious freedom restoration acts (RFRAs) took center stage (Griffin, 2016). Although many states had existing RFRA statutes, other states adopted laws far more protective of religious freedom than the federal RFRA. Other legislative efforts included state laws blocking local efforts to pass nondiscrimination ordinances that extended protections to the LGBT community.

According to the judicial backlash theory, courts striking down popular legislation to vindicate minority rights were not only ineffective but counterproductive. Judicial decisions "shutting down" politics (Rosenberg, 2008) could frustrate democratic majorities in ways that would produce more virulent politics than might have resulted if judges refused to intervene. In one of the dissenting opinions in *Obergefell*, Chief Justice Roberts pointed out "there will be consequences to shutting down the political process on an issue of such profound public significance."

In 2005 Professor Michael Klarman compared the response to *Goodridge*, the Massachusetts marriage decision, to the massive resistance to *Brown v. Board of Education* (1954). He asserted that "Court rulings such as *Brown* and *Goodridge* produce political backlashes for three principal reasons: They raise the salience of an issue, they incite anger over 'outside interference' or 'judicial activism,' and they alter the order in which social change would otherwise have occurred."

Klarman (2005) further argued that courts are poor vehicles for social change: "Judicially mandated social reform may mobilize greater resistance than change accomplished through legislatures or with the acquiescence of other democratically operated institutions." Loss through litigation especially enrages citizens accustomed to self-government: "Because [*Goodridge*] was a court decision, rather than a reform adopted by voters or popularly elected legislators, critics were able to deride it as the handiwork of arrogant 'activist judges' defying the will of the people" (Bumiller, 2004).

Obergefell grew out of innumerable court and legislative decisions, as appendices to the court's own opinion emphasized, with many of these decisions growing out of the Supreme Court's earlier decisions. The court's decision in *Obergefell* was possible not simply because public opinion changed, but also because the struggle in the courts helped change public opinion and forge new constitutional understandings.

Public support for gay marriage has risen dramatically over the last decade, but many Americans remain passionately opposed. And a plurality of citizens fiercely committed to views will make itself heard in ways a majority diffusely committed to views may not. For this reason, Americans opposed to same-sex marriage have mobilized to continue their fight, seeking control over the courts in campaigns for the presidency (Reilly, 2015; Tashman, 2016; Bomboy, 2016) and carrying their objections forward under the banner of conscience and religious liberty (NeJaime & Siegel, 2015). Just as *Brown* did not end the debate over racial segregation, *Obergefell* has not ended the debate over marriage but has instead channeled it into new forms.

Proponents of same-sex marriage persisted in the face of loss, and so too will its opponents. In what follows, I look back at backlash to same-sex marriage with attention to the ways in which the fight over the courts—and other sites of government decision making—was constructive, and not merely destructive, as backlash theory suggests. As conflict over same-sex marriage raged, citizens engaged in the struggle to influence government decision makers helped create new constitutional meanings—and in the process forged new relationships.

The first decisions recognizing same-sex marriage sparked conflict that in the short run produced immense setbacks. Judges who sought to impose new understandings of constitutional law saw their judgments quickly reversed. Yet it was precisely by amplifying the claims of despised minorities in the legislative process that courts changed the shape of the conflict over marriage and infused it with new meaning. Opponents in other jurisdictions mobilized to enact bans on same-sex marriage because they understood that court decisions recognizing the claim had imbued it with an increasing legitimacy. The countermobilization we call "backlash" was a response to the claim's growing authority (Cover, 1983).

Through these decisions, state courts began a conversation with the American people. Similarly, Alexander Bickel (1978) stated:

Virtually all-important decisions of the Supreme Court are the beginnings of conversations between the Court and the people and their representatives. . . . To say that the Supreme Court lays down the law of the land is to state the ultimate result, following upon a complex series of events, in some cases, and in others it is a form of speech only. The effectiveness of the judgment universalized depends on consent and administration.

The fight over marriage forged new meanings and altered relationships within movements, between movements, and in the public at large. Of course, the conflicts referred to as backlash are by no means caused by courts alone. Backlash arcs across the decades because there are natural incentives in democratic politics to appeal to those aggrieved by change, whether change transpires by judicial decision or the efforts of a local government. Backlash is best understood not as the repression of democratic politics but as one of its expressions. Backlash escalates as movements, parties, and officials embrace the cause of those who resent change in the hopes of winning their support (Siegel, 2017).

Backlash may involve courts, but it can also spread without courts. Conflict over abortion began before the Supreme Court ruled in *Roe*. It escalated as Republicans used the abortion issue to recruit conservative Democrats to join their party, a project that began before *Roe* and played out throughout the 1980s and 1990s (Greenhouse & Sigel, 2011).

The more the argument over marriage turned into a referendum on the equal status of gays in the community, the more the LGBT movement invested in the question. A movement that once understood itself as seeking sexual freedom came to understand itself through the institution of the family (Schacter, 2009).

As advocates attempted to persuade decision makers accountable to wider publics, each side was obliged to answer arguments of the other. In vying to persuade judges and the body politic, each side incorporated elements of the other's views. LGBT advocates responded to conservative arguments by espousing fidelity to family values, while defenders of traditional marriage responded to liberal arguments by espousing commitments to equality. These observations suggest some of the pathways through which even bitterly contested judicial decisions can shape conflict, even as the decisions provoke backlash and countermobilization. Judges could not resolve the debate over marriage, but the prospect of judicial intervention disciplined the argument.

Objections to same-sex marriage evolved in form, from gay-denigrating to gay-respecting modes of constitutional argument. In the 1980s and 1990s, it was commonplace to oppose same-sex marriage by depicting it as deviant and immoral. But in the aftermath of the Supreme Court decisions in *Romer* and *Lawrence*, which accorded gays rudimentary protections against discrimination, objections to same-sex marriage voiced in public settings began to shift into a gay-respecting mode.

In the 2000s, litigants and judges began to justify restricting marriage to different-sex couples in terms focused on the needs and vulnerabilities of heterosexuals. Heterosexual couples needed incentives to marry (the so-called "accidental procreation" argument, [Abrams & Brooks, 2009]), and children needed different-sex parents to model gender roles for them (the "dual gender" marriage argument, [Widiss, Rosenblatt & NeJaime, 2007]). Conservative opponents of same-sex marriage objected to being cast as "bigots" and asserted the importance of preserving traditional marriage to protect "religious liberty" (NeJaime & Siegel, 2015).

Publicly expressed opposition to same-sex marriage came to focus increasingly on a (gay-respecting) claim about the proper role of courts: There might in fact be a case for recognizing same-sex marriage, opponents argued, but in a constitutional democracy, that question is for determination by legislatures not courts.

FUTURE RESEARCH DIRECTIONS

Evolving objections to same-sex marriage signaled rising respect for gays among citizens, judges, and, possibly, opponents of same-sex marriage themselves. These changes in the grounds of constitutional argument illustrate how constitutional conflict can foster relationships, even among adversaries who fiercely disagree about the meaning of the constitutional norms to which they share fealty. An understanding of social change requires an analyst to look across time—paying attention to multiple instances across time. With attention to the understandings that guide participants in social conflicts, we can appreciate the ways in which struggles over the law are the locus of significant social differences, especially when conflict takes place over a longer timeframe. The issue of same-sex marriage is far from over, and continued research on how this modern-day social controversy continues to unfold will generate novel insights on social change.

CONCLUSION

The discussion in this chapter applied Stoddard's (1997) social change model to the issue of same-sex marriage. These interactions were examined through judicial decisions, public opinion, and media.

The social change that had seemed improbable decades earlier for the LGBT community was now the law of the land. With *Obergefell*, the public meaning of being gay was officially transformed from that of outlaws and outcasts to a legitimate category of U.S. citizen. During the two and a half hours of oral argument the label "homosexual" was never used.

Between 2003 and 2013 American society changed. In courts and legislative hearings as well as in the larger society, the public discourse around gays and lesbians was transformed. If we conceptualize change as a matter of changing hearts and minds, then social change in this instance would be categorized as how someone now talks about a person who is gay. Previously, courts, legislative hearings, and a larger society treated homosexuality as a matter of conduct, a "lifestyle" choice criticized for its immorality. Talking about sexual orientation as a matter of conduct has not disappeared entirely, but this discourse has lost ground. By 2013 treating sexual orientation as a matter of conduct had become morally problematic. Those who used this type of discourse were increasingly perceived as bigots. Public talk about gay marriage became talk about a person, an American citizen entitled to rights granted to other citizens.

For many, the legalization of marriage for same-sex couples was a desirable social change, a journey towards greater equality. Public engagement is a critical component to change, and this chapter incorporated it as a fifth factor to explain the rapidity of the cultural shift that occurred in various parts of the country since Stoddard's article regarding LGBT rights.

But with any change there are consequences. The chapter concluded with a discussion as to how change in many instances creates conflict that results in backlash. Consider how the backlash claims of progressives and conservatives diverged as the debate over marriage evolved. Over time, progressives shifted from whether a court should intervene on behalf of minority rights to claims about when and how they should intervene.

By contrast, conservatives have invoked backlash as a reason for courts to stay out of the marriage debate and leave its resolution to the political process. These various strands of backlash discourse are often tangled together. In Chief Justice Roberts' dissent in *Obergefell*, he cited Justice Ginsburg and the abortion debate as a reason why that the majority was wrong to recognize the constitutional rights of same-sex couples. These claims by both sides are a paradox-forming argument directed at the exercise of judicial power. Talk of backlash is just another legal argument that clarifies our understanding of judicial review.

REFERENCES

Abrams, K., & Brooks, P. (2009). Marriage as a message: Same-sex couples and the rhetoric of accidental procreation. *Yale Law Journal and Humanities*, *21*(1), 1–37.

Baehr v. Lewin, 74 Haw. 530 (1993).

Baker v. Carr, 369 U.S. 186 (1962).

Baker v. State, 170 Vt. 194 (1999).

Balkin, J. M. (2005). How social movements change (or fail to change) the Constitution: The case of the new departure. *Suffolk University Law Review*, *39*(27), 27–65.

Balkin, J. M. (2007). Original meaning and constitutional redemption. *University of Minnesota Law School*, *24*, 427–532.

Balkin, J. M., & Siegel, R. B. (2006). Principles, practices, and social movements. *University of Pennsylvania Law Review*, *154*(4), 927–950. doi:10.2307/40041288

Bickel, A. (1978). *The supreme court and the idea of progress*. New Haven, CT: Yale University Press.

Blinder, A., & Perez-Pena, R. (2015, September 1). Kentucky clerk denies same-sex marriage licenses, defying court. *New York Times*. Retrieved from https://www.nytimes.com/2015/09/02/us/same-sex-marriage-kentucky-kim-davis.html

Blinder, A., & Perez-Pena, R. (2015 September 8). Kim Davis, released from Kentucky jail, won't say if she will keep defying court. *New York Times*. Retrieved from https://www.nytimes.com/2015/09/09/us/kim-davis-same-sex-marriage.html

Bombay, S. (2015, December 16). The Supreme Court as a 2016 campaign issue. *Philly.com*.

Bonuato, M. L. (2005). Goodridge in context. *Harvard Civil Rights-Civil Liberties Law Review*, *40*(1), 1–69.

Brown v. Board of Education of Topeka, 347 U.S. 483 (1954).

Bumiller, E. (2004 February 25). Bush backs ban in constitution on gay marriage. *New York Times*. Retrieved from https://www.nytimes.com/2004/02/25/us/same-sex-marriage-the-president-bush-backs-ban-in-constitution-on-gay-marriage.html

Clendineu, D., & Nagourney, A. (1999). *Out for good: The struggle to build a gay rights movement in America*. Simon & Schuster.

Cover, R. M. (1983). The Supreme Court 1982 term—foreword: Nomos and narrative. *Harvard Law Review*, *97*(4), 4–69.

D'Emilio, J. (2002). *The world turned: Essays on gay history, politics and culture*. Durham, NC: Duke University Press. doi:10.1215/9780822383925

Dann, C., & Rafferty, A. (2016). Candidates react to Supreme Court's gay marriage ruling. *NBC News*. Retrieved from https://www.nbcnews.com/politics/2016-election/2016-candidates-react-supreme-courts-gay-marriage-ruling-n382441

Defense of Marriage Act Public Law 104-199, (1996).

Defense of Marriage Act Public of 1996: Hearing on H.R. 3396 Before the H. Comm. On the Judiciary, 104th Cong. (1996).

Goodridge v. Department of Public Health, 440 Mass. 309, 798 N.E. 2d 941 (2003).

Greenhouse, L., & Siegel, R. B. (2011). Before (and after) Roe v. Wade: New questions about backlash. *The Yale Law Journal*, *120*, 2028–2074.

Griffin, J. (2016, July 13). *State public accommodation laws.* National Conference of State Legislators. Retrieved from http://www.ncsl.org/research/civil-and-criminal-justice/state-public-accommodation-laws.aspx

Guinier, L. (2009). Courting the people: Demosprudence and the law/politics divide. *Baylor University Law Review, 89*, 539–561.

Hollingsworth v. Perry, 133 S. Ct. 2652 (2013).

Hunter, N. D. (1997). Lawyering for social justice. *New York University Law Review, 72*(5), 1009–1022.

Klarmen, M. (2005). Brown and Lawrence (and Goodridge*). Michigan Law Review, 104*(3), 431–490.

McLaughlin, E. C. (2015, June 30), Most states to abide by Supreme Court's same-sex marriage ruling, but. ... *CNN.* Retrieved from https://www.cnn.com/2015/06/29/us/same-sex-marriage-state-by-state/index.html

Moore, W. (1967). *Order and change: Essays in comparative sociology.* New York, NY: John Wiley & Sons.

NeJaime, D. (2012). The legal mobilization dilemma. *Emory Law Review, 61*, 663–737.

Obergefell v. Hodges, 135 S. Ct. 2584 (2015).

Perez, M. (2003). *Nationalizing same-sex marriage: Assessing the effect of Baehr v. Lewin on the Federal Defense of Marriage Act.* Colorado State University.

Pew Forum. (2014, September 22). *Public sees religion influence waning.* Retrieved from Pew Forum.

Pew Research Center. (2015). *Support for same-sex marriage.* Retrieved from http://www.people-press.org/files/2015/06/6-8-15-Same-sex-marriagerelease1.pdf

Pierceson, J. (2013). *Same-sex marriage in the United States: The road to the Supreme Court.* Lanham, MD: Rowan & Littlefield.

Pinello, D. R. (2003). *Gay rights and American law.* New York, NY: Cambridge University Press.

Post, R., & Siegel, R. (2007). Roe rage: Democratic constitutionalism and backlash. *Harvard Civil Rights-Civil Liberties Law Review*, *42*, 373–434.

Protect Thy Neighbor. (2016). *State legislative bill tracker*. Retrieved from http://www.protectthyneighbor.org/state-legislation-2016

Reilly, R. J. (2015, December 15). Marco Rubio suggests his Supreme Court would roll back marriage equality. *Huffington Post*.

Roe v. Wade, 410 U.S. 113 (1973).

Rosenberg, G. (2008). *The hollow hope: Can courts bring about social change?* (2nd ed.). Chicago, IL: University of Chicago Press. doi:10.7208/chicago/9780226726687.001.0001

Rosenberg, G. N. (2009). Romancing the court. *Baylor University Law Review*, *89*, 563–579.

Schacter, J. S. (2009). The other same-sex marriage debate. *Chicago-Kent Law Review*, *84*(2), 379–402.

Schaefer, R. T. (2006). *Sociology: A brief introduction* (6th ed.). Boston, MA: McGraw-Hill.

Siegel, R. B. (2017). Community in conflict: Same-sex marriage and backlash. *UCLA Law Review. University of California, Los Angeles, School of Law*, *64*, 1728–1769.

Smith, J. B. (2017, June 24). No courthouse weddings in Waco for same-sex couples 2 years after Supreme Court ruling. *Waco Tribune-Herald*. Retrieved from http://www.wacotrib.com/news/courts_and_trials/no-courthouse-weddings-in-waco-for-same-sex-couples-years/article_20244def-13f3-579f-a0d9-004618c56afb.html

Sobel, S. L. (2015). Culture shifting at warp speed: How the law, public engagement, and Will & Grace led to social change for LGBT people. *St. John's Law Review*, *89*(1), 143–194.

Stoddard, T. (1997). Bleeding heart: Reflections on using the law to make social change. *New York University Law Review*, *72*(5), 967–991.

Tashman, B. (2016 February 18). Donald Trump: Trust me to overturn the shocking gay marriage decision. *Right Wing Watch*. Retrieved from http://www.rightwingwatch.org/post/donald-trump-trust-me-to-overturn-the-shocking-gay-marriage-decision/

Torres, G. (2006). Some observations on the role of social change on the courts. *Drake Law Review*, *54*, 895–896.

Torres, G. (2007). Legal change. *Cleveland Law Review*, *55*, 137–138.

Torres, G., & Guinier, L. (2012). The constitutional imaginary: Just stories about we the people. *Maryland Law Review (Baltimore, Md.)*, *71*(4), 1052–1072.

Tracy, K. (2016). *Discourse, identity, and social change in the marriage equality debates. Oxford Studies in Language and Law*. Oxford University Press.

United States v. Windsor, 570 U. S. (2013) (ALITO, J., dissenting)

U.S. v. Windsor, 133 S. Ct. 2675 (2013).

Vaid, U. (1996). *Virtual equality: The mainstreaming of gay and lesbian liberation*. New York, NY: Doubleday.

Warbelow, S., & Diaz, B. (2016). *State equality index*. Washington, DC: Human Rights Campaign Foundation.

Washington v. Glucksberg, 521 U. S. 701, 720–721 (1997).

Widiss, D. A., & Rosenblatt, E. L. & NeJaime, D. (2007). Exposing sex stereotypes in recent same-sex marriage jurisprudence. *Harvard Journal of Law and Gender*, *30*, 461–492.

Wilson, R. F. (2014). Marriage of necessity: Same-sex marriage and religious liberty protections. *Case Western Reserve Law Review*, *64*(3), 1161–1268.

KEY TERMS AND DEFINITIONS

Amicus Brief: Literally, "friend of the court" (plural amici curiae); not a party to a case, who may or may not have been solicited by a party and who assists a court by offering information, expertise, or insight that has a bearing on the issues.

Backlash Theory: Denotes reactions to social or political change.

Social Change: The alteration of institutions, behaviors, or relations in a society.

Values: Collective conceptions of what is considered good, bad, or improper in a culture.

ENDNOTES

1 Fewer than two months before the *Obergefell* decision, a national opinion poll by the Pew Research Center (2015) found that 70 percent of white evangelical Protestants opposed allowing gays and lesbians to marry legally, with 43 percent describing their opposition as strong.

2 In the same opinion poll, 63 percent of Republicans and 54 percent of persons residing in the South-Central United States (Alabama, Arkansas, Kentucky, Louisiana, Mississippi, Oklahoma, Tennessee, and Texas) expressed opposition to marriage rights for gays and lesbians (Pew Research Center, 2015).

Chapter 3
Religious Liberty

ABSTRACT

This chapter places U.S. religious liberty principles in historical context. The 1960s to present day are examined, providing a provocative analysis of religious liberty cases and the ongoing role courts play in this debate, coupled with the legalization of same-sex marriage. A legal analysis is provided for Supreme Court cases.

INTRODUCTION

The role of religion in a free society, once a subject of benign and lofty discourse, has become a raging controversy in both the private and public realms. While few Americans challenge the multiple benefits of religion to the individual believer and to society, there are sharply divergent views as to the extent to which the idea of religious liberty immunizes religiously based conduct from sanction when it interferes with health, safety, and welfare, or the provision of goods and services.

Often with the assistance of legislatures and courts, religious entities have adopted a presumptive constitutional right to avoid the law pursuant to federal and state free exercise of religion guarantees, arguing that the First Amendment[1], the Due Process Clause[2], and separation of powers[3] render them immune from some legal requirements and precepts. Opponents have argued that this approach is at odds with American culture and with legal tradition.

DOI: 10.4018/978-1-5225-7961-8.ch003

On June 26, 2015, the U.S. Supreme Court issued a historic decision that extended the constitutionally protected fundamental right to marry to same-sex couples (*Obergefell v. Hodges*, 2015). The decision was a culmination of at least a four-decade-long legal war, but it hardly ended the accompanying legal and political battles. Those battles had started well before *Obergefell*, as states and sometimes municipalities enacted same-sex marriage per se[4] or some sort of marriage-like recognition of same-sex couples such as "reciprocal beneficiaries" or "civil unions." Opposition has come from state and local officials refusing to issue marriage licenses, perform weddings, issue documents listing same-sex spouses, etc. (Wetzstein, 2015) and from private businesses providing public accommodations such as wedding venues, photographers, and florists.

The court's decision triggered a new brand of anti-same-sex marriage activism. Opponents of same-sex marriage galvanized political support and successfully lobbied legislators to minimize or block the aftershock of an anticipated decision favoring same-sex marriage rights. These legislative responses took various forms. At the state level, state religious freedom restoration acts (RFRAs) took center stage (National Conference of State Legislatures, 2015). Although many states had existing RFRA statutes, other states adopted laws far more protective of religious freedom than the federal RFRA.

The backlash to the *Obergefell* decision is underway. Having lost in the courts, the opponents of same-sex marriage have altered their battle cry. Invoking religious freedom rather than defending their right to discriminate, they now claim to be the victims of discrimination. This chapter focuses on the tension between those advocating for LGBT-inclusive laws and those seeking protection from what they characterize as religious discrimination under state mini-RFRAs to resist the trend toward LGBT equal rights. It provides an analysis of key Supreme Court cases and examines how those cases intersect with marriage equality.

COURT RULINGS IN REVIEW

Supreme Court Cases

There has been an ongoing dialectic between religious entities, the law, and the public good for centuries, and it has tended from strong privileges for religious entities toward the application of the rule of law to them. There was a time in Anglo-American history when established religious entities were sovereign, and the clergy enjoyed special treatment under the law.

This was the case when the U.S. Supreme Court held that the Free Exercise Clause of the First Amendment required the government to demonstrate both a compelling interest and that the law in question be narrowly tailored before it denied unemployment compensation to someone fired because her job requirements substantially conflicted with her religion (*Sherbert v. Verner*, 1963). The case established the Sherbert test, requiring demonstration of a compelling interest and narrow tailoring in all Free Exercise cases in which a religious person was substantially burdened by a law. These conditions are the key components of what is called strict scrutiny.

In 1990 the Supreme Court decided that as a judicial constitutional analysis tool the Sherbert test was too broad when applied to all laws. With respect to religiously neutral, generally applicable laws that incidentally burden religious exercise, the Sherbert test was eliminated in the *Employment Division, Department of Human Resources of Oregon v. Smith* (1990) decision, which held that legislatures, not courts, are the appropriate branch to decide whether to create exceptions to neutral, generally applicable law(s). *Smith* took the courts' unbounded power to force religious accommodation and placed it in the hands of the legislature, where issues of fact and belief could be debated openly by various experts and no one need bear any burden of proof—because everyone in the process is intent on working toward an outcome consistent with public good.

The U.S. Supreme Court has been infrequently tasked with deciding on laws that discriminate against religious interests because legislatures have been generous toward those entities. As the court noted in *Smith*, " a society that believes in the negative protection accorded to religious belief can be expected to be solicitous of that value in its legislation."

The next leading case that addressed animus toward religion is the 1993 decision in *Church of the Lukumi Babalu Aye, Inc. v. Hialeah,* in which the city passed an ordinance outlawing animal sacrifice. The choice of language made clear to the court indicated that the city was not engaged in a neutral lawmaking effort but rather was targeting the one group in its jurisdiction that believed in the sacrifice of animals as part of its religious ritual, the Santerians. Moreover, the law was crafted to apply to Santerians only. The animus displayed was patent, and the court mandated not only strict scrutiny that required close judicial inspection of the law, but also seemed to imply that such animus was unconstitutional.

The court took language from *Smith* and *Lukumi*, first identifying generally applicable neutral laws and then distinguishing the generally applicable from the neutral. Religious groups have focused on the former term and co-opted the theory that the court must have meant *any* law creating an exception for one class of beneficiaries and not for religious individuals, or any law that singled out religious individuals, would be presumptively unconstitutional. In other words, any legislative distinction was enough to make a law constitutionally suspicious under the Free Exercise Clause, even without government hostility or animus toward religion. Therefore, the court would defer to legislative judgment. Of course, the exclusion of religious individuals or institutions from legal benefits could trigger strict scrutiny in later cases but only when the government was demonstrably hostile toward the religious group in question or religion in general.

When read together, *Smith* and *Lukumi* identified pivotal principles: first, that courts are to apply a default rule in favor of applying duly enacted, neutral, and generally applicable laws to religious conduct; second, this default rule is only overcome in the face of evidence of persecution of religion (Hamilton, 2005). In a small number of cases between 1963 and 1990, the court departed from its dominate approach to the Free Exercise Clause. This new approach mandated that neutral and generally applicable laws could be subjected to strict scrutiny (*Sherbert v. Verner*, 1963; *Wisconsin v. Yoder*, 1972). Thus, there were now three rules, the two listed above and a competing default rule that required strict scrutiny of neutral, generally applicable laws.

The court made its foray from dominate free exercise jurisprudence in the 1963 decision in *Sherbert v. Verner*, which addressed the question of whether a Sabbatarian could obtain unemployment compensation after refusing to work on the Sabbath. The case established the Sherbert test, requiring demonstration of a compelling interest and narrow tailoring in all Free Exercise cases in which a religious person was substantially burdened by a law. As mentioned previously, these conditions are the key components of strict scrutiny.

Sherbert was widely criticized after it was announced (Clark, 1969), because it was such a departure from bedrock constitutional principles. But by the late 1970s it was embraced (Greenwalt, 1984; Johnson, 1984). The idea that all neutral, generally applicable laws were presumptively unconstitutional when applied to religious entities opened the door for the most extreme libertarian arguments, including that churches should be immune from criminal liability[5]. However, the Supreme Court only extended *Sherbet*-type analysis to one other scenario—compulsory school laws. In *Wisconsin v. Yoder* (1972), the religious claimants were Amish and Mennonite parents who argued that compulsory education laws violated their religious principles. Even though the law was neutral on its face, the court held that it violated the Free Exercise Clause because the state had failed to prove a compelling interest in having the Amish children complete high school. In effect, the court weighed public policy and carved out an exemption from a generally applicable, neutral law solely for the Amish. The new doctrine that invalidated neutral, generally applicable laws in favor of religious conduct found enthusiastic support.

Michael McConnell's published article in the *Harvard Law Review*, with historical justification of the notion of mandatory exemption from legislative enactments described his conclusions:

The conclusions of this (article) are: (1) that exemptions were seen as a constitutionally permissible means for protecting religious freedom, (2) that constitutionally compelled exemptions were within the contemplation of the framers and ratifiers as a possible interpretation of the free exercise clause, and (3) that exemptions were consonant with popular American understanding of the interrelation between the claims of a limited government and a sovereign God. While the historical evidence may not be unequivocal (it seldom is), it does, on balance support Sherbet's interpretation of the free exercise clause. (McConnell, 1990a)

McConnell's (1990b) assessment of the historical record was rebuked by numerous scholars (Gedicks, 1998; West, 1989; Marshall, 1990; Hamburger, 1992) and if history supported mandatory exemptions, then what could the court have been thinking before and after 1963? The court chose between two competing rationales in the same year as *Employment Division v. Smith* (1990), and the rule of law was upheld. The case held that the state could deny unemployment benefits to a person fired for violating a state prohibition on the use of peyote, even though use of the drug was part of a religious ritual. Although states have the power to accommodate otherwise illegal acts performed in pursuit of religious beliefs, they are not required to do so. This case forced the court to choose between its two competing threads.

The enthusiastic reading of the *Sherbet* line of cases and *Yoder* would have applied strict scrutiny to Oregon's unemployment law, which by reference incorporated Oregon's narcotic laws. This is exactly what the counselor's lawyers argued. In other words, the law was presumptively unconstitutional. But the case was more in sync with the court's other free exercise cases, where the rule of law had been applied to a religious entity. In the end, the court could not support the overinflated reading of *Sherbet* and *Yoder* as repudiations of the rule of law as applied to religious entities, when it declared:

We have never held that an individual's religious beliefs excuse him from compliance with an otherwise valid law prohibiting conduct that the State is free to regulate. (Employment Division, Department of Human Resources of Oregon v. Smith, 1990)

Thus, neutral and generally applicable laws with the "incidental effect" of burdening religious conduct does not offend the First Amendment in *Smith*. The court did not close its decision with a simple rejection of the *Yoder* approach, but rather fit its religion clause jurisprudence into the larger structure of the Constitution and society. Religious entities were not required to abandon their desire to engage in religious conduct. They could not, however, find their solution in the courts. They were directed to the legislature, where they would have to justify their requests for exemption to the body charged with assessing and making public policy.

Values that are protected against government interference through enshrinement in the Bill of Rights are not thereby banished from the political process. Just as a society that believes in the negative protection accorded to the press by the First Amendment is likely to enact laws that affirmatively foster the dissemination of the printed word, so also a society that believes in the negative protection accorded to religious belief can be expected to be solicitous of that value in its legislation as well. It is therefore not surprising that several States have made an exception to their drug laws for sacramental peyote use.

But to say that a nondiscriminatory religious-practice exemption is permitted, or even that it is desirable, is not to say that it is constitutionally required, and that the appropriate occasions for its creation can be discerned by the courts. It may fairly be said that leaving accommodation to the political process will place at a relative disadvantage those religious practices that are not widely engaged in; but that unavoidable consequence of democratic government must be preferred to a system in which each conscience is a law unto itself or in which judges weigh the social importance of all laws against the centrality of all religious beliefs. (Employment Division, Department of Human Resources of Oregon v. Smith, 1990)

Many decried the idea that religious entities should be subjected to the political process. Douglas Laycock (1990) in *The Remnants of Free Exercise* criticized this idea in part because:

Legislators are under no obligation to be principled. Subject only to their oath to uphold the Constitution, they are free to reflect majority prejudices, to respond to the squeakiest wheel among minorities, to trade votes and make compromises, and to ignore problems that have no votes in them.

While the *Smith* court repositioned the court's free-exercise reasoning and firmly rejected the then-entrenched assumption that religious entities have a constitutional right to avoid the obligations of generally applicable, neutral laws, it did not overrule any case. Rather, it reframed the preceding cases that seemed to rest on a principle at odds with the dominate approach, casting them in a different light to show they were not inconsistent with the long-established principles the court reaffirmed. *Sherbet* was recast as a discrimination case, wherein the government had offered exemptions from the law for secular reasons but had not offered them for religious reasons. In effect, the court saw a difference in treatment to be a governmental retreat from sincere devotion to deterring harm. The government was willing to tolerate the harm in some circumstances, so there was reason to closely scrutinize the government's action in failing to permit religious individuals to avoid the law.

The court's attempt to incorporate the *Yoder* decision into its overarching jurisprudence was less convincing. The reasoning behind *Yoder* was directly at odds with the reasoning in *Smith.* Had the court overruled *Yoder*, the Amish would have had to approach their state legislatures to avoid upper-level compulsory education for their children.

After *Smith* was decided, a chorus argued the court had overturned a long-settled doctrine that required strict scrutiny of any law, no matter how neutral, which substantially burdened religious conduct. McConnell

(1990b), Laycock (1990), and others criticized the ruling as inconsistent with precedent. The intense response was not entirely because some had misread previous cases; to the contrary, the court invited the response by reaching an issue that was nether briefed nor argued. The petitioners in the case believed the case only addressed how *Sherbert*'s strict scrutiny applied, not whether it applied. Smith was, after all, another unemployment case, and the four preceding cases had applied strict scrutiny to the benefit of the religious entity. Most expected a similar response here, but the court looked beyond the unemployment compensation aspect of the case to its free exercise cases in other contexts and ultimately to the larger question of whether a generally applicable, neutral law is binding on religious entities. It would have been far better had the majority members in *Smith*, Justices Antonin Scalia, Byron White, John Paul Stevens, Anthony Kennedy, and Chief Justice Rehnquist let the parties know they were repudiating the approach in *Sherbert* and *Yoder* as it applied to religious entities.

The problem with the arguments against *Smith* were that the court had followed two paths of reasoning internally inconsistent in the free exercise cases between 1963 and 1990, not one. The preceding jurisprudence had employed what the critics saw as only one approach in free exercise in just a few cases, while the jurisprudence they found so shocking in *Smith* was in fact the dominate rule throughout the court's free exercise jurisprudence. The *Smith* court overturned the anomaly introduced by *Sherbert*.

The court had done nothing more than to reject a bad ruling used in a few cases. Congress responded to the objectors, and after three years of hearings passed the Religious Freedom Restoration Act (RFRA) in 1993, which required the application of strict scrutiny (Public Law 103–141, 1993). Religious and some secular groups turned to Congress to deliver what they claimed was their constitutional right—a return to strict scrutiny of every law in every free exercise case. At the House Judiciary Committee hearings, the Reverend Oliver S. Thomas, who appeared on behalf of the Baptist Joint Committee on Public Affairs, and the American Jewish Committee testified:

Since Smith was decided, governments throughout the U.S. have run roughshod over religious conviction. Churches have been zoned even out of commercial areas. Jews have been subjected to autopsies in violation of their families' faith. In time, every religion in America will suffer. (House Committee on Judiciary Hearing, 1990)

Others testified from diverse civil rights organizations and religious groups, underscoring RFRA's importance, including the American Jewish Congress, which offered that:

All religious minorities must be alarmed when the courts are stripped of the power to require government to accommodate those religious practices, to use Justice Scalia's phrase, 'not widely engaged in.' [RFRA] returns that power to the courts and, with it, ensures that government does not arbitrarily interfere with religious freedom. (House Committee on Judiciary Hearing, 1990)

The president of the ACLU stated that:

Members of minority religious groups should not have to depend on accidents of political process to protect their fundamental freedoms," and that without the passage of RFRA, religious liberty would be gravely threatened. (House Committee on the Judiciary Hearing, 1990)

Elder Dallin H. Oaks from the Church of Jesus Christ of Latter-day Saints (LDS Church) said:

Political power or impact must not be the measure of which religious practices can be forbidden by law. The Bill of Rights protects principles, not constituencies. (House Committee on the Judiciary, 1990)

Similarly, the Senate Report No. 103-111 (1990) accompanying RFRA indicated:

State and local legislative bodies cannot be relied upon to craft exceptions from laws of general application to protect the ability of the religious minorities to practice their faiths, an explicit fundamental constitutional right.

Under RFRA, every law was subject to strict scrutiny, whether neutral and generally applicable or not. RFRA provided:

(a) In General. Government shall not burden a person's exercise of religion even if the burden results from a rule of general applicability, except as provided in subsection (b).

(b) Exception. Government may burden a person's exercise of religion only if it demonstrates that application of the burden to the person.

(1) is in furtherance of a compelling governmental interest; and

(2) is the least restrictive means of furthering that compelling governmental interest. (Public Law 103–141, 1993)

In *Smith*, the court reinstituted the rule of law as applied to religious entities, but it encouraged them to go to the legislature for relief from laws imposing burdens on religious practice. But the positives were lost in the maelstrom against it. Ironically, the religious organizations did precisely what detractors seemed to believe they either could or should not do—they sought a legislative remedy proving the political feasibility of the decision. The court had articulated the relationship between religious entities, the government, and society. Its constitutional vision was based on fundamental principles of republican democracy: public good and the rule of no harm. The statute that was generated as a result, RFRA, raised the question of whether Congress could unilaterally rearrange the relationship between religious entities, the law, and the public good. If so, then democratic principles could be abandoned in favor of permitting religious entities to avoid most generally applicable, neutral laws.

The Supreme Court deferred to congressional exercises of power from the 1930s to 1995. Federalism all but disappeared, despite the plain meaning of the Constitution limiting its powers. Congress was supposed to be an institution of enumerated powers not plenary power. By 1995 the court began to draw some boundaries around what had become an arena that lacked limits (Post & Siegel, 2000; Kramer, 2000).

RFRA and *Boerne v. Flores* (1997) arrived at the court during this time. The country in the 1950s and 1960s was witnessing explosive social change in federal civil rights laws. It was a time of cataclysmic change for the rights of minorities. Between the states and the federal government, there was no question at that time that the federal government was the protector of liberty. Minorities were asking for a level playing field, but religious entities were not asking for equality under the law, rather the right to trump the law—to be treated better than others who were similarly situated and governed by the same law.

In *City of Boerne v. Flores* (1997), the court addressed the scope of Congress's enforcement power under Section 5 of the Fourteenth Amendment.

The basis for dispute arose when the Catholic Archbishop of San Antonio, Patrick Flores, applied for a building permit to enlarge the 1923 mission-style St. Peter's Church in Boerne, Texas (Miller, 1997). The building was in a historic district and considered a contributing property. Local zoning authorities denied the permit, citing an ordinance governing additions and new construction in a historic district. The archbishop sued, challenging the ruling under the Religious Freedom Restoration Act (RFRA) of 1993. *Flores* argued that his congregation had outgrown the existing structure, rendering the ruling a substantial burden on the free exercise of religion without a compelling state interest (Miller, 1997). The court's ruling (6-3) struck down RFRA as it applied to states as an unconstitutional use of Congress's enforcement powers. The majority opinion was delivered by Justice Kennedy:

Congress' power under § 5, however, extends only to enforcing the provisions of the Fourteenth Amendment. The Court has described this power as "remedial." The design of the Amendment and the text of § 5 are inconsistent with the suggestion that Congress has the power to decree the substance of the Fourteenth Amendment's restrictions on the States. Legislation which alters the meaning of the Free Exercise Clause cannot be said to be enforcing the Clause. Congress does not enforce a constitutional right by changing what the right is. It has been given the power "to enforce," not the power to determine what constitutes a constitutional violation. Were it not so, what Congress would be enforcing would no longer be, in any meaningful sense, the "provisions of [the Fourteenth Amendment].

Moreover, remedial or prophylactic legislation still had to show "congruence and proportionality" between the end it aimed to reach (that is, the violations it aimed to correct), and the means it chose to reach those ends—that is, the penalties or prohibitions it enacted to prevent or correct those violations. Because RFRA was not reasonably remedial or prophylactic, it was unconstitutional. (City of Boerne v. Flores, 1997)

In the wake of the *Flores* decision, where RFRA applies only to the federal government, many states around the country responded by passing state religious freedom restoration acts (state RFRAs), a trend that continues today. As Table 1 illustrates, since 1993, 21 states have enacted state RFRAs. These laws are intended to echo the federal RFRA but are not necessarily identical to the federal law. In 2016, 10 states considered legislation. Virginia amended its state RFRA, but otherwise no states have passed their legislation.

Table 1. States with Religious Freedom Restoration Acts as of 2015

Jurisdiction	Date of Passage	Statute
Alabama	1998	Ala. Const. Art. I, §3.01
Arizona	1999	Ariz. Rev. Stat. §41-1493.01
Arkansas		2015 SB 975, enacted April 2, 2015
Connecticut	1993	Conn. Gen. Stat. §52-571b
Florida	1998	Fla. Stat. §761.01, et seq.
Idaho	2000	Idaho Code §73-402
Illinois	1998	Ill. Rev. Stat. Ch. 775, §35/1, et seq.
Indiana	2015	2015 SB 101, enacted March 26, 2015; 2015 SB 50, enacted April 2, 2015
Kansas	2013	Kan. Stat. §60-5301, et seq.
Kentucky	2013	Ky. Rev. Stat. §446.350
Louisiana	2010	La. Rev. Stat. §13:5231, et seq.
Mississippi	2014	Miss. Code §11-61-1
Missouri	2003	Mo. Rev. Stat. §1.302
New Mexico	2000	N.M. Stat. §28-22-1, et seq.
Oklahoma	2000	Okla. Stat. tit. 51, §251, et seq.
Pennsylvania	2002	Pa. Stat. tit. 71, §2403
Rhode Island	1993	R.I. Gen. Laws §42-80.1-1, et seq.
South Carolina	1999	S.C. Code §1-32-10, et seq.
Tennessee	2009	Tenn. Code §4-1-407
Texas	1999	Tex. Civ. Prac. & Remedies Code §110.001, et seq.
Virginia	2007	Va. Code §57-2.02

(National Conference of State Legislators, 2017)

Many of the mini RFRAs mimic the federal RFRA by reinstating strict scrutiny review for challenges to government regulations that are alleged to substantially burden religious exercise. But other state RFRAs have key provisions that extend far beyond their federal parent. For example, some significantly dilute the substantial burden requirement (requiring only that the challenged law "burdens" or "restricts" religious exercise). Some envision the practice of religion to extend to any act or inaction that is tangentially related to a person's religious beliefs. And some even add a "clear and convincing" evidence requirement to satisfy strict scrutiny, making the government's burden of justifying the challenged law even more onerous.

Although both progressives and conservatives supported RFRA when it was enacted in 1993, much has changed in the ensuing decades. Since then,

RFRA has been exploited to justify discrimination and other harms to third parties, and courts have interpreted the law in ways its sponsors never intended. Religious exercise challenges increased, as states and municipalities began recognizing rights for nontraditional sexual choices and identities. Like a pendulum, the country has seen a swing in both directions of the civil rights continuum, with states almost universally banning same-sex marriage in the 1970s and 1980s to its legalization in *Obergefell*. Consequently, state RFRA laws and their variants have become the legal missile targeted at marriage equality.

Another recent court case in *Burwell v. Hobby Lobby Stores, Inc* (2014) painted a new landscape for free exercise claims. The court's decision opened the door for increased demands from private entities for accommodations or exemptions from neutral laws of general applicability with little regard to the problems of attenuation and harm to third parties. *Hobby Lobby* redesigned the terrain for free exercise claims, which could ultimately result in the protection of religious rights at the expense of LGBT rights. The court emphasized its broad interpretation of RFRA to provide the maximum protection to religious freedom permitted by the U.S. Constitution. This case challenged compliance with a law that may facilitate conduct by a third party that offended Hobby Lobby's religious beliefs. The insurance mandate only implicated Hobby Lobby's religious beliefs by potentially making Hobby Lobby complicit in a third party's immoral conduct.

Since the ruling in *Hobby Lobby*, there has been great consternation about what religious free exercise claims should protect and against whom (Laycock, 2014; Sibilia, 2015; Swindle, 2015; Thompson, 2015). The court upheld the corporation's RFRA claim that its free exercise rights were violated. The company objected to contraceptives that were abortifacients and stated that requiring its employer-provided insurance plan to pay for them violated its deeply held religious belief that life begins at conception.

In a 5–4 decision, the court agreed with *Hobby Lobby* and had no problem recognizing that a closely held corporation like Hobby Lobby had standing under RFRA to bring a free exercise claim. Turning to the government's burden under RFRA, the court held that because the government already had a mechanism for accommodating nonprofit religious institutions such as hospitals and universities, there were less restrictive means of meeting the government's interests, which the court assumed without deciding were compelling.

In her dissent, Justice Ginsburg argued that the majority distorted the coverage of RFRA far beyond its intended purpose, which was to reinstate pre-*Employment Division, Department of Human Resources of Oregon v. Smith* (1990) free exercise jurisprudence. She articulated a clear difference between a nonprofit religious organization and a for-profit corporation, and she opined that the latter had no standing under RFRA. Because there was no precedent pre-*Smith* for corporations other than churches to bring First Amendment free exercise claims, for-profit corporations should have no standing to bring a claim under RFRA.

In another case, *Trinity Lutheran Church of Columbia, Inc. v. Comer* (2017), the U.S. Supreme Court held that a Missouri program that denied funding that would be used for secular purposes to religious groups, which it provided to nonreligious groups, violated the First Amendment's guarantee of freedom of religious exercise known as the Free Exercise Clause (Savage, 2017; Moreau, 2017). Attorneys for *Trinity Lutheran Church of Columbia* (2017) had framed their arguments before the high court earlier when they stated that the Missouri Synod congregation wanted the funds to make its playground safer for children who attend the church preschool as well as the neighborhood families who use the playground when the preschool was closed. Who, they wondered, could possibly oppose that?

The bulk of current "religious liberty" litigation involves religious individuals and institutions seeking exemptions from state programs or requirements (most often from LGBT-inclusive nondiscrimination policies). In *Trinity Lutheran*, the roles are reversed. It's the church seeking access to a publicly funded grant, while the state counters it cannot provide funds to religious groups, lest it appear to be offering preferential treatment to one religious group over another.

This decision declared that religious institutions cannot be excluded from an "otherwise neutral and secular aid program" that could well serve as a stalking horse for religious institutions to then seek broad access to state and federal funds while simultaneously maintaining their tax-exempt status, and in some cases continuing to pursue (especially under the current administration) and be granted religious exemptions to otherwise neutral and generally applicable laws.

FUTURE RESEARCH DIRECTIONS

Some may argue that relabeling an individual's religious belief as offense trivializes religious freedom. Quite the contrary, recognizing a distinction between burdening religious freedom and causing offense preserves the important value placed on religious freedom. Just as all speech is not valued the same under the First Amendment's Free Speech Clause, not all free exercise claims are equal either. In determining which religious belief is sufficiently burdened to sustain the right of a proprietor of a public accommodation to deny service to LGBT patrons, a totality of factors should be considered. Further research on these factors should include: (1) how public the business is; (2) the nexus between the religious belief and the service denied; and (3) the harm done to third persons in denying the service.

CONCLUSION

In response to same-sex marriage rulings, there have been businesses refusing to extend their services to same-sex couples, local ordinances protecting sexual minorities against discrimination, and a now-rescinded Obama administration federal interpretation concerning school bathrooms for transgender students (U.S. Department of Justice, 2016). States have considered—and some have enacted—new versions of state religious freedom laws intended to protect such businesses. The governor of North Carolina, who signed such a law in March 2016, intended inter alia to nullify provisions in a Charlotte ordinance expanding protections for gays and lesbians (Harrison, 2016). A few days later, the governor of Georgia vetoed a similar measure that would have insulated businesses refusing service to same-sex couples on religious grounds (Telegraph Herald, 2016).

As applied in *Hobby Lobby*, RFRA requires the plaintiff to establish that the challenged action substantially burdens a religious practice or belief. Then, the burden shifts to the government to satisfy strict scrutiny. Under strict scrutiny review, the government must establish that its action furthers a compelling government interest and is the least restrictive means of serving that interest (*Hobby Lobby, 2014)*. However, the government's burden is not met by establishing the challenged action is the least restrictive means of serving "broadly formulated interests." Rather, RFRA requires a "'more focused' inquiry" and "requires the Government to demonstrate that the compelling interest test is satisfied through the application of the challenged law 'to the person'—the claimant whose sincere exercise of religion is being substantially burdened" (*Gonzales v. O Centro Espírita Beneficente União do Vegetal*, 2006).

This is a very deferential standard to the person or entity claiming a RFRA violation. It is a subjective test that is easily met, especially given the ease with which the plaintiff can satisfy its burden—namely, that the challenged action substantially burdens a sincerely held religious belief. In their recent *Yale Law Journal* article, Nejaime and Siegel (2015) characterized the RFRA claim in *Hobby Lobby* as a "complicity-based conscience claim." They point out the complicity-based conscience claim, as typified by *Hobby Lobby's* RFRA claim, has the "potential to inflict harms on specific third parties." This is the crux of concern about state RFRA claims and how they will be used to inflict harm by discriminating against third parties, specifically members of the LGBT community.

In their article, Nejaime and Siegel (2015) trace the history of this *Hobby Lobby*–type complicity-based conscience claims to health care refusal laws and the Church Amendment of 1973. Health care refusal laws provide exemptions to health care providers from treating potential patients (typically involving abortion services) based on religious objections. Eventually, these laws broadened their exemptions to cover persons and entities who were only tangentially involved with the potential patient seeking an abortion. Against this backdrop, *Hobby Lobby* seems like a natural extension of the health care refusal laws, granting the same type of protections to a broader group of individuals.

These protections have moved from medical facilities and providers to the board room and employers.

The next frontier is the business owner claiming conscience-based objections to serving LGBT persons. An extension of these conscience-based claims to providing services to LGBT couples and families threatens a slippery slope. There could be no end to religious claimants' objections to providing goods and services to the LGBT community, as is required by public accommodation laws and professional ethical standards based on complicity in or facilitation of morally objectionable conduct by third parties. Echoing the aftermath of *Roe*, the losing side on the same-sex marriage issue has and will continue to lobby state legislatures to pass robust RFRA laws as well as laws banning local nondiscrimination ordinances that extend protections to members of the LGBT community.

Having lost in the court, same-sex marriage opponents have garnered legislative support to impose their religious view of morally correct behavior on others. The next chapter of religious indignation claims will give license to discriminate. Although not framed as religious liberty versus freedom from discrimination, Justice Ginsburg parroted the concerns she raised in her *Hobby Lobby* dissent that in accommodating free exercise claims, courts should consider the harm caused to third persons who do not share the RFRA claimant's religious beliefs. Extending this principle to scenarios in which individuals and businesses refuse services to LGBT persons and families based on religious freedom, those discriminated against will certainly suffer harm.

Inference upon inference must be made to link the two. Originally RFRA was intended to reinstate free exercise analysis prior to *Smith.* It was not intended to be the basis on which private persons and companies could discriminate in public life by elevating their private religious beliefs above the rights of persons to be treated equally.

Even before the court published its *Obergefell* decision, opponents of same-sex marriage, who feared an unfavorable decision, marshaled their energies toward legislative rather than court support. Attempting to stem the tide of support for LGBT-expanding civil rights, the anti-same-sex marriage movement galvanized efforts to win legislative victories on the state level that would neutralize, or even block, this growing pro-LGBT rights trend. Those discriminating against LGBT individuals relabeled themselves as the "discriminated." Invoking religious freedom, citizens lobbied their state legislators to pass robust mini-RFRA laws and laws intended to nullify local nondiscrimination ordinances protecting the LGBT community.

Like the success of anti-abortion supporters who lobbied state and federal legislators to limit the effects of *Roe* by passing health refusal laws, the opponents to same-sex marriage have found a way to undermine *Obergefell* and stymie local LGBT antidiscrimination efforts through their legislative successes. With the rise of robust mini RFRAs and other laws protecting religious freedom at the expense of civil rights, the country is at a crossroads.

Indeed, robust state RFRA laws and state laws that intend to preempt local, LGBT-inclusive, nondiscrimination ordinances threaten to create a system that in the aggregate legally sanctions discrimination in the name of religious freedom. Emboldened by *Hobby Lobby*, public entities can now demand exemptions from public accommodation laws by refusing to provide services and goods to members of the LGBT community with conscience-based objections to same-sex marriage.

Groups of religious entities have pursued legislative exemptions from generally applicable laws on the theory that religious liberty demands freedom from the law. They have used the First Amendment for a presumptive constitutional right to avoid the law that pursuant to the federal and state free exercise of religion guarantees. They also have employed due process, ex post facto, and separation of power theories to argue that the law should not apply to them because they are religious. These wars of religious power have greatly intensified since the legalization of same-sex marriage.

REFERENCES

Burwell v. Hobby Lobby Stores, Inc., 134 S. Ct. 2751, 2762,2785 (2014).

Church of the Lukumi Babalu Aye, Inc. v. Hialeah, 508 U.S. 520 (1993).

City of Boerne v. Flores, 521 U.S. 507 (1997).

Clark, J. M. (1969). Guidelines for the free exercise clause. *Harvard Law Review, 83*(2), 300–329. doi:10.2307/1339673

Craig v. Masterpiece Cakeshop, Inc., 370 P.3d 272, 276, 280 (Colo. App. 2015).

Employment Division v. Smith, 494 U.S. 872 (1990).

Gedicks, F. M. (1998). A uniform foundation: The regrettable indefensibility of religious exemptions. *University of Arkansas at Little Rock Law Journal, 20*, 550–574.

Gonzales v. O Centro Espírita Beneficente União do Vegetal, 546 U.S. 418 (2006).

Greenwalt, K. (1984). Religion as a concept in constitutional law. *California Law Review, 72*(5), 753–816. doi:10.2307/3480329

Hamburger, P. A. (1992). A constitutional right of religious exemption: An historical perspective. *The George Washington Law Review, 60*, 915–948.

Hamilton, M. (2005). *God vs. the gavel: religion and the rule of law*. New York, NY: Cambridge University Press. doi:10.1017/CBO9780511511530

Harrison, S. (2016, March 23). N. C. gov Pat McCrory signs into law bill restricting LGBT protections. *Charlotte Observer*. Retrieved from http://www.charlotteobserver.com/news/local/arti cle67845317.html

Johnson, P. E. (1984). Concepts and compromise in First Amendment religious doctrine. *California Law Review, 72*(5), 817–846. doi:10.2307/3480330

Kramer, L. D. (2000, December 12). No surprise. It's an activist court. *New York Times*. Retrieved from https://www.nytimes.com/2000/12/12/opinion/no-surprise-it-s-an-activist-court.html

Laycock, D. (1990). The remnants of free exercise. *The Supreme Court Review*, *1990*, 1–68. doi:10.1086cr.1990.3109655

Laycock, D. (2014, July 1). Opinion, the religious freedom act worked the way it should. *New York Times*. Retrieved from https://www.nytimes.com/roomfordebate/2014/06/30/congress-religion-and-the-supreme-courts-hobby-lobby-decision/the-religious-freedom-act-worked-the-way-it-should

Marshall, W. P. (1990). The case against the constitutionally compelled free exercise exemption. *Case Western Reserve Law Review*, *40*, 357–412.

McConnell, M. W. (1990a). The origins and historical understandings of free exercise of religion. *Harvard Law Review*, *103*(7), 1400–1516. doi:10.2307/1341281

McConnell, M. W. (1990b). Free exercise revisionism and the Smith division. *The University of Chicago Law Review. University of Chicago. Law School*, *57*(4), 1100–1129. doi:10.2307/1599887

Miller, J. (1997). U.S. Supreme Court declares RFRA unconstitutional in Texas religious landmarking case. *Preservation Law Reporter*, *16*, 1053.

National Conference of State Legislatures. (2015). *State religious freedom restoration acts*. Retrieved from http://www.ncsl.org/research/civil-and-criminal-justice/2015-state-rfra-legislation.aspx

Nejaime, D., & Siegel, R. B. (2015). Conscience claims in religion and politics. *The Yale Law Journal*, *124*, 2510–2524.

Obergefell, 135 S. Ct. at 2607–08.

Post, R. C., & Siegel, R. B. (2000). Equal protection by law: Federal antidiscrimination legislation after Morrison and Kimel. *The Yale Law Journal*, *110*(3), 441–525. doi:10.2307/797522

Religious Freedom Restoration Act of 1991: Hearing on H.R. 5377 Before the Subcommittee on Civil and Constitutional Rights of the H. Comm. On the Judiciary, 101st Cong. (1990).

Religious Freedom Restoration Act of 1993, Pub. L. No. 103-141, 107 Stat. 1488 (1993).

S. Rep. No. 103-111 (1990).

Savage, D. (2013, March 1). Public opinion could sway Supreme Court ruling on gay marriage. *Los Angeles Times*. Retrieved from http://articles.latimes.com/2013/mar/01/nation/la-na-court-prop8-20130302

Sherbert v. Verner, 374 U.S. 398 (1963).

Sibilia, R. (2015). Play or pay: Interpreting the employer mandate of the patient protection and affordable care act as it relates to tribal employers. *American Indian Law Review*, *39*(1), 235–268.

Telegraph Herald. (2016, March 28). *Georgia governor vetoes religious exemption bill*. Retrieved from http://www.thonline.com/news/national_world/article_ce5d679a-f4fa-1 Ie5-ac9f-07236633ff48.html/

Thompson, E. S. (2015). Compromising equality: An analysis of the religious exemption in the employment non-discrimination act and its impact on LGBT workers. *Boston College Journal of Law & Social Justice*, *35*(2), 285–318.

U.S. Department of Justice. (2016, May 13). *Dear colleague letter on transgender students*. Retrieved from https://www2.ed.gov/about/offices/list/ocr/letters/colleague-201605-title-ix-transgender.pdf

West, E. (1989). The case against a right to religious-based exemptions. *Notre Dame Journal of Law, Ethics & Public Policy*, *4*, 590–624.

Wetzstein, C. (2015, July 6). States rebel against supreme court gay marriage ruling. *Washington Times*. Retrieved from http:/Avww.washingtontimes.com/news/2015/jul/6/states-rebel-against-supreme- court-gay-marriage-ru/

Wisconsin v. Yoder, 406 U.S. 205, 221 (1972).

KEY TERMS AND DEFINITIONS

Equal Protection Clause: Constitutional guarantee embodied in the Fourteenth Amendment to the Constitution.

Fourteenth Amendment: Guarantees citizens of the United States due process and equal protection of the laws. The due process clause has been the vehicle for applying nearly all the guarantees in the first 10 amendments to state action.

Procedural Due Process: Guarantees procedural fairness where the government would deprive someone of property or liberty.

Rational Basis: A method of constitutional analysis under the equal protection clause is used to determine whether a challenged law has a legitimate governmental objective. It is used when constitutional objection is raised regarding a law's reasonableness and not when constitutional rights violations are alleged.

Sherbert Test: A three-prong test for courts to use in determining whether the government has violated an individual's constitutionally protected right to the free exercise of religion. The first prong investigates whether government has burdened the individual's free exercise of religion. If government confronts an individual with a choice that pressures the individual to forego a religious practice, whether by imposing a penalty or withholding a benefit, then the government has burdened the individual's free exercise of religion. However, under this test not all burdens placed on religious exercise are constitutionally prohibited. If the first prong is passed, the government may still constitutionally impose the burden on the individual's free exercise, if the government can show: it possesses some compelling state interest that justifies the infringement (the compelling interest prong); and no alternative form of regulation can avoid the infringement and still achieve the state's end (the narrow-tailoring prong).

Strict Scrutiny: Involves determining whether the law violates the equal protection clause unless the state can show it is necessary to further a compelling government interest and is accomplished by the least intrusive means.

Substantive Due Process: Requires that all legislation further a legitimate governmental objective.

ENDNOTES

1 The first of 10 amendments added to the federal constitution in 1791 by the Bill of Rights. Originally intended to limit the power of the federal government, the various rights of political and religious freedom articulated in this amendment have been held applicable to the states through the due process clause of the Fourth Amendment. It contains two parts: the free exercise section guarantees against governmental compulsion in religious matters; while the establishment clause ensures that the government will maintain neutrality towards religion.

2 The phrase "nor shall any person be deprived of life, liberty, or property, without due process of law" was introduced in the Fifth Amendment to the federal constitution and was originally applicable to the actions of the federal government. The provision was made applicable to the states with adoption of the Fourteenth Amendment, Section 1. The meaning of the phrase is shaped by jurisprudential attitudes of fairness and is divided onto areas of substantive and procedural due process.

3 The doctrine prohibits one branch of government, either state or local, from infringing upon the powers belonging to another branch.

4 The first state to authorize same-sex marriage per se was Massachusetts because of two decisions by the Massachusetts Supreme Judicial Court: Goodridge v. Department of Public Health, 798 N.E.2d 941, 969 (Mass, 2003) and *In re* Ops. To the Senate, 802 N.E.2d 565, 577.

5 These arguments were raised in cases involving sexual abuse of children by clergy.

Section 3

Public Accommodations:

Discrimination and Sexual Orientation

Chapter 4
Public Accommodations: Discrimination and Sexual Orientation

ABSTRACT

The chapter examines potential issues posed by the wide variety of state public accommodation statutes in the context of sexual orientation and religious freedom. The historical approach to antidiscrimination will briefly be examined. A review of recent cases of discrimination due to the legalization of same-sex marriage are analyzed in the context of the arguments regarding freedom of speech and freedom of religion.

INTRODUCTION

Probably the most contentious issues surrounding same-sex marriage involve whether private individuals and companies can—primarily on religious grounds—legally refuse to provide services they generally provide to other couples (*Burwell v. Hobby Lobby Stores*, 2014). Can a private chapel or other venue refuse to host a same-sex wedding, a florist refuse to provide flowers, a bakery refuse to bake a wedding cake, a professional photographer refuse to photograph the reception, a transportation service refuse to rent a limo, a caterer refuse to provide food, a bridal boutique refuse to provide gowns, etc.? These issues were already cropping up around the United States well before *Obergefell v. Hodges* (2015) in those jurisdictions that permitted same-sex marriage and have since escalated (Wong, 2016).

DOI: 10.4018/978-1-5225-7961-8.ch004

Do the rights of freedom of speech and freedom of religion allow a business owner to refuse service to a potential customer or client because of the actual or perceived sexual orientation of that customer or client? Put another way, does the right to be free from discrimination of any kind override the business owner's rights to free speech or freedom of religion? Does one right trump another? The focus of this chapter is the change in our values and beliefs associated with the notion that all people, regardless of sexual orientation, have the right to be free from discrimination and how our courts are reconciling this notion with our fundamental First Amendment rights.

This chapter is divided into three parts. First, the historical approach to antidiscrimination will be briefly examined. Second, the facts and situations of recent cases of discrimination due to sexual orientation will be discussed. Finally, the arguments regarding freedom of speech and freedom of religion are analyzed in the context of the antidiscrimination laws.

ANTIDISCRIMINATION AND VALUE CHANGES

In 1964, for the first time since the end of Reconstruction, Congress enacted a law banning race discrimination in public accommodations, Title II of the Civil Rights Act of 1964. It is difficult today to understand why this law, which forbade hotels, restaurants, gas stations, and places of entertainment to discriminate based on race, color, or national origin, gave rise to such heated opposition and the longest filibuster in the history of the U.S. Senate. Landsberg (2015) in *Public Accommodations and the Civil Rights Act of 1964: A Surprising Success?* stated that "today, Title II gets little attention, while other non-discrimination laws, such as fair employment, fair housing, and voting rights legislation continue to produce litigation and garner public attention; yet, in 1963 and 1964, Title II was considered a key provision, as well as a very controversial one." This is certainly not the case today with the legalization of same-sex marriage. The ascendancy of gay rights has been accompanied by a rise in assertions of religious freedom. These assertions have primarily taken the form of state legislative initiatives (Barbaro & Eckholm, 2015; Eilperin, 2014). Supporters have cited perceived growing threats and hostility to religious liberty as a basis for such initiatives. As illustrated in an interview conducted by Kristina Torres (2015) in *Clergy Clash on 'Religious Liberty' Efforts at Capitol*, the executive director of the Georgia Baptist Convention, J. Robert White states:

. . . if there has been discrimination in this country, quite honestly, it has been against people of Christian faith, and it must stop.

Merriam-Webster dictionary defines *discrimination* as "the practice of unfairly treating a person or group of people differently from other people or groups of people." In the context of this paper, discrimination will be viewed based on sexual orientation. *Sexual orientation* is defined by Merriam-Webster as "a person's sexual preference or identity as bisexual, heterosexual, or homosexual."

State statutes also define sexual orientation. As illustrated in Table 1, currently 22 states and the District of Columbia prohibit businesses deemed to be public accommodations from refusing to serve prospective patrons based on sexual orientation. Therefore, sexual orientation discrimination would be the practice of unfairly treating a person differently because of his or her preference for heterosexuality, homosexuality, bisexuality, or perhaps even gender expression or identity. Another important aspect of the cases to be discussed pertains to where instances of discrimination take place. In all but one of the cases, the discrimination takes place in a public accommodation.

In U.S. law, public accommodations are generally defined as facilities, both public and private, used by the public. Examples include retail stores, rental establishments, and service establishments as well as educational institutions, recreational facilities, and service centers.

Federal law requires that a public accommodation be accessible to the handicapped and that it may not discriminate based on "race, color, religion, or national origin" (Civil Rights Act of 1964). Private clubs were specifically exempted under federal law as well as religious organizations[1]. The definition of public accommodation is limited to "any inn, hotel, motel, or other establishment which provides lodging to transient guests" in Title II of the Civil Rights Act, and so is inapplicable to churches. Section 12187 of the Americans with Disability Act of 1990 also exempts religious organizations from public accommodation laws, but religious organizations are encouraged to comply (Pubic Law 88–352, 78 Stat. 241).

The Civil Rights Act of 1964 is one of the most important pieces of legislation in our nation's history regarding antidiscrimination. After its enactment, a motel owner challenged the law based on the Fifth Amendment (*Heart of Atlanta Motel, Inc. v. United States*, 1964). The owner was opposed to renting the rooms to any but those of the Caucasian race as it was his right, he argued, to refuse service to anyone for any reason because it resulted in

Table 1. States with public accommodation statutes that include sexual orientation

State	Statute
California	Cal. Civil Code §§51-51.5 (2015) (adopted 2005)
Colorado	Colo. Rev. Stat. §24-34-601 (2015) (adopted 2008)
Connecticut	Conn. Gen. Stat. § § 46a-81 d, 46a-811 (2015) (adopted 1991)
Delaware	Del. Code Ann. tit. 6, §§ 4501-04 (2015) (adopted 2009)
Hawaii	Haw. Rev. Stat. §§489-2-5 (2015) (adopted 2006)
Illinois	775 III. Comp. Stat. 5/1-102-03, 5/5-101-03, 5/8A-104 (2015) (adopted 2006)
Iowa	Iowa Code § 216.7 (2015) (adopted 2007)
Maine	Me. Rev. Stat. Ann. tit. 5, §§ 4591-92(1) (2015) (adopted 2005)
Maryland	Md. Code Ann., State Gov't §§ 20-101,20-301-04 (West, 2015) (adopted 2009)
Massachusetts	Mass. Gen. Law sc Ii. 272, §§ 92A, 98 (2015) (adopted 1989)
Minnesota	Minn. Stat. §§ 363A.02-.03, 363A.11. 363A.24 (2015) (adopted 1993)
Nevada	Nev. Rev. Stat. §§ 233.010,651.050-.070 (2015) (adopted 2009)
New Hampshire	N.H. Rev. Stat. Ann. §§ 354-A: 16-17 (2015) (adopted 1998)
New Jersey	N.J. Stat. Ann. §§ 10:5-3-5 (2015) (adopted 1992)
New Mexico	N.M. Stat. §§ 28-1-2, 7-9 (2015) (adopted 2004)
New York	N.Y. Exec. Law §§ 290-96 (2015) (adopted 2002)
Oregon	Or. Rev. Stat. §§ 659A.003-.006, 659A.406-09, 659A.885 (2015) (adopted 2007)
Rhode Island	R.I. Gen. Laws §§11 -24-2-2.1 (2015) (adopted 1995)
Vermont	Vt. Stat. Ann tit. 9, § 4502 (2015) (adopted 1992)
Washington	Wash. Rev. Code §§49.60.030,49.60.215 (2015) (adopted 2006)
Wisconsin	Wis. Stat. §§ 106.52 (2015) (adopted 2009)

(Griffin, 2017)

a taking of liberty and property without due process of law and without just compensation (*Heart of Atlanta Motel, Inc. v. United States*, 1964).

Basically, the owner of the motel argued that he had the right to discriminate against African Americans and refuse to rent to them. The Supreme Court in *Heart of Atlanta* provided confirmation that Congress has the ability, through the Commerce Clause, to remove obstructions to interstate commerce caused by racial discrimination (Civil Rights Act, 1964). Although sexual orientation is not a protected class under the Civil Rights Act, the reasoning used by the court to prevent racial discrimination could be applied to preventing discrimination based on sexual orientation.

Many states had laws prohibiting the marriage of persons of different "races," which were thought to be one of the rights reserved to the states under the Tenth Amendment. *Loving v. Virginia* (1967) concerned Richard and Mildred Loving, an interracial couple who were arrested and charged with violation of this law. The trial judge's opinion in sentencing the couple confirmed that:

Almighty God created the races white, black, yellow, malay, and red, and he placed them on separate continents. And but for the interference with this arrangement there would be no cause for such marriages. The fact that he separated the races shows that he did not intend for the races to mix. (Loving v. Virginia, 1967)

It is easy to see from this quote that the judge used an argument based on his religious beliefs in making his judgment. The Supreme Court noted in *Loving* that the freedom to marry is a vital personal right essential to the pursuit of happiness and did not believe the argument that miscegenation laws applied to the Equal Protection Clause of the Fourteenth Amendment (*Loving v. Virginia,* 1967). Although this case centered on racial discrimination, its lesson is important: "…the Equal Protection Clause requires consideration of whether the classifications drawn by any statute constitutes an arbitrary and invidious discrimination" (*Loving v. Virginia,* 1967). This case demonstrates a change in the values and beliefs of our society regarding marriage and interracial relationships. At the time, 16 states had miscegenation laws.

Race discrimination is the paradigmatic civil rights violation in America, and religious objections have arisen to marriage between people of different races, as they have to marriage between people of the same sex or gender (Oleske, 2015). Sepper (2014) contends that historically, as now, religious opposition emerged in response to race, religion, or gender nondiscrimination requirements. Outcry around interracial marriage followed a pattern much like those in objections to same-sex marriage today.

Could a religious organization receive an exemption from public accommodation laws so it could exclude access to a couple because of its sincere theological opposition to interracial marriage? Almost certainly not, as the court in *Newman v. Piggie Park Enterprises, Inc.* (1968) called "patently frivolous" the claim by a restaurant owner that an antidiscrimination law "was invalid because it 'contravenes the will of God'" and constitutes an interference with the 'free exercise of the [owner's] religion.'"

Civil rights laws in the United States virtually never permit that sort of exemption. That is true even though religious objections to interracial marriage have long been heard. Is religious objection to interracial marriage different from religious objection to same-sex marriage, so that the two cannot be compared?

Kent Greenawalt (2013) in *Religious Toleration and Claims of Conscience* maintains that the practice of limiting civil marriage to one man and one woman has been universal among cultures and religions. Second, he observes that "without modern technology, it takes a union of a male and a female to produce children." While neither of these points is enough to defend exclusions from civil marriage, they do suggest that "such unions are 'unnatural' or 'less natural.'" Whether prohibitions on interracial and same-sex marriage have been widespread is a matter for historians. Certainly, interracial marriages also have been considered unnatural, as noted in the *Loving* opinions, and in other places (Oleske, 2015).

Greenawalt might suggest that the opposition to interracial marriage is not comprehensible, despite its grounding in history and biology, and therefore that it is less worthy of accommodation, even though that opposition has been rooted in religion (Tebbe, 2015). If that is so, then some reason other than history and biology must be found for saying that opposition to racial intermarriage is incomprehensible but opposition to LGBT marriage is not. Perhaps a reason can be found, although it does not come to mind. Reasonable people surely do disagree today on whether the race analogy works (Carpenter, 2013).

Even if the race analogy is complicated, comparison to prohibitions on differentiation based on marital status and religion itself point to the same result—that a prohibition on religion exemptions in public accommodation laws does seem to cohere with scenarios in antidiscrimination law about which there is a high degree of confidence. In other words, the principles of fundamental rights and equal citizenship, as discussed in the next section, suggest that we should hesitate to allow a religious exemption that generates exclusion of same-sex couples from public accommodations.

Fundamental Principles

The first principle as identified by the Supreme Court throughout the constitutional amendments is that all people possess certain fundamental rights. These rights have been defined by the court over the years as a "principle of justice so rooted in the traditions and conscience of our people as to be ranked as fundamental" (*Snyder v. Massachusetts*, 1934). The United States Supreme Court in *Obergefell* reiterated "under the Due Process Clause of the Fourteenth Amendment, no State shall 'deprive any person of life, liberty, or property, without due process of law.'" The fundamental liberties protected by this clause include most of the rights enumerated in the Bill of Rights (*Obergefell v. Hodges*, 2015). The Supreme Court also has recognized family, the right to vote, interstate travel, and privacy as fundamental rights (*Planned Parenthood of Se. Pa. v. Casey*, 1992). A fundamental right is not subject to the vote of people and is protected by the Constitution.

The second principle is equal citizenship. Under this commitment, all members of the political community enjoy equal standing before the government. This principle is independent of the first. Even a person able to exercise all the basic rights that belong to citizens is also protected from being constituted as an essentially different sort of American. To take a religion example, the government could not declare "America is a Christian nation," regardless of whether it otherwise impeded the exercise of basic freedoms. Justice Kagan explained this in her dissent:

[T]he Constitution guarantees that however people worship, they count as full and equal American citizens. . . .they stand in the same relationship with [their] country. . . . When each person performs the duties or seeks the benefits of citizenship, she does so not as an adherent to one or another religion, but simply as an American. (Town of Greece, N.Y. v. Galloway, 2014)

How do religious accommodations in marriage equality laws fare under these principles? And how do they cohere with cases in antidiscrimination law? Let us begin with a simple example situation: private individuals may decide whether to solemnize a marriage on theological grounds, even if that decision involves discrimination on a prohibited basis in violation of public accommodations law (Lupu & Tuttle, 2010). That is true, even though clergy are empowered to preside over weddings that result in civil marriages as well as religious marriages. So, statutory accommodations of these decisions are defensible. They are also unnecessary because they duplicate basic constitutional law under free exercise and the freedom of expressive association (Wilson, 2014).

Clergy and congregations have a constitutional right to shape private marriage according to their beliefs. Conversely, no state could constitutionally require religious groups to perform such weddings once they became eligible for civil recognition in a state with marriage equality (Tebbe, 2015). Similar reasoning allows those congregations to decide who may use their sanctuaries for weddings, as long as the buildings are not held open to the public. While it is possible to imagine a law that deputizes clergy to perform civil weddings only on the condition that they not discriminate on protected grounds (Lupu & Tuttle, 2010), the practice of allowing clergy to perform civil marriages is so widespread and longstanding in the United States, that conditioning it on nondiscrimination would be an affront to religious freedom understandings that are universal today (Tebbe, 2008).

Beyond these constitutional basics, religion accommodations quickly become contested. For example, since 2015, as illustrated in Table 2, the states of Louisiana, Oklahoma, Texas, and Utah each have exemptions that allow religiously affiliated nonprofit organizations to close their facilities to all weddings and receptions that offend their religious beliefs, even if those facilities are public accommodations under general antidiscrimination law. (None of these states have protections for sexual orientation). Applying the principle of full citizenship highlights an immediate problem, which is that the accommodation appears to impinge on the liberties of others, namely the ability of LGBT people to access facilities for the celebration of their union in a community.

This type of systematic exclusion could significantly impact the economic wherewithal of same-sex couples. Even if the exclusion is not widespread and alternative facilities exist, the principle of equal citizenship weighs against allowing public accommodations to exclude people based on sexual orientation or marital status. One of the basic purposes of antidiscrimination law is to preserve the equal standing of members of minority groups in the economy and in society, as in politics. In *Roberts v. United States Jaycees* (1984), for example, the Supreme Court noted that gender discrimination carries many of the same ill effects of racial discrimination:

In upholding Title II of the Civil Rights Act of 1964, which forbids race discrimination in public accommodations, we emphasized that its fundamental object was to vindicate the deprivation of personal dignity that surely accompanies denials of equal access to public establishments. That stigmatizing injury, and the denial of equal opportunities that accompanies it, is surely felt as strongly by persons suffering discrimination based on their sex as by those treated differently because of their race.

A person's relationship with the community can be altered with respect to equal citizenship, even if adequate alternative venues exist. A fundamental insight of antidiscrimination law is that equal citizenship in a community can be infringed not just by government discrimination but also by exclusion from nongovernmental public accommodations tolerated by a legal regime. Some might argue against this application of principles of natural rights regarding full and equal citizenship by distinguishing between status and conduct. Discrimination against LGBT people, as such, is morally reprehensible and legally punishable, the argument might go, but objection to the act of marriage is understandable and should be accommodated (Bernstein 2014).

Yet this distinction does not perfectly track social meanings or practices. Marriage, like intimate sexual conduct, may well be too closely associated with LGBT identity to be separately proscribed without damaging citizenship interests. Justice O'Connor rejected the distinction between act and identity in the context of intimate sexual relations (*Lawrence v. Texas*, 2003), and recently the New Mexico Supreme Court rejected it in the context of unions between people of the same sex (*Elane Photography v. Willock*, 2013).

Scholars have questioned the distinction for similar reasons (NeJaime, 2012; Sepper, 2014; Dorf, 2011). Citizenship concerns are difficult to avoid in the context of marriage, once they are recognized as relating to sexual orientation itself.

Changes in Values and Beliefs: The *Obergefell* Decision

In the 1990s, anti-marriage-equality ballot initiative efforts and pro-equality state legislative efforts began to build significant momentum. It was not unusual at that time for legislators to state they did not have any LGBT constituents or to state they never heard from constituents who supported LGBT issues (Culhane & Sobel, 2005). As LGBT advocates engaged in more legislative activities, they incorporated grassroots efforts to affect legislative outcomes.

Using social media to stage protests and celebrations related to LGBT litigation victories (Browning, 2009), both advocates and opponents engaged in grassroots campaigns related to ballot and legislative initiatives. Some scholars criticize the use of direct democracy employed in ballot initiative efforts (Varona, 2010), describing the process as a discriminatory one that oppresses and marginalizes minority communities (Chemerinsky, 2007) and demonstrated by all the ballot losses for the LGBT community prior to 2012.

Even though the initiative battles were all lost until 2012, the tide turned. The ballot initiative process forced individuals to confront the issues and engage in a conversation on LGBT issues and marriage. The media campaign against California's Proposition 8 was vigorously criticized by scholars and advocates (Varona, 2010), yet the 2008 initiative ultimately forced the public to consider marriage equality when many people would not otherwise have been exposed to the issue. These conversations had an impact on public opinion and ultimately led to victories.

The last several years have been characterized by enormous strides toward equality for the LGBT community. The U.S. Supreme Court opinion in *United States v. Windsor* (2013), holding that Section 3 of the Defense of Marriage Act denying federal recognition of same-sex marriages was a violation of the Fifth Amendment's Due Process Clause, was followed by an almost uninterrupted string of victories on the issue of marriage equality in federal and state courts. These opinions led to the U.S. Supreme Court's opinion in *Obergefell v. Hodges* in June 2015. In *Obergefell*, Justice Kennedy began his opinion with the following:

The Constitution promises liberty to all within its reach, a liberty that includes certain specific rights that allow persons, within a lawful realm, to define and express their identity . . . concluding that by prohibiting same-sex marriage, gays and lesbians were demeaned, determined unequal, and stigmatized. (Obergefell v. Hodges, 2015)

The court determined this should no longer be the case. However, the ascendancy of gay rights has been accompanied by a rise in assertions of religious freedom. These assertions have primarily taken the form of state legislative initiatives (Eilperin, 2014). Supporters have cited perceived growing threats and hostility to religious liberty as a basis for such initiatives.

Since *Obergefell*, legislative measures have been introduced across the country in numerous statehouses, representing a backlash to the ruling, as indicated in Table 2, which has revived state legislative religious freedom restoration efforts that had been relatively stagnant since the late 1990s (Lund, 2010; Ledewitz, 2014). Although most of these efforts failed, 21 states, as demonstrated in Table 3, currently have legislative provisions purporting to protect the free exercise of religion (Griffin, 2017). Ledewitz (2014) predicts that the demands of "religious believers for exemptions will increase," resulting in increased societal conflict.

Table 2. States that permit discrimination against same-sex couples since 2015

State	RFRA	Public Accommodation	Rel. Org.			Non-Profit Org.		For-Profit Bus. and Gov. Official		Bill No.
			1	2	3	1	2	1	2	
LA	La. Rev. Stat. §13:5231, et seq.	La. Rev. Stat. §51:2247	x	x	x	x	x	x	x	Executive Order BJ 15-8 Marriage & Conscience 05/19/15
MI	State Constitution Mich.Const. Art. 1 §4	Mich. Comp. Laws. §§ 37.1102, 2302	4							HB 4188 9/9/15
NC	No RFRA	*							x	SB 2S.L. 2015-75 6/11/15
OK	Okla. Stat. tit. 51, §251, et seq.	Okla Stat. tit. 25, §1401	x	x		x				HB 1007 11/1/15
TX	Tex. Civ. Prac. & Remedies Code §110.001, et seq.	*	x	x		x				SB 2065 6/11/15
UT	Religious Land Use Act Utah Code Ann. §63L-5-101 to 403	*	x	x		x			x	SB 297/S.L. Ch.046 5/12/15

(Griffin, 2017; National Conference of State Legislators, 2017)

* Some of the states listed do have public accommodation statutes but do not cover sexual orientation. It is implicit that all states will comply with the provisions contained within Title II of the Civil Rights Act of 1964.

Religious Organizations

1. Religious leaders/houses of worship exempted from performing same-sex marriage.
2. Religious entities can refuse to provide marriage-related services to same-sex married couples.
3. Religious employer can refuse at least some benefits to same-sex married couples.
4. Faith-based adoption agencies can refuse services to same-sex married couples.

Nonprofit Organizations

1. Nonprofits can refuse to provide marriage-related services to same-sex married couples.
2. Nonprofit employers can refuse at least some benefits to same-sex married couples.

For-Profit Businesses and Government Officials

1. For-profit businesses can refuse to accept same-sex married couples as customers.
2. Government officials exempted from performing or assisting with same-sex marriage.

One of the sources of perceived threats to religious freedom are public accommodation statutes. States have nonuniform laws that provide for nondiscrimination based on sexual orientation in public accommodations, as sexual orientation is not a protected class under federal law. As of 2016, comparing data in Table 3, 28 states do not have antidiscrimination legislation that protects sexual orientation, and 22 states do protect sexual orientation in public accommodations (Dhooge, 2016). The inclusion of sexual orientation within the antidiscrimination statutes suggests that beliefs and values are changing in some areas of the country and not others. Application of these statutes in well-publicized cases involving religious objections to providing goods and services to same-sex couples celebrating marriages have been the source of considerable controversy.

But there is another type of problem for existing exemptions not mentioned above, namely constitutional concerns under the Establishment Clause. These raise a distinctive set of normative considerations as well as legal concerns.

The principle holds that governments may voluntarily lift regulatory burdens from religious actors but not if accommodating them shifts burdens onto third parties. Driving that rule is the normative principle that shifting burdens in this way would improperly impose the faith of one private party on another in violation of the government's obligation of evenhandedness in the face of religious differences among citizens. It is possible to understand this commitment as connected to both fundamental rights and equal citizenship—fundamental rights because, here, protecting the religious liberty rights of one party against the government would in fact impose on the liberty of others in violation of Justice Jackson's maxim (*Prince v. Massachusetts*, 1944) that:

Table 3. States with religious freedom restoration and public accommodations statutes

Jurisdiction	Religious Freedom Statute	Public Accommodation Statute
Alabama	Ala. Const. Art. I, §3.01	*
Arizona	Ariz. Rev. Stat. §41-1493.01	*
Arkansas	2015 SB 975, enacted April 2, 2015	*
Connecticut	Conn. Gen. Stat. §52-571b	Conn. Gen. Stat. §§ 46a-81 d, 46a-811 (2015) (adopted 1991);
Florida	Fla. Stat. §761.01, et seq.	*
Idaho	Idaho Code §73-402	*
Illinois	Ill. Rev. Stat. Ch. 775, §35/1, et seq.	Conn. Gen. Stat. §§ 46a-81 d, 46a-811 (2015) (adopted 1991);
Indiana	2015 SB 101, enacted March 26, 2015; 2015 SB 50, enacted April 2, 2015	*
Kansas	Kan. Stat. §60-5301, et seq.	*
Kentucky	Ky. Rev. Stat. §446.350	*
Louisiana	La. Rev. Stat. §13:5231, et seq.	*
Mississippi	Miss. Code §11-61-1	*
Missouri	Mo. Rev. Stat. §1.302	*
New Mexico	N.M. Stat. §28-22-1, et seq.	N.M. Stat. §§ 28-1-2, 7-9 (2015) (adopted 2004);
Oklahoma	Okla. Stat. tit. 51, §251, et seq.	*
Pennsylvania	Pa. Stat. tit. 71, §2403	*
Rhode Island	R.I. Gen. Laws §42-80.1-1, et seq.	R.I. Gen. Laws §§ 11-24-2-2.1 (2015) (adopted 1995);
South Carolina	S.C. Code §1-32-10, et seq.	*
Tennessee	Tenn. Code §4-1-407	*
Texas	Tex. Civ. Prac. & Remedies Code §110.001, et seq.	*
Virginia	Va. Code §57-2.02	*

(Griffin, 2017; National Conference of State Legislators, 2017)

* Some of the states listed do have public accommodation statutes but do not cover sexual orientation. It is implicit that all states will comply with the provisions contained within Title II of the Civil Rights Act of 1964.

Religious activities which concern only members of the faith are and ought to be free—as nearly free as anything can be. But nonreligious activities, such as when religious organizations engage in secular businesses to raise money from nonbelievers, are "Caesar's affairs, and may be regulated by the state so long as it does not discriminate against one because he is doing them for a religious purpose and the regulation is not arbitrary and capricious, in violation of other provisions of the Constitution.

Also, this would impact equal citizenship, because voluntary accommodations that work by imposing the religious beliefs of one party on another impermissibly align the government with the religious convictions of some citizens over others. When it comes to an identity characteristic as socially salient as religion, government favoritism of that sort works constitutional harm (Eisgruber & Sager, 2007; Tebbe, 2013). Court precedent gives the principle against burden, shifting the force of law. In *Estate of Thornton v. Caldor, Inc.* (1985), for instance, the court reasoned that "the First Amendment . . . gives no one the right to insist that in pursuit of their own interests, others must conform their conduct to his own religious necessities."

Ignoring that principle risks the religious freedom rights of third parties. The court's decision in *Burwell v. Hobby Lobby Stores, Inc.* (2014) must not be read to abrogate this longstanding rule. Here, statutory exemptions for religious actors in marriage equality laws run up against this basic rule of constitutional law and the principle of political morality it embodies. To see how, the cases below are provided.

RECENT CASES

No reasonable person would seriously contend that an American religious body can be ordered by any civil authority to perform weddings in violation of the tenets of that religion. But the issue becomes a clouded one when owners or operators of a wedding chapel open to the public decide to pick and choose what marriages they will and will not host or perform. These types of cases have percolated through the lower courts for nearly a decade: can small business owners, such as photographers, florists, and bakers be exempted from state antidiscrimination laws based on their religious beliefs about same-sex marriage?

Idaho, Nevada, New York, and Wedding Chapels

In Idaho, a married couple who assert both partners are "ordained ministers with the International Church of the Foursquare Gospel" and operate the for-profit Hitching Post Wedding Chapel were confronted with a local nondiscrimination ordinance (Ford, 2014). After the Ninth Circuit Court of Appeals struck down Idaho's ban on same-sex marriage, they temporarily closed the chapel and have since refused to perform or allow same-sex weddings on the premises

(*Knapp v. City of Coeur d'Alene*, 2016). Although the ordinance contained a religious exemption, and the city contended the religious exemption would apply to them, they sued in federal court, asserting they were in fear of its enforcement. On March 25, 2016, the federal district judge dismissed all their claims except for economic injuries for the single day of October 15, 2014, when they might have had a reasonable fear of enforcement in *Knapp*.

Other private wedding chapels also have refused to permit or perform same-sex weddings (Rodgers, 2015). Even some Elvis-themed chapels in Las Vegas have refused on religious grounds (Sieczkowski, 2014). Although the issue of wedding venue refusal to perform or permit same-sex marriage has been widespread, it appears there has been only one reported merits decision on the subject to date. Cynthia and Robert Gifford own and operate Liberty Ridge Farm, LLC in New York and rent out part of the farm for both religious and secular wedding ceremonies and receptions (*Gifford v. McCarthy*, 2016).

In October 2011, they refused to host a wedding of two women on religious grounds. The women filed a discrimination complaint with the New York State Division of Human Rights, which awarded each of them $1,500 in compensatory damages, imposed a $10,000 fine, and ordered the Gifford's to cease and desist their discriminatory practices. The New York State Supreme Court, Appellate Division, upheld the Divisions of Human Rights judgment against multiple challenges, including one asserting the Gifford's free exercise of religion (*Gifford v. McCarthy*, 2016).

New Mexico and the Wedding Photographer

There appears to be only one reported judicial decision on the refusal of a wedding photographer to be hired for a same-sex ceremony. In *Elane Photography v. Willock* (2013), a private company in New Mexico that acknowledged it is a public accommodation, refused to be hired for a same-sex "commitment ceremony." (This was not a wedding per se, as the state of New Mexico had not yet authorized same-sex marriages). One of the women who had been denied service filed a discrimination complaint with the New Mexico Human Rights Commission, which ruled in her favor. *Elane Photography* appealed through the state courts to the New Mexico Supreme Court, which upheld the decision. *Elane* argued that compelling her to photograph a same-sex couple's ceremony would violate New Mexico's Religious Freedom Restoration Act (NMRFRA).

The New Mexico Supreme Court disagreed, because the NMRFRA (N.M. Stat. §28-22-1, et seq) was not meant to apply to suits between private litigants but rather is a restriction on actions by government agencies that interfere with free exercise (*Elane Photography v. Willock*, 2013). The court said simply because a business is for-profit does not strip the business of its First Amendment speech protections, and the antidiscrimination laws simply required businesses to offer services to the public without regard to a potential client's membership in a protected class such as sexual orientation. The New Mexico Supreme Court reasoned from *West Virginia State Board of Education v. Barnette* (1943), a case that established the right to refrain from speaking. The reasoning in this case is important in demonstrating that one citizen's rights must end where another's begins.

Washington and the Florist

In February 2017 the Washington State Supreme Court upheld damages and an injunction against a flower shop and its owner for refusal to provide flowers for a same-sex wedding *(Washington State v. Arlene's Flowers, Inc.*, 2017). The court rejected the owner's claims of violation of her rights to free speech (i.e., against "compelled speech"), free exercise of religion, and free association.

The Bakers and the Supreme Court

The Oregon Bureau of Labor and Industry ordered bakery owners to pay an astonishing $135,000 in damages for emotional suffering to a same-sex couple to whom they had denied service *(Sweet Cakes by Melissa v. Oregon Bureau of Labor and Industries,* 2015)[2]. While such a large fine seems grossly disproportionate, it was clearly meant to send a signal to business owners in general not to discriminate against same-sex couples or risk grave consequences (Parks, 2015).

These cases culminated in *Craig* v. *Masterpiece Cakeshop* (2018), in which a Colorado court of appeals upheld the decision of that state's Human Rights Commission that a "cakeshop" violated that state's Anti-Discrimination Act by refusing to design and create a cake to celebrate a same-sex wedding. Phillips, the cakeshop owner, had asserted that requiring him to do so violated his rights to free exercise of religion and free speech—in this case, his alleged right not to be compelled to speak (i.e., tacitly approve of the wedding). The

U.S. Supreme Court agreed to hear the case and ordered a reversal of the decision made by the Colorado Civil Rights Commission.

The majority opinion written by Justice Kennedy stated that although a baker in his capacity as the owner of a business serving the public, "might have his right to the free exercise of his religion limited by generally applicable laws," a state decision in an adjudication "in which religious hostility on the part of the State itself" is a factor that violates the "State's obligation of religious neutrality" under the Free Exercise Clause of the First Amendment to the Constitution (*Craig v. Masterpiece Cakeshop,* 2018).

The opinion observed that there was hostility towards Phillips' religious views in the commission's review of his case. The commission compared Phillips' religious beliefs to the defense of slavery or the Holocaust. Kennedy found such comparisons "inappropriate for a Commission charged with the solemn responsibility of fair and neutral enforcement of Colorado's anti-discrimination law" in *Masterpiece Cakeshop*, further noting that the court may have been inclined to rule in favor of the commission if they had remained religiously neutral in their evaluation.

The court affirmed that there remains protection of same-sex couples and gay rights, which states can still enforce through antidiscrimination laws, but avoided ruling broadly on the intersection of antidiscrimination laws and rights to free exercise because of the existence of this hostility in the current case, stating that:

the outcome of cases like this in other circumstances must await further elaboration in the courts, all in the context of recognizing that these disputes must be resolved with tolerance, without undue disrespect to sincere religious beliefs, and without subjecting gay persons to indignities when they seek goods and services in an open market." (Craig v. Masterpiece Cakeshop, 2018)

Scholars and commentators emphasized that the court's opinion was narrowly concerned with neutrality in the adjudication of religious exemption claims (Epstein, 2018; Liptak, 2018). But as Douglas NeJaime and Reva Siegel (2018) show in *Religious Exemptions and Antidiscrimination Law in Masterpiece Cakeshop*, the court provided more guidance on the relationship between religious exemptions and antidiscrimination law than has been acknowledged. In the decade before *Masterpiece Cakeshop*, and in the litigation itself, advocates asserted that courts and legislatures should treat sexual orientation differently than race for purposes of exemptions from antidiscrimination law. They argued that whereas courts have rightly resisted religious exemptions from laws prohibiting race discrimination, courts should adopt a two-tiered framework and grant religious exemptions from laws prohibiting sexual orientation discrimination. Advocates for broad religious exemptions urge courts and legislatures to think about accommodating conscience claims for LGBT citizens based on the model of abortion rather than race. There were multiple amicus briefs filed in support; Ryan Anderson's brief connected abortion to LGBT rights in the same passage that distinguished race from sexual orientation. For Anderson,

pro-life conscience protections do not undermine Roe or women's equality. Neither do conscience protections for conjugal marriage supporters undermine Obergefell or gay equality. By contrast, conscience protections for opponents of interracial marriage could undermine the purposes of Loving, Brown, and the Civil Rights Act of 1964: racial equality. (Amicus Brief, 2018)

The comparison to abortion is not merely an analogy employed in courts; it is a call to activists to secure exemptions protecting a right to refuse to deal with same-sex couples in many settings. Emphasizing that opponents of abortion had secured expansive "religious liberty and conscience rights," Anderson (2015) has urged his fellow opponents of same-sex marriage . . .

to do the same: Ensure that we have freedom from government coercion to lead our lives, rear our children, and operate our businesses and charities in accord with our beliefs—the truth—about marriage.

These arguments for broad religious exemptions—the two-tiered antidiscrimination model and the unconstrained refusals model—work together. They point the nation away from an antidiscrimination regime that has tolerated relatively limited religious exemptions (Sepper, 2016) and toward a refusal regime with little court oversight that authorizes ever-expanding religious exemptions, seemingly without regard to their impact on those who do not share the objector's beliefs (NeJaime & Siegel, 2015).

The majority opinion rejects these arguments. Rather than carve out a special (and lesser) place for sexual orientation, *Masterpiece Cakeshop* treats lesbian and gay individuals as full members of the community deserving of equal protection from discrimination. The court accomplished this by analyzing the case as presenting an ordinary question of public accommodations law. At the outset of its opinion, the court invoked the "general rule" that religious objections "do not allow business owners and other actors in the economy and in society to deny protected persons equal access to goods and services under a neutral and generally applicable public accommodations law." In so doing, the court cites the leading precedent rejecting a free exercise claim in the public accommodations context—*Piggie Park*, which denied a business owner's claim for an exemption from the race nondiscrimination mandate of the 1964 Civil Rights Act.

The court did not endorse a two-tiered system of antidiscrimination law, in which some groups get full protection and others get less. Instead, it adopted one public accommodations framework in which government "can protect gay persons, just as it can protect other classes of individuals, in acquiring whatever products and services they choose on the same terms and conditions as are offered to other members of the public" in *Masterpiece Cakeshop*. The citation to *Piggie Park* provides more than doctrinal authority, it reaffirms the concept of public accommodations against conservative challenge. In recent years, some religious conservatives have criticized the concept of public accommodations and argued that business owners should be free to act on their religious convictions in the marketplace, as well as in the public square, by discriminating in their business dealings (Colombo, 2013).

One way to understand the wave of recent wedding-cake litigation is as an insurgent challenge to the public settlement, dating to the lunch-counter sit-ins of the civil rights era, which limited the prerogatives of business owners on the understanding that equal citizenship includes a customer's equal right to participate in commerce (Singer, 2015). In the wake of the sit-ins of the mid-20th century, the nation no longer allows business owners to invoke property rights as a reason to refuse service to minorities as they once commonly did (Schmidt, 2018). It now enforces public accommodation laws on terms that require business owners, whatever their personal convictions, to run their businesses in a nondiscriminatory fashion. A framework of this kind facilitates unimpeded access to the market for those who have long been subject to discrimination and who do not share the business owners' beliefs. That is a primary aim of public accommodation laws—an aim the court has repeatedly recognized as "compelling" (*Roberts v. United States Jaycees*, 1984).

The court makes clear that exemptions must be limited in order to protect gays and lesbians not only from material but also from dignitary harm. Second, the court is concerned to limit exemptions with the potential to be asserted by "a long list of persons" who might inflict "community-wide stigma." Claims by those who object to facilitating a marriage have exactly that potential to expand in numbers. As described by NeJaime & Siegel (2015), complicity-based claims vastly expand the universe of objectors, and accommodating them makes it far more difficult to protect third parties from harm.

The court required the government to address religious objectors evenhandedly, and with respect, when the government adjudicates religious exemption claims. At the same time, the court stated that the government can enforce public accommodation laws that protect gays and lesbians "in acquiring whatever products and services they choose on the same terms and conditions as are offered to other members of the public," and that the government may restrict religious exemptions from such laws in order to achieve that purpose in *Masterpiece Cakeshop*.

In recent years, some religious conservatives have challenged the role imposed on market participants by public accommodation laws. Paul Horwitz (2014) describes this as seeking to "upend" the conventional "picture of the marketplace as a neutral space." The court rejected this challenge. A public accommodation law can require a seller to act in the market in accordance with this role and provide "protected persons equal access to goods and services," while treating the seller's religious beliefs with respect (Lessing, 1995). The concluding passage directs the government to adjudicate disputes involving religious claimants evenhandedly, even as it reaffirms the importance of limiting religious exemptions in public accommodations. Some advocates insist that legislation that would prohibit LGBT discrimination should be conditioned on the availability of expansive religious exemptions (Goldstein, 2015). Robin Fretwell Wilson (2018) in *Religious Freedom v. Anti-Discrimination Laws: Can Rights Be Reconciled?* says,

[A]dvocates for antidiscrimination law covering sexual orientation will have to provide religious exemptions of the kind Phillips sought if they hope to pass antidiscrimination protections in Republican-dominated jurisdictions. But if we're going to have SOGI [sexual orientation and gender identity] nondiscrimination laws in the rest of America, we're going to have to leave room for religious people . . . . we're going to have to find ways in these new laws to live together, and that means leaving room for people like Phillips. And I'm sorry that I don't have a map with me, but those thirty-two states that don't now have sexual-orientation gender identity nondiscrimination laws are, not surprisingly, all Republican. Every single state house is controlled by Republicans. There are Republican governors in every single one of those states except two. And they rank among the most religious in America. So, at some point there's going to have to be room left there for religious people in the public square, too. . . .

Many statutes simply authorize religious refusals, without providing any nondiscrimination protections for LGBT people. Some of these statutes aim broadly. Others target specific services. These laws are deeply at odds with the understanding of religious accommodation that guides the court's reasoning in *Masterpiece Cakeshop*.

FUTURE RESEARCH DIRECTIONS

The varied outcomes in these cases demonstrate that public accommodation laws are ill-prepared to address sexual orientation, let alone same-sex marriage. This is due in part to the many different forms public accommodation statutes take throughout the country. Further complicating this area is the wide variety of terminology, definitions (or the absence thereof), coverage, and prohibited practices among these statutes. These differences have the potential to create uncertainty, confusion, and disparate treatment with respect to access to public accommodations for the LGBT community.

CONCLUSION

The focus of this chapter is the change in our values and beliefs associated with the notion that all people, regardless of his or her sexual orientation, have the right to be free from discrimination, and how our courts are reconciling this notion with our fundamental First Amendment Rights. This chapter addressed some historical aspects of antidiscrimination. The facts of recent cases of discrimination were reviewed due to sexual orientation in the context of antidiscrimination laws.

In 1964, for the first time since the end of Reconstruction, Congress enacted a law banning race discrimination in public accommodations, Title II of the Civil Rights Act of 1964. It is difficult today to understand why this law, which forbade hotels, restaurants, gas stations, and places of entertainment to discriminate based on race, color, or national origin, gave rise to such heated opposition and the longest filibuster in the history of the U.S. Senate.

Advocates for the rights of sexual minorities quite reasonably want the same rights—on the same terms—as everyone else. Unquestionably, that wish runs counter to many persons' sincerely held religious or moral beliefs. Either side can—and often does—take an absolutist approach (Feldblum, 2006). Sexual minorities often want to compel all people to recognize and deal with them as equals in all matters, including matters with religious overtones (Feldblum, 2006). People who object for sincere religious reasons (or possibly less sincere and less religious reasons) often want to not only refuse to accommodate sexual minorities but also prevent others from doing so.

Cogent arguments can be made on each side of this divide. Sexual minorities may justifiably argue that private prejudices can never be the basis for public policy (*Palmore v. Sidoti*, 1984).

They may assert that public officials are sworn to uphold the law and, if they feel they cannot do so, their duty is to resign. They may argue that private individuals or entities, for-profit or otherwise, that enter the stream of commerce must make their services available to all individuals on an equal basis. Further, should it become acceptable for public officials or private entities providing public accommodations to discriminate based on sexuality, this will readily lead to other forms of divisive discrimination. For instance, could a baker refuse to bake a cake, or a florist refuse to provide flowers, for a marriage involving an interracial couple, an interfaith couple, a Jewish or Muslim or Greek couple, a second marriage, a marriage in which the parties are "living in sin," a marriage that has already produced a child, a marriage where the bride is pregnant, a marriage where one of the parties is not a virgin, etc.?

Recognizing that prejudice will not end overnight, with or without a Supreme Court decision, is it not better to enforce nondiscrimination with the hope that, over time, prejudice will dissipate? Probably relatively few Americans today really believe stores should be allowed to refuse service based on race or religion, or that black Americans should have to sit in the back of the bus, as was the law in many places until our country took a firm stand on these matters a half century ago in *Brown v. Board of Education*, 1954.

On the other side, persons of certain religious beliefs may assert that they should not be compelled to commit acts that force them to commit what they believe to be sin, nor be complicit in sin, and that the Free Exercise Clause was specifically designed to prevent such a result. They may assert that at least if sexual minorities have other options readily available to them to achieve their desired ends, those with religious objections should be allowed to adhere to their sincere beliefs. They may assert that they should be protected against compelled speech they find objectionable (*Glickman v. Wileman Bros. & Elliott, Inc.*, 1997).

They might ask, if they can be forced to bake a cake for a same-sex marriage, could a bakery owned by a same-sex couple be compelled to bake a cake with an anti-gay message[3]? They may assert that compelling individuals to act against their sincere beliefs, or risk a heavy fine, or go out of business, will only heighten antagonisms not diffuse them.

As this chapter illustrated in *Elane*, Justice Bosson, in his concurring opinion, stated that tolerance and compromise in the beliefs held by Americans is an important "glue" to our nation. He went on to say that the "sense of respect we owe others, whether or not we believe as they do, illuminates this country, setting it apart from the discord that afflicts much of the rest of the world. It is the price of citizenship."

As such, when values and beliefs of that society change and grow, so too do the laws that govern its citizens. Our country has experienced this changing and growing throughout its history, especially with regards to equality for its citizens, from slavery to the civil rights movement, to gender equality and, more recently, sexual orientation and transgender issues. However, what happens when the idea of equality clashes with an individual's fundamental rights? That is when these changing values and beliefs hurl our justice system into a balancing act within the gray area of the law.

REFERENCES

American with Disabilities Act, Public Law 88–352, 78 Stat. 241 (1990).

Anderson, R. (2015, July 14). Will marriage dissidents be treated as bigots or pro-lifers? *Federalist.* Retrieved from http://thefederalist.com/2015/07/14/will-marriage-dissidents-treated-bigots-pro-lifers/

Barbaro, M., & Eckholm, E. (2015, March 27). Indiana law denounced as invitation to discriminate against gays. *New York Times*. Retrieved from http://www.nytimes.com/2015/03/28/us/politics/indiana-law-denounced-as-invitation-to-discriminate

Bernstein, D. (2014, February 27). The Volokh conspiracy: Guest post from Prof. Doug Laycock: What Arizona SB1062 actually said. *Washington Post.* Retrieved from http://perma.cc/GR5W-ZYAX

Brief for Ryan T. Anderson, PhD, and African-American & Civil Rights Leaders as Amici Curiae, p.22, Supporting, Masterpiece Cakeshop v. Colorado Civil Rights Commission, 138 S.Ct. 1719 (2018).

Brown v. Board of Education, 347 U.S. 483, 495 (1954).

Browning, B. (2009, May-June). Politics at lighting speed. *Gay and Lesbian Review*.

Burwell v. Hobby Lobby Stores, Inc., 134 S. Ct. 2751, 2762,2785 (2014).

Carpenter, D. (2013, October 23). *Letter from Dale Carpenter*. University of Minnesota Law School. Retrieved from http://perma.cc/GY4V-UG48

Chemerinsky, E. (2007). Challenging direct democracy. *Detroit College of Law at Michigan State University Law Review*, 293–308.

Civil Rights Act of 1964, Public Law. 88–352, 78 Stat. 241 (1964)

Colombo, R. J. (2013). The naked private square. *Houston Law Review*, *51*(1), 18–107.

Craig v. Masterpiece Cakeshop, Inc., 370 P.3d 272, 276, 280 (Colo. App. 2015).

Dhooge, L. J. (2016). Public accommodation statues, sexual orientation and religious liberty: Free access or free exercise? *University of Florida Law and Public Policy*, *27*, 1–58.

Discrimination. (2018). In *Merriam – Webster dictionary online*. Retrieved from http://www.merriamwebster.com/dictionary/discrimination

Dorf, M. C. (2011). Same-sex marriage, second-class citizenship, and law's social meanings. *Virginia Law Review*, *97*, 1260–1314.

Eilperin, J. (2014, February 27). After veto in Arizona, conservatives vow to fight for religious liberties. *Washington Post*. Retrieved from http://www.washingtonpost.com/politics/after-veto-in-arizona-conservatives-vow-to-fight

Eisgruber, C. L., & Sager, L. A. (2007). *Religious freedom and the Constitution*. Cambridge, MA: Harvard University Press. doi:10.4159/9780674034457

Elane Photography v. Willock, 309 P.3d 53, 58-59, 61 (N.M. 2013).

Epstein, R. A. (2018, June 4). The worst form of judicial minimalism: Masterpiece cakeshop deserved a full vindication for its claims of religious liberty and free speech. *SCOTUSblog*. Retrieved from http://www.scotusblog.com/2018/06/symposium-the-worst-form-of-judicial-minimalism-masterpiece-cakeshop-deserved-a-full-vindication-for-its-claims-of-religious-liberty-and-free-speech/

Estate of Thornton v. Caldor, Inc., 472 U.S. 703 (1985).

Feldblum, C. R. (2006). Moral conflict and liberty: Gay rights and religion. *Brooklyn Law Review*, *72*, 61–123.

Ford, Z. (2014, October 20). For-profit wedding chapel sues after Idaho legalizes same-sex marriage. *Think Progress*. Retrieved from http://thinkprogress.org/lgbt/2014/10/20/3581733 /idaho-marriage-chapel-adf/

Gifford v. McCarthy, 137 A.D.3d 30, 33 (N.Y. App. Div. 2016).

Glickman v. Wileman Bros. & Elliott, Inc., 512 U.S. 457, 470-72 (1997).

Greenawalt, K. (2013). Religious toleration and claims of conscience. *Journal of Law and Policy*, *28*, 91–113.

Griffin, J. (2016, July 13). *State public accommodation laws*. National Conference of State Legislators. Retrieved from http://www.ncsl.org/research/civil-and-criminal-justice/state-public-accommodation-laws.aspx

Heart of Atlanta Motel, Inc. v. United States, 379 U.S. 241 (1964).

Knapp v. City of Coeur d'Alene, 172 F. Supp. 3d 1118, 1133, 1135 (D. Idaho 2016).

Lansburg, B. K. (2015). Public accommodations and the civil rights act of 1964: A surprising success. *Hamline University School of Law Journal of Public Law and Policy*, *36*(1), 1–25.

Lawrence v. Texas, 539 U.S. 558, 583 (2003) (O'Connor, J., concurring).

Ledewitz, B. (2014). Experimenting with religious liberty: The quasi-constitutional status of religious exemptions. *Elon Law Review*, *6*(37), 72–73.

Lessig, L. (1995). The regulation of social meaning. *The University of Chicago Law Review. University of Chicago. Law School*, *62*(3), 943–966. doi:10.2307/1600054

Liptak, A. (2018, June 4). In narrow decision, split sides with Baker who turned away gay couple. *New York Times.* Retrieved from https://www.nytimes.com/2018/06/04/us/politics/supreme-court-sides-with-baker-who-turned-away-gay-couple.html

Liptak, A. (2018, June 4). Supreme Court sides with baker who turned away gay couple. *New York Times*. Retrieved from https://www.theguardian.com/law/2018/jun/04/gay-cake-ruling-supreme-court-same-sex-wedding-colorado-baker-decision-latest

Loving v. Virginia, 388 U.S. 1 (1967).

Lund, C. (2010). Religious liberty after Gonzales: A look at state RFRAs. *South Dakota Law Review*, *55*, 466–475.

Lupu, I. C., & Tuttle, R. W. (2010). Same-sex family equality and religious freedom. *Northwestern Journal of Law and Social Policy*, *5*(2), 274–306.

Masterpiece Cakeshop, Ltd. v. Colorado Civil Rights Commission 138 S. Ct. 1719 (2018).

National Conference of State Legislatures. (2017). *Religious freedom restoration act legislation.* Retrieved from http://www.ncsl.org/research/civil-and-criminal-justice/2017-religious-freedom-restoration-act-legislation.aspx#

NeJaime, D. (2012). Marriage inequality: Same-sex relationships, religious exemptions, and the production of sexual orientation discrimination. *California Law Review*, *100*, 1160–1192.

NeJaime, D., & Siegel, R. B. (2018). Religious exemption and antidiscrimination law in Masterpiece Cakeshop. *The Yale Law Journal Forum*, 201-225.

Newman v. Piggie Park Enters., Inc., 390 U.S. 400, 402 n.5 (1968).

Obergefell v. Hodges, 135 S. Ct. 2584 (2015).

Oleske, J. (2015). The evolution of accommodation: Comparing the unequal treatment of religious objections to interracial and same-sex marriage. *Harvard Civil Rights-Civil Liberties Law Review*, *50*, 100–154.

Palmore v. Sidoti, 466 U.S. 429, 433 (1984).

Parks, C. (2016, August 25). Oregon Lawyers: Sweet Cakes by Melissa $135,000 damage award was justified. *Oregonian*. Retrieved from https://www.oregonlive.com/portland/index.ssf/2016/08/oregon_lawyers_sweet_cakes_by.html

Planned Parenthood of Se. Pa. v. Casey, 505 U.S. 833 (1992).

Prince v. Massachusetts, 321 U.S. 158, 177 (1944) (Jackson, J., concurring).

Roberts v. Jaycees, 468 U.S. 609, 625 (1984).

Rodgers, G. (2015, January 28). Grimes' Gortz Haus to stop all weddings in wake of discrimination complaint. *Des Moines Register*. Retrieved from http://www.desmoinesregister.com/story/news/investigations/2015/01/28/gortz-haus-owners-decide-stop-weddings/22492677/

Schmidt, C. W. (2018). *The sit in: Protest and legal changes in the civil rights era*. Chicago: The University of Chicago Press. doi:10.7208/chicago/9780226522586.001.0001

Sepper, E. (2014). Doctoring discrimination in the same-sex marriage debates. *Indiana Law Journal (Indianapolis, Ind.)*, *89*, 700–714.

Sepper, E. (2016). Substantiating the burdens of compliance. *University of Illinois Law Review*, 53.

Sexual Orientation. (2018). In *Merriam – Webster dictionary online*. Retrieved from http://www.merriamwebster.com/dictionary/sexual%20orientation

Sieczkowski, C. (2014, October 20). Elvis-themed Las Vegas chapel refuses to hold gay weddings. *Huffington Post.* Retrieved from http://www.huffmgtonpost.eom/2014/10/20/elvis- themed-vegas-gay-weddings_n_6014550.html

Singer, J. W. (2015). We don't serve your kind here: Public accommodations and the mark of Sodom. *Baylor University Law Review*, *95*, 925–947.

Snyder v. Massachusetts, 291 U.S. 97, 105 (1934).

State v. Arlene's Flowers, Inc., 389 P.3d 543, 548, 568 (Wash. 2017).

Sweet Cakes by Melissa, v. Oregon Bureau of Labor and Industries, Final Order, Nos. 44-14 & 44-15 (BOLI, 2015).

Tebbe, N. (2008). Excluding religion. *University of Pennsylvania Law Review*, *156*, 1263–1339.

Tebbe, N. (2015). Religion and marriage equality statutes. *Harvard Law & Policy Review*, *9*, 25–61.

Town of Greece v. Galloway, 572 U.S. (2014).

U.S. v. Windsor, 133 S. Ct. 2675 (2013).

Varona, A. (2010). Taking initiatives: Reconciling race, religion, media and democracy in the quest for marriage equality. *Columbia Journal of Gender and Law*, *19*(3), 805–866.

Washington State v. Arlene's Flowers, Inc., P.3d (Wash. 2017).

West Virginia State Board of Education v. Barnette, 319 U.S. 624 (1943).

Wilson, R. F. (2014). Marriage of necessity: Same-sex marriage and religious liberty protections. *Case Western Reserve Law Review*, *64*(3), 1161–1268.

Wong, C. M. (2016, February 2). Pennsylvania's W. W. Bridal Boutique under fire for reportedly turning away lesbian brides-to-be. *Huffington Post*. Retrieved from http://www.huffmgtonpost.eom/2014/08/l l/ww-bridal-boutique-lesbia_n_5668645.html

KEY TERMS AND DEFINITIONS

Civil Rights Act of 1964: Federal act passed to amend statutes passed after the Civil War to provide stronger protections for constitutional rights.

Compelled Speech: Transmission of expression required by law.

Fourteenth Amendment: Guarantees citizens of the United States due process and equal protection of the laws. The Supreme Court expanded the concepts to any societal function involving state action to prevent discrimination against individuals on the grounds of race, sex, religion, or age.

Invidious Discrimination: The treatment of a class of people unequally in a manner that is malicious, hostile, or damaging.

Miscegenation: People of different races having children together.

Public Accommodations: Defined as entities that are used by the public, whether they are publicly or privately operated. Examples include retail stores, rental establishments and service establishments, educational institutions, and recreational facilities. States with fully inclusive public accommodations discrimination protections have laws indicating that LGBT people may use these establishments like all other members of the public. Some states have laws protecting only LGB people from this kind of discrimination.

ENDNOTES

1 Religious organizations and institutions were not mentioned in Title II of the Civil Rights Act of 1964, but they received an exemption under Title VII.

2 In re Klein case.

3 The Colorado Court of Appeals in the *Masterpiece Cakeshop* case distinguished prior decisions of the Colorado Civil Rights Division that bakeries had not violated the Colorado Anti-Discrimination Act when they had refused, for example, to bake bible-shaped cakes with inscriptions such as "Homosexuality is a detestable sin. Leviticus 8:2." Craig v. Masterpiece Cakeshop, 370 P.3d272,282 n.8 (Col. App. 2015).

Chapter 5
Social Change:
The Power of Place

ABSTRACT

The differences between states and within states are profound, and while that has long been true, it is much more consequential to LGBT individuals since the legalization of same-sex marriage. Social change relating to LGBT issues were originally addressed in a 1997 article written by Thomas Stoddard titled "Bleeding Heart: Reflections on Using the Law to Make Social Change." This chapter uses his framework and examines legislative responses to the legalization of same-sex marriage focusing on place.

INTRODUCTION

In our everyday lives, we typically do not think about place and are therefore unaware and unconcerned by the increasingly placeless character of the contemporary world. The primacy of place in experience—that everything and everyone is in place—is that place is an essential precondition for the existence of anything. Societies are not only shaped by their places, their places shape them, and these places are experienced as communities and a shared culture.

Place is experienced in the buildings we inhabit and in those daily rituals of dwelling that bind us to a place as home, which constructs a community through shared cultivation. Our globalized way of life, now epitomized by the contemporary business traveler and the tourist, is one in which place is

DOI: 10.4018/978-1-5225-7961-8.ch005

more important than it was when people were rooted to one place. We cannot know how far we have gone or how different the places or the people are we have visited without reference to the permanent place that is our home. Our ability to judge, our ethical foundation, is founded in our place. Places do not only orient us as physical, experiencing bodies on the earth, they also orient us as acting, ethical beings in the world.

Differences in place produce varied political cultures that construct different values, beliefs, attitudes, and expectations of citizens toward the political system and as participants in it. In the U.S., these beliefs are increasingly codified by both demographics and geographical location. Political systems and actors are now characterized as either "red" or "blue," which translates into legislative decision making and electorate voting behavior (Pallay, 2013).

Each color represents a different paradigm that extends beyond politics and reveals divergent social worlds. The idea of red (Republican) and blue (Democrat) states, places within a state, or individuals has become commonplace. The general understanding is that *blue* denotes the politically liberal, while *red* is characterized as conservative. Red areas adhere to traditional values and are often opposed to what they believe to be radical social changes such as granting or extending LGBT rights. These regions tend to be rural and people tend to be more religious, less educated, and not mobile. In contrast, blue communities have taken hold in urban areas and along the coasts and are increasingly Democratic, where the presence and importance of choice, diversity, and change is commonplace.

The realities of these differences are far more complicated than the simple contrast between red and blue. At the core of these distinctions are deep social divisions over changing values and lifestyles that shape and are expressed in the politics of place. Recognizing that red and blue families live different lives has dominated legal and political debates for some time. Ideologically, legislators from a red or a blue state have different worldviews that influence and mold their decision making. Rights for an LGBT individual vary from region to region, state-to-state, and even within states, shaped by a variety of factors from partisanship, to public opinion, to migration and immigration, all of which influence the content of laws and policies. Each of these elements offers examples of their dynamic and interactive nature on social and political processes, wherein particular relationships are established, reproduced, or transformed.

THE FRAMEWORK APPLIED TO LGBT ISSUES

Thomas Stoddard's 1997 article, "Bleeding Heart: Reflections on Using the Law to Make Social Change" ("Bleeding Heart"), offers a framework for social change—four factors necessary for a culture shift to occur. Hunter (1997) and Sobel (2015) added a fifth dimension of social change—public engagement, which explains the speed at which cultural transformation occurs. Using these elements of change, this chapter examines the links between place and inequality:

(1) A change that is very broad or profound; (2) Public awareness of that change; (3) General sense of the legitimacy (or validity) of the change; (4) Overall, continuous enforcement of the change (Stoddard, 1997); and (5) Public engagement. (Hunter, 1997; Sobel, 2015)

The human significance of space and place invoke the concepts of attachment, identity, and belonging, each influencing the political significance of people's psychological representations of space. These shape people's understandings of who belongs, the rights and freedoms that people may claim and exercise, decisions about where we feel "at home" or "out of place," where we may move or avoid, and much more. The social and political significance of place and its psychological representation may (ironically) lead us to underestimate the degree to which place and space have political significance for our daily routines and decision making.

In countless everyday settings and mundane social interactions, representations of place and space matter. They impact who can be where, affect how people are included or excluded from public spaces, and shape the ways in which people relate to one another. In short, place and space play a central role in the ways that large-scale and abstract social categories such as "nation," "class," "race," and "gay or straight" impact lived experience and are reproduced through it. For all these reasons, a key issue facing members of the LGBT community is the everyday construction of place and space.

In the sections of the chapter to follow, an overview of the factors that influence an elected official's interactions include describing the differences in various state cultures that are supportive and not supportive of LGBT equality. The links between place and inequality are powerful. What does an unsupportive "political culture" mean for LGBT citizens in the United States?

Broad and Profound Change

This chapter applies Stoddard's (1997) framework as well as a theoretical discussion on place to determine whether a rule shift on LGBT issues has been accompanied by a corresponding culture change. The intersection of place and the gay rights movement intensified after the *Obergefell* decision. But beginning in 2000, one such shift occurred, when Vermont gay couples were granted the legal benefits of marriage through civil unions—the state stopping short of calling it marriage. Then again in 2003, the Massachusetts Supreme Court ruled that under the state's constitution, gay couples have the right to marry (*Goodridge v. Department of Public Health*, 2003). This breach of formal norms rippled throughout the United States, where marriage between people of the same-sex was prohibited elsewhere.

Relationship recognition laws have changed through the centuries. Throughout U.S. history, the laws of each state defined marriage. Since the founding of the Republic, without exception, marriage had been a matter of state concern and control until 1996, when Democratic President Bill Clinton signed into law the Defense of Marriage Act (DOMA), which forbade the federal government and states to recognize same-sex marriages (Public Law 104-199, 1996).

It was in 2010 that polling data first found that a narrow majority of Americans supported marriage equality (Sant'Ambrogio & Law, 2011). By 2012, Silver (2013) noted, only seven states showed support below 39% and a total of 30 states had support below 50%. This compared to 1996, when only 27% of Americans believed that marriages between same-sex couples should be legally recognized and provide the same rights as traditional marriages (Jones, 2013). By 2004, that percentage grew to 42%, before falling to 37% the next year, but, nonetheless, this continued an upward trend (Jones, 2013).

Until 2012, same-sex marriage opponents had "won" 29 consecutive constitutional amendment fights—excluding Arizona's 2006 failed constitutional amendment to ban same-sex marriage. That streak ended in 2012, when opponents lost the referendum in the State of Washington (Michelson, 2012), and Maryland passed a same-sex marriage law (Robinson, 2012; Linskey, 2012); when they failed to secure a constitutional amendment in Minnesota (Michelson, 2012) and Maine voters enacted same-sex marriage at the ballot box (Bangor Daily News, 2012). All of these occurred after the tide of national public opinion had shifted in favor of same-sex marriage.

By 2020, according to Silver (2013), support for same-sex marriage will be overwhelming in every state except Mississippi, where support remains below 39%. In all states but six (South Carolina, Arkansas, Georgia, Louisiana, Alabama, and Mississippi) most voters are projected to support same-sex marriage. In four of the latter states (South Carolina, Arkansas, Georgia, Louisiana), support is expected to be within two percentage points of a majority. The rule-shifting movement to prohibit sexual orientation discrimination was engaged in earlier than the marriage equality movement, and 21 states passed nondiscrimination laws. Those states that provide statewide protections against employment discrimination are largely clustered in the Northeast and Pacific regions of the United States, leaving most LGBT people in the Midwest, South, and Mountain states with limited legal options to workplace discrimination (Hasenbush et al., 2014).

More LGBT people live in the 29 states without state nondiscrimination laws. However, a large percentage of Americans, 63%, support LGBT-inclusive nondiscrimination laws that would make it illegal to discriminate in the workplace based on sexual orientation or gender identity (Newport, 2013; Gelman, 2013). The difficulty is, despite the broadness of the change (Klarman, 2005; Carroll, 2007), there are still many areas where relatively no change has occurred.

Public Awareness of the Change

Repeated court cases, legislative battles, and ballot initiatives, coupled with the portrayal of LGBT people on television (Tropiano, 2002) has resulted in long-term public exposure to and awareness of LGBT issues. Rule shifting related to LGBT rights has become mainstream news. In fact, 75% of Americans already believe there is a federal law prohibiting employment discrimination based on sexual orientation, when no such protection exists (Jones, 2013). This misinformed belief demonstrates that culture has shifted in some areas to the point in which citizens believe the laws have already changed (Newport, 2013; Gelman, 2013).

Validity of Change

Even though rule shifting toward equality is not embraced by all, it is recognized as a valid part of the movement's legal landscape. Stoddard (1997) looked at the process of rule shifting as it applied to this prong. He examined the timing and venue of the change—legislation versus litigation—as impacting the legitimacy of the legal change.

LGBT advocates availed themselves of the judicial system because of the long-held belief that the courts were the best option for disadvantaged groups to protect their rights (*Chambers v. State*, 1940). Some scholars also have acknowledged that litigation is an attractive option for disadvantaged groups rather than the political process because courts are generally obligated to consider legal claims when lawmakers are not inclined to address a group's concerns (NeJaime, 2012). Others have criticized the role of the court as a savior or its ability to play the role of the "counter-majoritarian hero" (Klarmen, 1996).

It is difficult to get legislators to address LGBT concerns. Even legislators who are supportive of equality are more likely to avoid the issue than to introduce or move legislation (Culhane & Sobel, 2005). Consequently, litigation became a primary focus for LGBT advocates and organizations engaged in a purposeful legal strategy (NaJaime, 2012). Some of this litigation, filed by lawyers who were not part of the movement, had significant impact. The *Baehr v. Lewin* (1993) case was represented by a single private-practice lawyer and "substantially altered the course of the LGBT movement and single-handedly changed the national conversation on LGBT rights" (Cummings & NaJaime, 2010).

For advocacy organizations, marriage litigation took priority (Ball, 2014). The strategy was to pick states that had constitutional provisions and judicial personnel likely to rule in favor of marriage equality. One of the biggest differences in the location of successes among efforts to gain recognition of legal rights for LGBT people versus other equality movements was both the vertical and horizontal nature of the activity (Hunter, 1997).

There has been much greater activity at the state level than at the federal level on LGBT issues, whether one examines legislation or litigation. For example, the first three states to allow gay marriage did so because of court rulings (Massachusetts, 2003; Connecticut, 2008; and Iowa, 2009), rather than through legislative action or putting the issue to voters to decide. But by mid-2009, six states had approved gay marriage laws by passing laws in state legislatures (Vermont, 2009; New Hampshire, 2009; New York, 2011; Rhode Island, 2013; Delaware, 2013; and Minnesota, 2013) and three states by ballot initiatives (Maine, 2012; Maryland, 2012; Washington, 2012). Similarly, the breakthroughs on functional family recognition and domestic partner benefits occurred first at the state and local levels. And virtually all employment and public accommodations successes have occurred at the state level (Hunter, 1997).

Many state-related advances followed the path of incremental change by pursing rights in a predetermined sequence of legislation that decriminalized sodomy; punished hate crimes against LGBT people; created nondiscrimination laws in employment, housing, and public accommodations; provided limited relationship recognition for same-sex couples; and then advocated for full marriage equality (Keck, 2009). These legislative efforts were often engaged while litigation was pending on the same issues in state courts. The validity of the change on LGBT issues is not based in a litigation versus legislation debate but in the fact that LGBT advocates used all types of tactics to push for change.

Some perceive social change through litigation as less valid than change derived legislatively. Chief Justice Roberts' dissent in the *Obergefell v. Hodges* (2015) expressed those concerns:

Petitioners make strong arguments rooted in social policy and considerations of fairness. They contend that same-sex couples should be allowed to affirm their love and commitment through marriage, just like opposite-sex couples. That position has undeniable appeal; over the past six years, voters and legislators in eleven States and the District of Columbia have revised their laws to allow marriage between two people of the same sex.

But this Court is not a legislature. Whether same-sex marriage is a good idea should be of no concern to us. Under the Constitution, judges have power to say what the law is, not what it should be. The people who ratified the Constitution authorized courts to exercise "neither force nor will but merely judgment." Although the policy arguments for extending marriage to same-sex couples may be compelling, the legal arguments for requiring such an extension are not. The fundamental right to marry does not include a right to make a State change its definition of marriage. And a State's decision to maintain the meaning of marriage that has persisted in every culture throughout human history can hardly be called irrational. In short, our Constitution does not enact any one theory of marriage. The people of a State are free to expand marriage to include same-sex couples, or to retain the historic definition.

Today, however, the Court takes the extraordinary step of ordering every State to license and recognize same-sex marriage. Many people will rejoice at this decision, and I begrudge none their celebration. But for those who believe in a government of laws, not of men, the majority's approach is deeply disheartening. Supporters of same-sex marriage have achieved considerable success persuading their fellow citizens—through the democratic process—to adopt their view. That ends today. Five lawyers have closed the debate and enacted their own vision of marriage as a matter of constitutional law. Stealing this issue from the people will for many cast a cloud over same-sex marriage, making a dramatic social change that much more difficult to accept.

Enforcement

The enforcement prong of Stoddard's (1997) test does appear to be an issue in certain parts of the country. The states that have passed legislation or had a court decision granting relationship recognition to same-sex couples have enforced the law. Even though there may be people who were displeased with the results, it appears compliance with the new laws and court decisions have been commonplace (Keck, 2009).

There are several instances where local clerks have refused to issue marriage licenses (Kaplan, 2001; Meyers, 2013; Phillips, 2015) and, conversely, there are several instances where state attorneys general have refused to defend state bans on marriage equality (Eilperin, 2013). In those instances, in which government officials have not followed rule changes, or when the reach of a case was not clear, the courts have forced compliance with the new rules. This was the case when the chief justice of the Alabama Supreme Court, Roy Moore, released a letter addressed to Alabama Governor Robert J. Bentley, in which he said:

Our State Constitution and our morality are under attack by a federal court decision that has no basis in the Constitution of the United States. Nothing in the United States Constitution grants to the Federal Government the authority to redefine the institution of marriage. The laws of this state have always recognized the Biblical admonition stated by our Lord:

But from the beginning of the creation God made them male and female. For this cause shall a man leave father and mother and cleave to his wife; And they twain shall be one flesh: so, then they are no more twain, but one flesh. What therefore God hath joined together, let not man put asunder (Mark 10:6-9).

As of this date, 44 federal courts have imposed by judicial fiat same-sex marriages in 21 states of the Union, overturning the express will of the people in those states. If we are to preserve that "reverent morality which our source of all beneficent progress in social and political, improvement then we must act to oppose such tyranny! (Associated Press, 2016)

Moore warned any judge who might issue a marriage license to a same-sex couple that "the issuance of such licenses would be in defiance of the laws and Constitution of Alabama." Saying that his court was not bound by U.S. District Court rulings, he wrote to the governor: "Be advised that I stand with you to stop judicial tyranny and any unlawful opinions issued without constitutional authority." The governor responded:

The people of Alabama voted in a constitutional amendment to define marriage as being between man and woman. As Governor, I must uphold the Constitution. I am disappointed in the ruling, and I will continue to oppose this ruling. The Federal Government must not infringe on the rights of states. (Associated Press, 2016)

Shortly after the *Obergefell* decision was announced, the Alabama House of Representatives voted 53–36 in favor of a bill that sought to do away with marriage licenses issued by the state, effectively taking Alabama out of the marriage business. Supporters of the bill claimed it would protect probate judges who oppose issuing marriage licenses to same-sex couples. However, the bill failed because it needed a two-thirds majority in favor. The sole sponsor of House Bill 41 was Republican Representative Jim Hill:

Under existing law, marriage licenses are issued by the judge of probate. This bill would provide that judges of probate would no longer issue marriage licenses upon proof of eligibility for marriage, but instead, will be statutorily required to receive and record civil contracts of marriage presented by parties to the civil contract. This bill would require the judge of probate to transmit a copy of each civil contract filed with the judge of probate during the preceding calendar month to the Office of Vital Statistics on or before the fifth day of the following calendar month. This bill would remove the requirement of marriage licenses.

This bill would provide that parties desiring to enter a marital union may enter a civil contract for marriage to be known as a civil contract. This bill would provide that it shall be the responsibility of the parties to the contract for marriage to record the civil contract with the judge of probate as evidence of their marital union. The bill would specify that the judge of probate would have no authority or responsibility to make determinations of the eligibility of the parties to the contract for marriage, other than age determination, which shall be proved by submission of a consent form by the parents or guardians of a minor to the marriage contract. This bill would provide that a religious, civil, or independent ceremony of marriage, or other officiation, or administration of the vows, may, but need not be, conducted or engaged in by the parties to the civil contract as a condition of the contract of marriage. This bill would provide that the state shall have no role in the independent or religious ceremony of marriage.

Less than a year later, another Republican, Senator Greg Albritton, introduced a similar measure to do away with state-issued marriage licenses. The Alabama Senate approved it in a 23–3 vote. The bill died without a vote in the House. Representative Patricia Todd, a Democrat, and the only openly gay legislator in the state, called the bill unnecessary, saying, "The probate judges should do their job and issue licenses" (Williams, 2015).

Public Engagement

Stoddard's (1997) original framework did not include public engagement. Hunter (1997) and Sobel (2015) added this dimension of social change, which explains the speed at which cultural transformation occurs. These changes would not likely have occurred so quickly if LGBT advocacy organizations alone directed the pace of rule shifting. The efforts of LGBT rights opponents prompted the rapidity of change by enacting backlash through related legislation and ballot initiatives. These efforts brought public engagement into what had mostly been a litigation-driven and organization-dominated strategy. By asking people to weigh in on the issue of marriage equality, ordinary citizens were confronted with the issue and many of them likely engaged in a dialogue that would never have occurred without the impetus of a ballot initiative or legislative action.

Scholars disagree about the impact backlash had on LGBT equality efforts (Keck, 2009). Some believe that what may have appeared to be legal victories for LGBT people in reality made the situation worse for them through backlash legislation and ballot initiatives (Rosenberg, 2008). While litigation often has been the catalyst for rule shifting on marriage equality (Sant'Ambrogio

& Law, 2011), associated decisions also have led to legislative and voter-initiated backlash. The legal battle started with the Hawaii's litigation in *Baehr v. Lewin* (1993) and continued after Massachusetts's highest court granted full marriage equality in *Goodridge, v. Department of Public Health* (2003), culminating in the *Obergefell* decision.

The litigation produced publicity, public education, and public policy opportunities for advocates (NaJaime, 2012), and benefits for movement constituents may have also produced indirect effects to mobilize and empower constituents, aid fundraising, gain publicity, obtain leverage with government officials, and move the public and elites on an issue (McCann, 2004). Some believe the scholarly examination and rejection of the court's reasoning and conclusion in *Bowers v. Hardwick* (1986) directly led to favorable attention of the gay rights movement and, ultimately, the court's decision to overturn *Bowers* in *Lawrence v. Texas* (2003). Others, however, believe "broad societal change, not just additional scholarly research and legal commentary, was vital to bringing about the *Lawrence* decision," and that grassroots organizations like the National Gay and Lesbian Task Force ("NGLTF") helped produce the change by using *Bowers* as a galvanizing force to help repeal remaining sodomy laws and result in the *Lawrence* decision.

Similarly, the *Goodridge* decision resulted in both backlash and opportunity for LGBT advocates. There was backlash from state legislators when they introduced 51 separate anti-LGBT pieces of legislation in 2004 (Culbane & Sobel, 2005). Because of the increase in the number of anti-LGBT legislation, activists across the country began to form larger and more diverse coalitions to work on behalf of the LGBT community. The next section of the chapter explores the elements of place.

THE POWER OF PLACE

In many areas of social scientific inquiry, the significance of place remains neglected. Often construed in simple physical terms, places typically feature as mere passive containers in which social life happens to unfold.

Gradually the limits of this "minimalist" (Stokols, 1990) conception of our human relationship to environment was incorporated into research. Unsurprisingly, geographers have been among the first to attempt to recover the lived experiences implied in phrases such as "sense of place," "rootedness," and "place attachment." Relph (1976) argues that to be human "is to live in a world that is filled with significant places: to be human is to have and know your place." He described how our connection with, and experience of, place can range from "existential insidedness" (an "unselfconscious and authentic experience of place as central to existence") to a much more superficial ("inauthentic") experience of place (Relph, 1976, p. 142). If in the latter we are outsiders, looking upon a place "as a traveler might look down upon a town from a distance," in the former we are insiders who can fully experience a place, being "surrounded by it and part of it" (p. 49). Indeed, it is here we feel "at home."

Members of the LGBT community from the 1950s through the 1980s were subjected to the consistently crafted rhetoric that was (and is) used by anti-LGBT individuals to pathologize and demonize LGBT people as diseased and as pedophiles and child molesters. The clinical history of the word homosexual is aggressively used by anti-gay extremists to suggest gay people are somehow diseased or psychologically and emotionally disordered.

As such, concepts such as identity, attachment, and belonging feature prominently in the everyday vocabulary of place-making rhetoric and practice, and in the ways in which these constructs have been used to politically prosecute the LGBT community through naturalizing certain person-place relationships.

Thus, the analytic framework and concepts must capture both the representation and experience of place and the social and political dynamic to their production. Following World War II, discrimination against gays ramped up. Presidents Truman and Eisenhower supported measures to purge the government and armed forces of all homosexuals. Underlying some versions of the humanistic tradition in human geography is the assumption that one becomes an "existential insider" by uncovering the "authentic" meaning of a place. Furthermore, such a perspective often assumes that this meaning can be grasped independently of wider discursive and political practices of representation (Hopkins & Dixon, 2006). In many instances, public sentiment aligned with the disparaging rhetoric. For example, in the late 1950s Congress issued a report titled "Employment of Homosexuals and Other Sex Perverts in Government" in response to what was known as the "Lavender Scare"—a purging of 5,000 government workers from federal employment. The report described LGBT people as ones who "engage in overt acts of perversion [and] lack the emotional stability of normal persons."

In 1952 the American Psychiatric Association included homosexuality as a "sociopathic personality disturbance" in its first publication of the *Diagnostic and Statistical Manual of Mental Disorders*, a description that remained there until 1973. In 1953 President Eisenhower issued an executive order banning

LGBT people from federal employment as well as from employment with any private contractor working for the federal government. He reasoned that homosexuals were "security risks," along with alcoholics and neurotics.

Bonauto and Bonnes (2000) theorized the concept of social identity (Tajfel & Turner, 1979) to explain the role of collective processes in the place-identity relationship. This concept emphasizes the idea that our sense of who we are is fundamentally social and based on our identification with various social group memberships. In drawing upon this literature, researchers interested in space and place make the point that many social identities incorporate a spatial dimension. Most obviously, national identities are typically spatialized (such that it becomes possible to speak of the "the United States [as a] Christian nation") and reproduced through boundary-making practices. In the 1970s, Anita Bryant, a nationally known singer and spokesperson for Florida orange juice and a prominent Baptist (Medley, 2009), led the "Save our Children" campaign to repeal a Dade County, Florida, ordinance preventing discrimination based on sexual orientation. Bryant used hateful anti-LGBT rhetoric in her campaign. She said:

As a mother, I know that homosexuals cannot biologically reproduce children; therefore, they must recruit our children and if gays are granted rights, next we'll have to give rights to prostitutes and to people who sleep with Saint Bernards and to nail biters. (Medley, 2009)

A full-page newspaper advertisement was taken out by Save Our Children, warning that the:

OTHER SIDE OF THE HOMOSEXUAL COIN IS A HAIR-RAISING PATTERN OF RECRUITMENT AND OUTRIGHT SEDUCTION AND MOLESTATION. (Medley, 2009)

In the 1980s, then-Congressman William Dannemyer wrote a book titled *Shadow in the Land: Homosexuality in America*, in which he described LGBT people as "the ultimate enemy" and described the LGBT civil rights movement as a "blitzkrieg" that was "better planned and better executed than Hitler's."

Who Belongs? Citizenship and the Identity of Place

To observe that different groups may construe the same space in different ways does not mean all are equally placed to act based on their understandings.

Often particular constructions predominate and are so effective in shaping people's spatial behavior that we are blind to their operation. Indeed, it is only when we are faced with people or practices that appear strangely "out of place" that we become aware of the degree to which spatial behavior is controlled by conceptions of place. Save Our Children's anti-LGBT victory had a ripple effect. The day after the Dade County vote, Florida's governor signed into law a ban on adoption by gay men and lesbians, which was the first statewide adoption prohibition in the United States.

Klinsman (1995) illustrates the point that issues of place and space lie at the heart of contemporary analyses of citizenship. Indeed, in their introduction to a special issue on citizenship in the journal *Political Geography*, Painter and Philo (1995) observe that many questions have shifted from the more traditional issue of an individual's relationship with an overarching political body "to a more diffuse 'social-cultural' form of citizenship wrapped up in questions of who is accepted as a worthy, valuable, and responsible member of an everyday community of living and working" (p. 115). Thus, while institutional arrangements remain important, more informal notions of citizenship also are crucial and have a social dynamic of their own in which place and space are central. As they put it:

[If] citizenship is to mean anything in an everyday sense it should mean the ability of individuals to occupy public spaces in a manner that does not compromise their self-identity, let alone obstruct, threaten or even harm them more materially. If people cannot be present in public spaces (streets, squares, parks, cinemas, churches, town halls) without feeling uncomfortable, victimized, and basically "out of place," then it must be questionable whether or not these people can be regarded as citizens at all: or, at least, whether they will regard themselves as full citizens of their host community able to exist on an equal footing with other people who seem perfectly "at home" when moving about in public spaces. (Painter & Philo, 1995)

The struggles over space are key arenas where citizenship rights are negotiated is well illustrated in the controversies surrounding same-sex marriage. When opponents argue LGBT rights would compromise traditional values, behind these developments is a struggle over the symbolic definition of space, place, and belonging, and these clashes evoke and imply different conceptualizations of who belongs and on what terms (Isin & Siemiatycki, 2002).

However, even in more mundane settings it is possible to discern related struggles, and Dixon, Levine, and McAuley (2006) explore how a place's identity is constructed through reference to people's evaluations of the moral meanings of everyday behavior and consideration for what this means for ordinary people's conceptions of who does or does not really have a place in the public sphere. They argue that people are not merely the passive recipients of socially shared representations but are actively engaged in deliberating upon wider ideological dilemmas (Billig, Condor, Edwards, Gane, Middleton, & Radley, 1988) concerning the balance between freedom and control in public space. The significance for political culture is that it illustrates and explicates the connections between an individual's deliberations and wider social beliefs and ideologies, and hints at how we conceptualize individuals' thinking on place and citizenship.

The narrative of an LGBT person or the community has changed from a crime, to a disease, to a sin. From prosecution and arrest to persecution and parades. During the McCarthy era, homosexuals were assumed to be communists. By the second decade of the 21st century, the use of phrases that included "homosexual activities" and "gay lifestyle" came to be taken as signs of bigotry. In fact, by 2010 it had become common for speakers to pair an argument for same-sex marriage with an appeal to be "on the right side of history." Public talk had changed. Homosexuality became a matter of identity—gay or lesbian—and not a name for a set of activities in which a person engaged. At least that's true in court rooms or legislative chambers, but not in other places that LGBT people live like Kansas or Texas or Tennessee.

Partisanship

A byproduct of place in politics is partisanship. A partisan is a person who strongly supports the principles of a specific party. America is dominated by two major parties, Republican and Democrat. For American voters, party affiliation is a way to expressly support the social groups and issues they represent (Taub, 2017). This partisan loyalty is a form of political identity used by the public to determine whether someone fits into their political ingroup or outgroup and is therefore deserving of respect or derogation (Haidt & Hetherington, 2012). A core assumption is that political identity has universal meaning; what one person understands to be a conservative or liberal is what another person understands to be a conservative or liberal.

Morgan, Skitika, and Wisneski, (2014) suggest that judgments about ourselves typically involve social comparison and a shared understanding of what it means to be part of a group. Choosing a political identity does not occur in a vacuum; instead it reflects what one's social environment tacitly defines as liberalism and conservatism. It stands to reason, then, that when people determine where they fall on the political ideology spectrum, they will rely on the perceptions of those around them. If this is the case, then where individuals live should have an important impact on how they identify politically, because different locations diverge in how left or right leaning they tend to be, and thus should exert different social influences. For example, "moderately liberal" might mean something different to someone in a relatively Republican region of the country than it does to someone in a Democratic region.

Feibberg, Tullett, Mensch, Hart, and Gottlieb, (2017) hypothesize that the political "blueness" or "redness" of people's locations will influence where they view themselves on the political spectrum. Using two competing hypotheses:

The first was the "identity conformity hypothesis," which addressed if it were possible that people feel pressure to conform to the identity prevalent in their location (Asch, 1951). In other words, one might have to hold particularly liberal views to resist conformity and identify as a liberal in a red state or particularly conservative views to identity as a conservative in a blue state. If this were the case, then location should "pull" people's identities out of alignment with their views. As states get bluer, the same identity would be associated with more right-leaning views, and as states get redder, the same identity would be associated with more left-leaning views.

Second, is it possible that people use the identity of those around them as a "political reference point"—a point with which to compare themselves and adjust accordingly (Festinger, 1954)? In red locations, if individuals perceive their political stances to be to the left of most of those around them, they may identify as strongly liberal, even though their positions (nationwide) are not nearly as extreme as those individuals identifying as strong liberals who live in blue locations. In contrast, individuals in blue locations who perceive their politics to be to the right of those around them will be more likely to identify as strongly conservative, even though their positions (nationwide) are much more moderate than those identifying as strongly conservative in red locations.

In other words, the political reference point in blue and red locations differs, and when individuals determine where they stand on the political spectrum, they will compare themselves to their respective reference points.

Both alternatives share an important implication: how a person identifies on the political ideology spectrum takes on different meaning, depending on where people live. The findings highlight how the meaning of political identity is not objective but rather socially determined—a point rarely considered by researchers or the lay public. Along these lines, the results may also align with theories about political ideology having both symbolic and operational components (Page & Shapiro, 1992; Stimson, 2004). The first refers to more abstract categories and stereotypes, and the latter refers to more concrete policy positions. Although direct claims about causality are lacking, using California, Tennessee, North Carolina, and Texas as examples that location affects the relationship between policy preferences can serve as usual examples.

California

An exception to Republican domination is Democratically controlled California. In 2015 it boasted a $2.44 trillion economy—the sixth largest in the world (Lang, 2014). In the wake of the 2016 presidential election, the state pushed by referendum for secession from the United States with its “Yes California” campaign. Shortly, after the “Calexit” secession effort failed, the Golden State shifted its legislative agenda outward, passing legislation that banned government employees from “traveling” to states that have anti-LGBT laws under consideration in their legislatures.

Admonishing the actions of another state is common; sister states frequently pass policy resolutions condemning the actions of another. However, California was the first state in the nation to flex its statutory and economic muscle. As stated by Democrat State Representative Evan Low, who led the LGBT caucus and was the sponsor of Assembly Bill 1887, The Prohibition on State-Funded and State-Sponsored Travel to States with Discriminatory Laws of 2017, “Public taxpayer dollars should not subsidize discrimination, period . . . the allocation of our tax dollars is an expression of our values” (Greenblatt, 2017). The law does not target any specific state but lays out in detail whether a state will be impacted. Travel is forbidden to any state that has passed a law that explicitly discriminates against LGBT people, or that has passed a law voiding or repealing state or local protections for LGBT people and is enacted as follows:

(1) California is a leader in protecting civil rights and preventing discrimination.

(2) California's robust nondiscrimination laws include protections on the basis of sexual orientation, gender identity, and gender expression, among other characteristics.

(3) Religious freedom is a cornerstone of law and public policy in the United States, and the Legislature strongly supports and affirms this important freedom.

(4) The exercise of religious freedom should not be a justification for discrimination.

(5) California must take action to avoid supporting or financing discrimination against lesbian, gay, bisexual, and transgender people.

(6) It is the policy of the State of California to promote fairness and equality and to combat discrimination. (Assembly Bill No. 1887, 2016–2017)

The statute further required that the attorney general maintain a list of the states that would qualify and issue an opinion to determine which states have laws that discriminate against LGBT individuals (Greenblatt, 2017). The prohibition on state-funded travel was to continue while any law that discriminates based on sexual orientation, gender identity, or gender expression remained in effect. Further clarifying that a state is subject to the travel prohibition if, after June 26, 2015,

. . . it has enacted a law that voids or repeals, or has the effect of voiding or repealing, existing state or local protections against discrimination on the basis of sexual orientation, gender identity, or gender expression, or has enacted a law that authorizes or requires discrimination against same-sex couples or their families or on the basis of sexual orientation, gender identity, or gender expression, including any law that creates an exemption to antidiscrimination laws in order to permit discrimination against same-sex couples or their families or on the basis of sexual orientation, gender identity, or gender expression. (Gov. Code, § 11139.8, subd. (b))

The original states impacted by the travel ban were Kansas, Mississippi, North Carolina, and Tennessee. Republican legislators in each of these states sponsored and passed anti-LGBT laws[1].

Tennessee

In 2011 the Metropolitan Government of Nashville and Davidson County amended Chapter 4.28 of the Metropolitan Code, adding sexual orientation and gender identity to the classes of persons protected by equal opportunity provisions applicable to government contractors. Within months of its enactment, Republican State Representative Glen Casada responded with House Bill 600 creating the Equal Access to Intrastate Commerce Act. The measure prohibited local governments from extending protections exceeding those recognized by state law and defined "sex" as the designation indicated on an individual's birth certificate (Public Chapter 278). Following Tennessee, two additional states, Arkansas in 2015 and North Carolina in 2016, passed statutory preemption in the areas of discrimination.

North Carolina

In 2016 North Carolina Representative Dan Bishop passed House Bill 2, the Public Facilities Privacy and Security Act, commonly known as the "Charlotte bathroom bill," which removed local authority on several issues including regulating access of public facilities (Public Chapter 278). The bill was passed in a one-day special called session in direct response to nondiscrimination ordinance 7056 passed by the Charlotte City Council that prohibited sex discrimination in public facilities and nullified the workplace and public accommodations discrimination ordinances of more than a dozen North Carolina cities (Gordon, Price & Peralta, 2016). A notable provision within the bill served as an olive branch to business interests because it included language that eliminated the power of a local authority to increase the minimum wage. Even though North Carolina municipalities had never set different wages, businesses supported the preemption of such authority. Gaining business support was necessary, as these interests in other states have stopped similar antidiscrimination laws from being passed or signed. A veiled attempt was made to repeal the law during another special legislative session, but the agreement between the state legislature and the Charlotte City Council failed, keeping provisions of the bill intact.

While many preemption bills do not explicitly mention religion, they often are introduced alongside religious exemption laws. These "religious freedom" bills would allow businesses and individuals to exempt themselves from general legal requirements based on religious grounds. These laws often preempt local governments from regulating in this area. In some places where religious freedom bills have been passed, city ordinances stand in opposition to these state-imposed limitations.

As prodigies of the state, there is little that cities can do to counteract state action. However, a 1996 Supreme Court ruling in *Romer v. Evans* (1996) could be a beacon for cities. In that decision, the court struck down a state constitutional amendment that prohibited localities from designating "homosexual, lesbian, or bisexual orientation" as a protected class (Casuga & Rose, 2016). Most of the justices found the amendment violated the equal protection clause of the Constitution because it was based on bias toward a group of individuals and not related to a legitimate government interest (*Romer v. Evans*, 1996). In the future, if cities can argue the goal of the preemption is to harm people or treat groups differently, then they may have some leverage against preemptive state actions.

These splintering and fracturing forces dominate today's social and political life, as illustrated by North Carolina, Tennessee, and Arkansas. Conservative state legislators' efforts to address progressive city policies where the majority party in the legislature holds different values from the city have passed preemption efforts.

There are still regions across the United States that, despite increasing amounts of public focus, acceptance and rights for LGBT people have not changed. This separation along geographic lines means different value orientations have become more partisan—resulting in the intractability between the two perspectives now dominating the political debate.

More About Place (The List Expands)

The efforts to win marriage equality in the courts has created a vast body of new anti-gay measures. It was clear from the outset that many of the Supreme Court rulings would generate backlash. The California travel ban highlights something already clear, that is, different states have different values, even though not all individuals within a state agree on what those values should be. Judging the culture of other states through policy or statute is evidence that social derision is rampant.

In 2016 Tennessee passed Senate Bill 1556, a law that allows professional therapists and counselors who have "sincerely held beliefs" at odds with their clients' goals to reject LGBT clients. It also requires counselors who do so to refer the client to another professional and blocks such moves if there is an imminent danger of clients doing harm to themselves or others.

In response to California, Tennessee lawmakers wrote a blistering response, led by Republican Senator Mike Bell. The Senate Joint Resolution 111 urged 48 other states "to refrain from imposing their unfounded moral judgment on their sister states as California has done to prevent escalating foolishness" (Sher, 2017), calling California's AB 1887 a "type of blackmail."

A RESOLUTION relative to state travel bans. WHEREAS, California has passed legislation banning state-sponsored travel to Tennessee and certain other states;

WHEREAS, the ban stems from legislation enacted by Tennessee that allows counselors to refer patients to other counselors who can better meet their goals, which the California State Legislature has judged to be morally reprehensible;

WHEREAS, California's attempt to influence public policy in our state is akin to Tennessee expressing its disapproval of California's exorbitant taxes, spiraling budget deficits, runaway social welfare programs, and rampant illegal immigration; and

WHEREAS, Tennessee is pleasantly surprised that California will not be sending its economic development teams to Tennessee to recruit our businesses, but we can still send our teams to recruit their businesses;

WHEREAS, Tennessee is puzzled why California thinks it is a good idea to prohibit its state colleges and universities from participating in athletic competition in Tennessee (March Madness comes to Memphis this year via the South Regional), Kansas, Mississippi, and North Carolina;

WHEREAS, this type of ban, the result of legitimate disagreements about government policy, is neither persuasive nor productive for either party and will lead to economic warfare among states, as one sovereign entity attempts to tell an equally sovereign entity how to conduct its affairs by restricting travel thereto;

WHEREAS, the United States Constitution provides for a strong federal government for the common defense, but the Tenth Amendment grants the several states sovereignty in SJR0111 003256 -2- addressing issues solely within their jurisdiction, and all states should respect this most basic precept of American government;

WHEREAS, if states such as California persist in banning travel to Tennessee as a punitive action for this body conducting its constitutionally mandated duties as its members see fit, our state leaders should consider strong reciprocal action in banning state-sponsored travel to those misguided states;

BE IT RESOLVED BY THE SENATE OF THE ONE HUNDRED TENTH GENERAL ASSEMBLY OF THE STATE OF TENNESSEE, THE HOUSE OF REPRESENTATIVES CONCURRING, that we urge and encourage the Governor, the Speaker of the Senate, and the Speaker of the House of Representatives to ban state-sponsored and state-funded travel within their respective jurisdictions to any state of the Union that has banned state-sponsored travel to Tennessee in a selective way, so that the other states feel the pain and not Tennessee.

BE IT FURTHER RESOLVED, that we urge the other forty-eight states to refrain from imposing their unfounded moral judgment on their sister states as California has done in order to prevent escalating foolishness.

BE IT FURTHER RESOLVED, that a certified copy of this resolution be transmitted to the National Conference of State Legislatures, the Council of State Governments, and the American Legislative Exchange Council and that a certified copy of this resolution be sent electronically to each member of each state legislative body in the nation, so they may also consider taking action against this type of blackmail.

Texas

In the case of Texas, California officials cited HB 3859, a new state law allowing child welfare providers to deny adoptions based on "sincerely held religious beliefs," much like laws passed in South Dakota and Alabama, which were also added to California's travel ban list. In each of these illustrations, states are acting to safeguard individuals' deeply held religious beliefs.

What remains clear is that each of us possesses certain foundational beliefs—narratives about the self, ideas about social order—that essentially cannot be violated. To contradict them would call into question our own self-worth. As such, these views demand fealty from other opinions. And any other information gleaned from the world is amended, distorted, diminished, or forgotten to make sure these sacrosanct beliefs remain whole and unharmed. Political beliefs cross over into the realm of the sacrosanct as demonstrated in the differences between California and the states it has banned travel to.

California's travel ban effectively does very little, since it contains ample exceptions. But what it lacks in substance, it makes up for in moral preening, casting states that pass bathroom bills or religious freedom protections as hate-filled backwaters that the Golden State will not deign to visit.

California's expanded travel ban is timely, since the most recent U.S. Supreme Court decision in the case of *Craig v. Masterpiece Cakeshop* (2018) overturned the ruling of the Colorado Civil Rights Commission. A Colorado baker declined to bake a wedding cake for a gay couple, citing religious convictions about marriage. The baker was ordered by the Colorado Civil Rights Commission to create cakes that celebrate same-sex weddings, reeducate employees, and file quarterly "compliance" reports for two years. The case centered on whether creative businesses can refuse service based on First Amendment rights of free speech and free exercise of religion in light of public accommodation laws that hold that public and private facilities open to the public cannot discriminate (Colorado is one of 21 states that prohibit discrimination based on sexual orientation).

Many of the states on California's list landed there because they passed laws designed to protect people like the baker. Some report North Carolina's bathroom bill as inspiration for the travel ban, but the California lawmaker said he decided to act after Indiana signed Senate Bill 50, the Religious Freedom Restoration Act (RFRA), into law in 2015. Twenty other states have similar RFRAs on the books like Indiana's, and there are currently eight states on the travel ban list.

Other states now on California's list include: Alabama (HB 24), South Dakota (SB 149), and Texas (HB 3859), which in 2017 passed legislation that could prevent LGBT parents from adopting or fostering children. Kentucky passed a religious freedom bill (SB 17), which would allow students to exclude LGBT classmates from campus groups.

Polarization

A second element of place is polarization. Political parties unified internally but ideologically distant from the opposing party are described as polarized. The country has seen increasing partisan polarization since the 1970s (McCarthy, Poole, & Rosenthal, 2006) as both politicians and political parties have become more ideologically extreme at the national level and in the states. Mann and Orstein (2012) offer that this increasing polarization is a central problem in modern-day politics, and the divisiveness is not only between parties but within parties (Boulard, 2011). Others observe there is more at stake than ideology. The divides are not just about politics, but it's where we live that impacts who we are as people.

In *Putting Inequality in its Place: Rural Consciousness and the Power of Perspective*, Katherine Walsh shows how place consciousness serves as a its own perspective through which people interpret politics.

The analyses examined how this framework structures perceptions of the distribution of power, resources, and values. The study argues the significance for politics for rural residents is not just that people in rural areas have a different demographic profile, or that different experiences in rural areas result in different attitudes. It also goes beyond the argument that rural/urban divides are manifestations of class conflict or over material resources. Instead, it shows how consciousness of being a rural resident itself can make preferences for limited government obvious, appropriate, and expected, even among low-income people.

To understand why rural consciousness is likely important for political understanding, it is necessary to recognize the psychology behind understanding in general, and the importance of place in this process. Psychology tells us that in order for people to make sense of the world, they categorize (Chi, Feltovich, & Glaser 1981; Medin & Cooley, 1998). In politics, a particularly powerful act of categorization is the parsing of people into "us" and "them" (Tajfel, 1981; Turner, et al. 1987).

Identities as members of social groups, whether friendship groups or society-wide categories, serve as reference points for social comparison and boundaries of allegiance; help guide notions of appropriate behavior and attitudes; and influence what messages people pay attention to and incorporate into prior beliefs (Brewer & Miller, 1984; Sears & Kinder,1985; Tajfeletal, 1971). Social group identities play a central role in the way individuals interpret the political world, influencing political attitudes and behaviors

(Conover, 1984, 1988; Huddy, 2003). Group consciousness literature has taught us that when social identities are imbued with notions of distributive justice, they are particularly important for political behavior.

Place matters for political understanding in the form of group consciousness for many reasons. Representation, and thus resources, are allocated by geography in the United States. Therefore, individuals' perceptions of distributive justice are likely related to place, especially among those who perceive their communities as being relatively deprived. Even though there is contention over how *rural* is defined, studies of rural communities suggest the term carries a great deal of meaning for people who identify with it (Mellow, 2005). Moreover, the conflicts between rural and urban areas within states are intensifying (Gimpel & Schuknecht, 2003), suggesting even more sensitivity to inequalities across these areas.

As noted by in the *Politics of Resentment*, this widening gap between rural and urban communities creates resentment about who gets what (Cramer, 2016). These perceptions of place and justice also correlate to who has power and how it is exercised (Hayward, 2000). The connections between place, justice, fairness, and inequality are powerful, because they involve conflicting perspectives on life. Demographic and economic shifts in the nexus of family, home, and the marketplace have resulted in a redefinition of gender roles. During this time the idea of marriage began to shift as well. Supporters of both paradigms feel threatened and are critical of the other points of view and vote for individuals and policies that reflect these differences. These competing groups struggle for dominance in American political culture, geographic boundaries, and individual lives (Wuthnow, 1989).

As Kansas Republican Senator John Vratil, a seasoned veteran of the state's politics, proudly stated: "The legislator who revels in bipartisanship and moderation has been on the outs. The person who is more confrontational has become a driving force and gets all the attention" (Boulard, 2011).

The country now seems polarized and embattled to the point of dysfunction.

This geographical separation in political culture is significant in red and blue areas regarding the enactment of pro-LGBT legislation. For example, states that have passed favorable same-sex marriage legislation have been exclusively blue. These cultural clashes between red and blue states manifest in the types of bills legislators sponsor and are distinguishable by region, especially when related to bills that have protected the idea of traditional marriage or have expanded LGBT rights.

Taking a deeper look at jurisdictions that previously enacted same-sex marriage measures, it is no surprise that they share a cluster of characteristics: Democrats controlled both houses of the legislature, a Democratic governor, and populations that rank among the least religious (Newport, 2013) but most educated (U.S. Census, 2011).

This short list of demographic factors likely created a favorable environment for same-sex marriage recognition. In those states, some legislators also saw same-sex marriage legislation as "a reasonable extension" of existing nondiscrimination laws that provided open access for LGBT persons to housing, hiring, and public accommodations (McKinley, 2010). Not surprisingly, every jurisdiction that prohibited sexual-orientation discrimination in housing, employment, and public accommodations did so well before recognizing same-sex marriage.

But unlike those jurisdictions prior to the *Obergefell* (2015) decision, there were 31 states where the demographic characteristics favoring marriage equality fragment. In addition to being largely Republican controlled, these states have constituents who are more religious. The levels of formal education in these states are strikingly lower in those that enacted anti-LGBT laws, and they rank in the bottom for educational attainment.

These states' absence of a statewide guarantee of nondiscrimination is significant: it means legislators crafting accommodations for same-sex marriage will be writing on a blank slate when deciding how much—or little—latitude to give those who are opposed. If nothing in state or local law prohibits discrimination based on sexual orientation, dissenters will not need protections. In this difficult political terrain, especially in states in which legislators are accountable and consist of more "very religious" people, one might reasonably expect legislators will tip the balance regarding marriage equality in favor of same-sex marriage objectors. The onslaught of anti-LGBT legislation since the 2015 *Obergefell* decision has steadily increased and is designed to protect religious objectors by allowing individuals and businesses to deny service and employment to LGBT people based on a professed "religious belief" (Human Rights Campaign, 2017). States took varying approaches in 2016 to legislate restrictions on the LGBT community. Some, like Tennessee and Oklahoma, introduced dozens of single-issue bills.

The *Obergefell* (2015) court held that the Constitution does not permit states to ban same-sex couples from marriage on the same terms as opposite-sex couples. While the court decision did result in a momentous step forward for same-sex couples, and the rules related to LGBT people in the United

States have advanced since "*Bleeding Heart,*" whether a person's rights are protected is still reliant on place.

These differences across states and regions are the causes and effects of economic, family, and health disparities between LGBT people and their non-LGBT counterparts (Hasenbush, et al., 2014). The social climate of each geographic region towards LGBT people reflects the legal differences across regions and the degree of security that LGBT people may possess in order to be fully visible. The level of acceptance and belonging for lesbian, gay, and bisexual people likely reflects how policies and legal statuses differ among states. The policy landscape in the United States for LGBT people indicates there are substantial differences among the states regarding the degree to which their public policies are LGBT-inclusive.

A Nation in Flux

In an article published in 2005, Michael Klarman compared the response to *Goodridge*, the Massachusetts marriage decision, to the massive resistance to *Brown v. Board of Education*, asserting that court rulings produce political backlashes for three principal reasons:

They raise the salience of an issue, they incite anger over 'outside interference' or 'judicial activism,' and they alter the order in which social change would otherwise have occurred.

Klarrman (2013) qualified his views, suggesting that whether action derives from legislatures or courts seems to be relatively unimportant—political backlash results from government action that contravenes public opinion. Courts are more likely than legislatures to take action that deviates from public opinion, and that generates powerful backlash.

Rosenberg (2008) pointed out that court decisions could consolidate social change but could not prompt social change, pointing to the many laws and amendments enacted to ban same-sex marriage. Concern about backlash to court decisions recognizing the right to marry has not been limited to academics. Faced with litigation losses and warnings of backlash, gay rights litigators assumed a self-consciously cautious litigation strategy (Bonauto, 2016; Cummings & NeJaime, 2010), seeking to avoid suits unless necessary (Cummings & NeJaime, 2010; Yoshino, 2015). In 2008, when lawyers unaffiliated with the gay rights movement prepared to challenge state marriage bans under the federal Constitution in *Hollingsworth v. Perry* (2013), movement lawyers worked to stop them from bringing the case forth (NeJaime, 2012). How would the public respond to a court decision recognizing the constitutional right of same-sex couples to marry that changed the law in all states? When unable to dissuade the lawyers in the *Perry* case, the movement worked to shape the litigation of the case (NeJaime, 2012).

Judges began to speak openly about backlash as the *Perry* litigation progressed. The district judge in Perry asked the plaintiffs' lawyers about the risk of backlash before conducting a lengthy trial and ruling in their favor. As the *Perry* case made its way toward the Supreme Court—along with the *United States v. Windsor* case challenging the constitutionality of the federal Defense of Marriage Act—a variety of academics and advocates urged judges to narrow scope or to avoid decision in the cases, warning the Supreme Court that a court decision striking down state same-sex marriage bans could trigger powerful backlash. Even Supreme Court justices joined the conversation. In several public interviews in 2012 and 2013, Justice Ginsburg offered not-so-veiled warnings about the dangers of a Supreme Court decision in *Perry* by reiterating her view that an early and overbroad ruling in *Roe* had caused backlash.

The court should not move "too far too fast," she cautioned. When the Supreme Court struck down the Defense of Marriage Act in *Windsor* but ruled that the parties in *Perry* lacked standing to bring the case, Justice Kennedy objected that the court should not have avoided the merits and adverted to judicial concerns about backlash. Instead, *Perry* sent the decision back to the lower federal and state courts.

FUTURE RESEARCH DIRECTIONS

Future research that follows individuals who move from strongly blue to red, or red to blue, locations would help provide insight into exactly how people's surroundings influence the relationship between political identity and policy stances.

CONCLUSION

This chapter applied Stoddard's (1997) model of social change to the same-sex policy debate suggesting geography matters in American politics today above all (Green & Silk, 2004). There are ideological differences associated with red and blue maps. Socially shared, intensely felt values are a fundamental part of our lives in the United States.

Each generation works with the political cultural template left by the previous generation and makes its own adjustments, either minor or major, of what is permissible and impermissible, proper and improper, in American politics and government. This remarkable mosaic of culture is redefined and reshaped. With the historic *Obergefell* ruling comes new and advanced challenges to full inclusion of LGBT communities into American society. New legal and legislative battles are underway, political campaigns are being organized, and social protests planned.

In Stoddard's (1997) view, legislative change is preferred to litigation due to the greater likelihood that it will result in a culture shift. Currently, various places across the United States have undergone a cultural transformation, and other areas are currently in a period of cultural lag, still struggling to adapt to new conditions.

However, in a globalized world, many social identities, from those associated with small face-to-face communities to those of nations, often have a spatial referent such that as group members move from one place to another, they may not only experience a change in physical place but a change in their social environment. Individuals' understanding of what such changes mean for their identity may be an important aspect of place attachment. Put simply, people may feel attached to a place not only because of the meanings associated with the location itself but also because of their ability to "be themselves" when there.

The wider implications illustrate the significance of social identity concerns regarding how people deliberate upon spatial behavior such as the crossing of an identity-relevant (in this case, national) boundary. Furthermore, it illustrates the complexity of place attachment. How one orients to place seems shaped in part by the spatial distribution of people and identities and one's understanding of what this means in practice for the ability to live out our various identities. Everywhere, constructions of place are both politically charged and psychologically relevant, for as Edward Said (1993) said:

Just as none of us is outside or beyond geography, none of us is completely free from the struggle over geography. That struggle is complex and interesting because it is not only about soldiers and cannons but also about ideas, about forms, about images and imaginings. (p. 6)

REFERENCES

American Psychiatric Association Diagnostic and Statistical Manual. (1952). *Mental Disorders*. Retrieved fromhttp://www.turkpsikiyatri.org/arsiv/dsm-1952.pdf

Andrews, K. (2001). Social movements and policy implementation: The Mississippi civil rights movement and the war on poverty, 1965–1971. *American Sociological Review*, *66*(1), 71–95. doi:10.2307/2657394

Asch, S. E. (1951). Effects of group pressure upon the modification and distortion of judgements. In H. Guestskow (Ed.), *Groups, leadership and men* (pp. 222–236). Oxford, UK: Carnegie Press Groups.

Associated Press. (2016). *Alabama Senate approves replacing marriage licenses with contracts*. Retrieved from http://www.al.com/news/index.ssf/2016/03/alabama_senate_approves_replac.html

Baehr v. Lewin, 74 Haw. 530 (1993).

Ball, C. A. (2014). *Same-sex marriage and children: A tale of history*. New York, NY: Oxford University Press. doi:10.1093/acprof:oso/9780199977871.001.0001

Bangor Daily News. (2012, November 14). *General election results for Maine*. Retrieved from https://bangordailynews.com/2012/11/06/politics/both-sides-of-gay-marriage-question-optimistic-as-polls-close/

Billig, M., Condor, S., Edwards, D., Gane, M., Middleton, D., & Radley, A. (1988). *Ideological dilemmas: A social psychology of everyday thinking*. London: Sage.

Bonauto, M., & Bonnes, M. (2000). Social psychological approaches in environment behavior studies: Identity theories and the discursive approach. In S. Wapner, J. Demick, T. Yamamoto, & H. Minami (Eds.), *Theoretical perspectives on environment-behavior research* (pp. 67–78). New York, NY: Plenum. doi:10.1007/978-1-4615-4701-3_7

Bonauto, M. L. (2016). Equality and the impossible—state constitutions and marriage. *Rutgers University Law Review*, *68*, 1481–1507.

Bowers v. Hardwick, 478 U.S. 186 (1986).

Brewer, M., & Miller, N. (1984). Beyond the contact hypothesis: Theoretical perspectives on desegregation. In N. Miller & M. B. Brewer (Eds.), *Groups in contact: The psychology of desegregation* (pp. 281–302). Orlando, FL: Academic Press. doi:10.1016/B978-0-12-497780-8.50019-X

Brown v. Board of Education of Topeka, 347 U.S. 483 (1954).

Carroll, J. (2007 August 16). Most Americans approve of interracial marriages. *Gallup*.

Casuga, J. B., & Rose, M. R. (2016, July 19). Are state workplace preemption laws on the rise? *Bloomberg BNA*. Retrieved from https://www.bna.com/state-workplacepreemption-n73014444995/

Chambers v. Florida, 309 U.S. 227 (1940).

Chi, M., Paul, T. H., Feltovich, J., & Glaser, R. (1981). Categorization and representation of physics problems by experts and novices. *Cognitive Science*, *5*(2), 121–152. doi:10.120715516709cog0502_2

Conover, P. J. (1984). The influence of group identifications on political perception and evaluation. *The Journal of Politics*, *46*(3), 760–785. doi:10.2307/2130855

Craig v. Masterpiece Cakeshop, Inc., 370 P.3d 272, 276, 280 (Colo. App. 2015).

Cramer, K. J. (2016). *The politics of resentment*. Chicago, IL: The University of Chicago Press. doi:10.7208/chicago/9780226349251.001.0001

Cumming, S. & NeJaime, D. (2010). Lawyering for marriage equality. *University California Los Angeles Law Review*, *1235*, 1550–1552.

D'Emilio, J. (2002). *The world turned: Essays on gay history, politics and culture*. Durham, NC: Duke University Press. doi:10.1215/9780822383925

Defense of Marriage Act Public Law 104-199, (1996).

Feinberg, M., Tullerr, A. M., & Mensch, Z., Hart., W., & Gottlieb, S. (2017). The political reference point: How geography shapes political identity. *PLoS One*, *12*(2), 1–13.

Festinger, L. A. (1954). A theory of social comparison process. *Human Relations*, *7*(2), 117–140. doi:10.1177/001872675400700202

Gay History. (2009, August 13). *Anita Bryant and the Save the Children campaign*. Retrieved from http://gayhistory4u.blogspot.com/2009/08/religious-right-has-been-on-attack.html

Gellman, A. (2013). *Polls say ENDA remarkably close to public sentiment*. Gallup.

Gimpel, J. G., & Schuknecht, J. E. (2003). *Patchwork nation: Sectionalism and political change in American politics*. Ann Arbor, MI: University of Michigan Press. doi:10.3998/mpub.17820

Goodridge v. Department of Public Health, 440 Mass. 309, 798 N.E. 2d 941 (2003).

Greenblatt, A. (2017, September). Some states are treating others like foreign countries. *Governing*. Retrieved from http://www.governing.com/topics/mgmt/gov-state-laws-travel-blocks-california-bathroom-bills.html

Haidt, J., & Hetherinton, M. J. (2012). Campaign stops: Look how far we've come apart. . *New York Time*. Retrieved from https://campaignstops.blogs.nytimes.com/2012/09/17/look-how-far-weve-come-apart/?mtrref=www.google.com&gwh=F3B7189E77AA58A64C33E14F52903DFA&gwt=pay&assetType=opinion

Hasenbush, A., Flores, A. R., Kastanis, A., Sears, B., & Gates, G. J. (2014). The LGBT divide: A data portrait of LGBT people in the Midwestern, Mountain & Southern States. *The Williams Institute*. Retrieved from http://williamsinstitute.law.ucla.edu/research/lgbt-divide-dec-2014/

Hollingsworth v. Perry, 133 S. Ct. 2652 (2013).

Hopkins, N., & Dixon, J. (2006). Space, place and identity: Issues for political psychology. *Political Psychology*, *27*(2), 173–185. doi:10.1111/j.1467-9221.2006.00001.x

Huddy, L. (2003). Group identity and political cohesion. In D. O. Sears, L. Huddy, & R. Jervis (Eds.), *Oxford handbook of political psychology* (pp. 511–558). New York: Oxford University Press.

Human Rights Campaign. (2016, January 28). *Cities and counties with non-discrimination ordinances that include gender identity*. Retrieved from http://www.hrc.org/resources/cities-andcounties-with-non-discrimination-ordinances-that-includegender

Hunter, N. D. (1997). Lawyering for social justice. *New York University Law Review*, *72*(5), 1009–1022.

Isin, E. F., & Siemiatycki, M. (2002). Making space for mosques: Struggles for urban citizenship in immigrant Toronto. In S. Razack (Ed.), *Race, space and the law: Unmapping a white settler society* (pp. 185–210). Toronto: Between the Lines Press.

Johnson, T. (2017, Jan/Feb). Cultural competence to represent LGBTQ Clients post-Obergefell. *GPSolo*. Retrieved from https://www.americanbar.org/groups/gpsolo/publications/gp_solo/2017/january-february/cultural-competence-represent-lgbtq-clients-post-obergefell/

Jones, J. (2013, May 13). Same-sex marriage support solidifies above 50% in U.S. *Gallup Politics*. Retrieved from http://news.gallup.com/poll/162398/sex-marriage-support-solidifies-above.aspx

Kaplan, T. (2011, September 27). Rights Collide as town clerk sidesteps role in gay marriages. *New York Times*. Retrieved from https://www.nytimes.com/2011/09/28/nyregion/rights-clash-as-town-clerk-rejects-her-role-in-gay-marriages.html?mtrref=www.google.com&gwh=1447C02D00F338E47AB86C5277C91D6A&gwt=pay

Keck, T. (2009). Beyond backlash: Assessing the impact of judicial decision on LGBT rights. *Law and Society Review*, *43*, 151-170.

Klarmen, M. J. (1996). Rethinking the civil rights and civil liberties revolution. *Virginia Law Review*, *82*(1), 2–25.

Klarmen, M. J. (2005). Brown and Lawrence (and Goodridge). *Michigan Law Review*, *431*, 439–440.

Klarmen, M. J. (2013). *From the closet to the altar: Courts, backlash, and the struggle for same-sex marriage*. Oxford University Press.

Klinsman, P. (1995). Landscape, race and national identity: The photography of Ingrid Pollard. *Area*, *27*(4), 300–310.

Landsbaum, C. (2016, November 11). The future of LGBT rights under President Trump is not pretty. *The Cut*. Retrieved from https://www.thecut.com/2016/11/what-will-lgbt-rights-look-like-under-president-trump.html

Lang, N. (2014, November 24). The 5 worst states for LGBT people. *Rolling Stone*. Retrieved from https://www.rollingstone.com/politics/news/the-5-worst-states-for-lgbt-people-20141124

Lawrence v. Texas, 539 U.S. 558 (2003)

Mann, T., & Ornstein, N. (2012). *It's even worse than it looks: How the American constitutional system collided with the new politics of extremism*. New York: Basic Books.

McCann, M. (2004). Rights at work: Pay equity reform and the politics of legal mobilization. In A. Sarat (Ed.), *The Blackwell companion to law and society* (pp. 5–121). Wiley Blackwell Publishing.

Medley, R. (2009). Anita Bryant: Sunny side of life. *NewsOK*. Retrieved from http://ndepth.newsok.com/anita-bryant

Mellow, M. (2005). The work of rural professionals: Doing Gemeinschaft-Gesellschaft Gavotte. *Rural Sociology*, *70*(1), 50–69. doi:10.1526/0036011053294637

Meyers, D. (2013, December 23). Utah County refuses to issue same-sex marriage licenses. *Salt Lake Tribune*. Retrieved from http://archive.sltrib.com/article.php?id=57302479&itype=CMSID

Michelson, N. (2012, November 7). Minnesota Amendment 1 Same-sex marriage ballot measure fails. *Huffington Post*. Retrieved from https://www.huffingtonpost.com/2012/11/07/minnesota-amendment-1-results-2012_n_2050310.html

Morgan, G. S., Skitika, L. J., & Wisneski, D. C. (2014). Political ideology is contextually variable and flexible rather than fixed. *Behavioral and Brain Sciences*, *37*(3), 321–322. doi:10.1017/S0140525X13002665 PMID:24970444

NeJaime, D. (2012). The legal mobilization dilemma. *Emory Law Review*, *6*, 663–684.

Newport, F. (2013, July 30). Public Shifts to more conservative stance on gay rights. *Gallup*.

Obergefell v. Hodges, 135 S. Ct. 2584 (2015).

Page, B. I., & Shapiro, R. Y. (1992). *The rational public: Fifty years of trends in American's policy preferences*. Chicago: University of Chicago Press. doi:10.7208/chicago/9780226644806.001.0001

Painter, J., & Philo, C. (1995). Spaces of citizenship: An introduction. *Political Geography, 14*(2), 107–120. doi:10.1016/0962-6298(95)91659-R

Pally, G. (2013). Who runs the states: Part 1: Partisanship of the 50 states between 1992–2013? *Ballotepidia*. Retrieved from https://www.heartland.org/publications-resources/publications/who-runs-the-states-part-1-partisanship-of-the-50-states-between-1992-2013

Phillips, A. (2015, January 3). As Gay marriage approaches, several county clerks opt out of wedding ceremonies. *Tampa Bay Times*. Retrieved from http://www.tampabay.com/news/courts/in-north-florida-a-views-collide-over-gay-weddings-as-many-clerks-opt-out/2212297

Relph, E. (1976). *Place and placelessness*. London: Pion.

Richardson, L. E., Konisky, D. M., & Milyo, J. (2012). Public approval of state legislatures. *State Politics & Policy Quarterly, 37*, 99–116.

Robinson, G. (2012, October 10). Liberty and justice for all in Maryland. *On Faith*. Retrieved from https://www.onfaith.co/onfaith/2012/10/10/liberty-and-justice-for-all-in-maryland/10097?tid=a_mcntx

Roe v. Wade, 410 U.S. 113 (1973).

Romer v. Evans, 517 U.S. 620 (1996).

Rosenberg, G. N. (2008). *The hollow hope: Can courts bring about social change?* (2nd ed.). Chicago, IL: University Chicago Press. doi:10.7208/chicago/9780226726687.001.0001

Ryan, K. (2017, August 28). *New Data reveals best and worst places to be gay in America*. Retrieved from https://www.good.is/articles/best-worst-states-lgbt

Said, E. (1993). *Culture and imperialism*. Knopf.

Sant'Ambrogio, M., & Law, S. (2011). Baehr v. Lewin and the long road to marriage equality. *University of Hawaii Law Review, 705*, 740.

Sears, D. O., & Kinder, D. R. (1985). Whites opposition to busing: On conceptualizing and operationalizing group conflict. *Journal of Personality and Social Psychology, 48*(5), 1141–1147. doi:10.1037/0022-3514.48.5.1148.a

Sher, A. (2017, February 13). Tennessee Republicans denounce 'absurdity' of California travel ban. *Times Free Press*. Retrieved from http://www.timesfreepress.com/news/politics/state/story/2017/feb/13/tennessee-republicans-set-retaliate-against-california-after-travel-ban/412639/

Silver, N. (2013, March 26). How opinion on same-sex marriage is changing, and what it means. *New York Times*. Retrieved from https://fivethirtyeight.blogs.nytimes.com/2013/03/26/how-opinion-on-same-sex-marriage-is-changing-and-what-it-means/

Sobel, S. L. (2015). Culture shifting at warp speed: How the law, public engagement, and Will & Grace led to social change for LGBT people. *St. John's Law Review*, *89*(1), 143–194.

Stimson, J. A. (2004). *Tides of consent: How public opinion shapes American politics*. New York, NY: Cambridge University Press. doi:10.1017/CBO9780511791024

Stoddard, T. (1997). Bleeding heart: Reflections on using the law to make social change. *New York University Law Review*, *72*(5), 967–991.

Stokols, D. (1990). Instrumental and spiritual views of people-environment relations. *The American Psychologist*, *45*(5), 641–646. doi:10.1037/0003-066X.45.5.641

Tajfel, H., & Turner, J. C. (1979). An integrative theory of intergroup conflict. In W. G. Austin & S. Worchel (Eds.), *The social psychology of intergroup relations* (pp. 33–47). Monterey, CA: Brooks/Cole.

Taub, A. (2017, May 12). Comey firing tests strength of the guardrails of democracy. *The New York Times: The Upshot*. Retrieved from https://www.nytimes.com/2017/05/12/upshot/comeys-firing-tests-strength-of-the-guardrails-of-democracy.html

Tropiano, S. (2002). *The prime-time closet: A history of gays and lesbians on tv*. New York: Applause Theatre & Cinema.

U.S. v. Windsor, 133 S. Ct. 2675 (2013).

Walsh, K. C. (2012). Putting inequality in its place: Rural consciousness and the power of perspective. *The American Political Science Review*, *106*(3), 517–532. doi:10.1017/S0003055412000305

Williams, A. (2015, September 17). Alabama marriage license vote. *WTOK.com*. Retrieved from http://www.wtok.com/home/headlines/Alabama-Marriage-License-Vote-328051831.html

Wuthnow, R. (1989). *The struggle for America's soul: Evangelicals, liberals and secularism*. Grand Rapids, MI: Eerdmans.

Yoshino, K. (2015). *Speak now: Marriage equality on trial the story of Hollingsworth v. Perry*. New York, NY: Crown.

KEY TERMS AND DEFINITIONS

Belonging: Acceptance as a member or part that adds value in life and assists in coping.

Change: The act or process of making something different.

Citizenship: The status of a person recognized under the law as being a legal member of a sovereign state or belonging to a nation.

Judicial Review: The power of the judiciary to interpret and overturn actions taken by the legislative and executive branches of government.

Polarization: Political parties or groups that are unified internally but ideologically distant from those in other parties or groups.

ENDNOTE

1 Kansas passed Senate Bill 175 (2016), which allows religious student groups the ability to bar individuals who don't share a group's beliefs. Mississippi enacted House Bill 1523 Protecting Freedom of Conscience from Government Discrimination Act (2016); North Carolina passed House Bill 2 the Public Facilities Privacy and Security Act (2016); Tennessee passed Senate Bill 1556 (2016), a law that allows professional therapists and counselors who have "sincerely held beliefs" at odds with their clients' goals to reject LGBT clients. It also requires counselors who do so to refer the client to another professional and blocks such moves if there is imminent danger of clients doing harm to themselves or others.

Section 4

The Future of LGBT Rights

Chapter 6
The Future of LGBT Politics

ABSTRACT

This chapter summarizes the role of the U.S. Supreme Court in national policymaking. In the United States there exists a nationally shared set of beliefs, values, and customs, or cultural universals. However, these shared attributes vary according to place and political affiliation. Extending the right to marry to same-sex couples through judicial means precipitated a backlash in which religious groups and individuals turned to legislative solutions to contest the court's decision and their obligation to recognize marriage equality. As the final arbiter of law in the United States, the nine unelected justices of the U.S. Supreme Court play a significant role in policymaking, and their attitudes and decisions regarding policy are tied to the political selection of justices. In the future, decision making from the court to further extend the rights of LGBT citizens may be directly tied to the increasingly partisan selection process for justices.

INTRODUCTION

Alexis de Tocqueville said about American society in the early 19th century that Americans tend to transform almost every important political question into a legal one. The major issues of American political life, perhaps even more so today than in Tocqueville's time, frequently find their way into court. Contemporary issues such as same-sex marriage, abortion, gun rights, religious freedom, and a host of others have found their way into courtrooms. There can be little doubt that courts have played and continue to play a major role in shaping and influencing political and social life in the United States.

DOI: 10.4018/978-1-5225-7961-8.ch006

Judicial policymaking raises questions in the minds of many people as to whether it is fair for judges, rather than elected representatives, to make certain types of decisions and, even more important, whether judges are competent to decide on complex issues of public policy. Other critics maintain the major problem with contemporary courts is not that judges are engaged in policymaking but that the policy made is unjust (Tushnet, 1979).

There has been an increasingly strident chorus that asserts the United States has been secularized and religion has lost its force in the culture. Stephen Carter's (1994) widely read book, *The Culture of Disbelief: How American Law and Politics Trivialize Religious Devotion*, fed into this narrative. The book portrays religion as a diminishing influence in society. Ironically, the secularization thesis has permitted organized religion to don the garb of the underdog, when in fact its political power has been quite potent, even behind the scenes. Religion's double role of downtrodden and politically powerful was transparent when Utah Senator Orin Hatch justified the Religious Freedom Restoration Act of 1993, which put religious individuals and institutions in the position of being able to challenge every neutral and generally applicable law in the country, by saying, "Government too often views religion with deep skepticism, and our popular culture too often treats religious belief with contempt" (Statement of Senator Hatch, 1993). Indeed, the *Culture of Disbelief* and viewpoint it fostered aided religious entities in their lobbying efforts, because few would suspect that such "weak" political actors could be as busy and successful the religious "lobby" has been in the both legislative and judicial contexts (Carter, 1994).

The truth is, the clear majority of Americans are religious believers and attend religious services—and religious viewpoints fill the public square. In recent decades, religious entities have worked hard to immunize their actions from the law, either by obtaining legislative exemptions or by forcing the courts to invalidate any law substantially burdening religious conduct that was unnecessary. These religious actors have always waved the banner of "religious liberty," and few Americans have stopped to question them. What could be more important in a free society than religious liberty? When left in the abstract, it is hard to fathom anything more important.

But when one scrutinizes the facts, there are all types of interests that trump religious conduct in a just and free society. Every citizen has as much right to be free from harm as a religious entity has to be free from government regulation.

An underlying assumption throughout this book is that courts—as active and frequent makers of public policy—make a great deal of difference in American life. Theories of law wax and wane and have shifting emphases subject to developments at the time and place of their formulation. This includes broad influences such as a period of social turmoil or rapid social change as well as more immediate influences within the intellectual settings in which legal theories are developed—academic specialization, institutional support, and current scholarly norms or fads.

One of the more striking features of same-sex litigation in the United States was the prominent role of social science in addressing factual issues germane to legal arguments on both sides. It is impossible to say with certainty whether social science played a decisive role—whether it influenced legal outcomes in litigation. It is also difficult to gauge indirect influences such as impacts on legal decisions that served as precedent in later court cases. Each side's use of social science evidence in the legal contests over same-sex marriage were a series of credibility contests. On issue after issue judges were required to assess the weight and credibility of each side's evidence.

Whether or not it did, should social science have played a decisive role in marriage equality litigation? Certainly, the cases could have been decided based on legal principles alone, without reference to social science evidence. Indeed, significant prior Supreme Court jurisprudence on marriage (including dismantling interracial marriage bans and protecting the legal status of nonmarital offspring) disregarded social science evidence in favor of broad legal principles of equal treatment and nondiscrimination (Ball, 2014, pp.126–27).

By incorporating social science into its justification for marriage equality, the courts may have set a dangerous precedent by making a group's "access to constitutional rights contingent on tests not imposed on other groups, such as the ability to produce child outcomes equivalent to the gold standard of intact biological parent families" (Ball, 2014; Meadow, 2013).

The United States exists in a common culture that reflects the country's basic values, beliefs, and customs, also known as cultural universals. These practices vary geographically, resulting in differing political, economic, and social conditions. These value variations have created regional concepts of what is culturally considered good, desirable, and proper or bad, undesirable, and improper.

Culture shifts relating to LGBT rights were originally addressed in a 1997 article written by Thomas Stoddard titled "Bleeding Heart: Reflections on Using the Law to Make Social Change" ("Bleeding Heart"). The framework for social change was examined as to how rule shifting and cultural shifts interact with the legalization of same-sex marriage. These interactions were examined through judicial decisions, public opinion, and media. The social change that had once seemed improbable decades earlier for the LGBT community was now law of the land. On June 26, 2015, the U.S. Supreme Court issued a historic decision that extended the constitutionally protected fundamental right to marry to same-sex couples (*Obergefell v. Hodges*, 2015). The decision was a culmination of at least a four-decade-long legal war, but it hardly ended the accompanying legal and political battles. The public perception of gay Americans was officially transformed from that of outlaws and outcasts to a legitimate category of U.S. citizen.

For many, the legalization of marriage for same-sex couples was a desirable social change—a journey towards greater equality. Public engagement was a critical component to the change that contributed to the cultural shift that took place in various parts of the country since Stoddard's article.

But change brings consequences. Opponents of same-sex marriage galvanized political support and successfully lobbied legislators to minimize or block the aftershock of an anticipated decision favoring same-sex marriage rights.

Probably the most contentious issues surrounding same-sex marriage involve whether private individuals and companies can—primarily on religious grounds—legally refuse to provide services they generally provide to heterosexual couples (*Burwell v. Hobby Lobby Stores*, 2014). Can a private chapel or other venue refuse to host a same-sex wedding, a florist refuse to provide flowers, a bakery refuse to bake a wedding cake, a professional photographer refuse to photograph a reception, a transportation service refuse to rent a limo, a caterer refuse to provide food, or a bridal boutique refuse to provide gowns? These issues were already cropping up around the United States before *Obergefell* in jurisdictions that permitted same-sex marriage and have since escalated (Wong, 2016).

Legislative responses opposing *Obergefell* have taken various forms. Conservatives across the country invoked backlash as a reason for courts to stay out of the marriage debate and leave its resolution to the political process. These various strands of backlash discourse are often tangled together. In Chief Justice Roberts' dissent in *Obergefell,* he cited Justice Ginsburg and the abortion debate as a reason why that the majority was wrong to recognize the constitutional rights of same-sex couples. These claims by both sides are a paradox-forming argument directed at the exercise of judicial power.

Do the rights of freedom of speech and freedom of religion allow a business owner to refuse service to a potential customer or client because of the actual or perceived sexual orientation of that customer or client? Put another way, does the right to be free from discrimination of any kind override a business owner's rights to free speech or freedom of religion? Does one right trump another?

A focus within this book has been to address these questions and the changes in our values and beliefs associated with the notion that all people—regardless of sexual orientation—have the right to be free from discrimination. Another focus is how our courts are reconciling this notion with our fundamental First Amendment rights and the variation of these rights as it relates to place.

In our everyday lives, we typically do not think about place and are therefore unaware and unconcerned by the increasingly placeless character of the contemporary world. The primacy of place in experience—that everything and everyone has a place—is that place is an essential precondition for the existence of anything. Societies are not only shaped by their places, rather their places shape them, and these places are experienced as communities and a shared culture.

Changes in place produce varied political cultures that construct different values, beliefs, attitudes, and expectations of citizens toward the political system and as participants in it. In the U.S., these beliefs are increasingly codified by both demographics and geographical location. Political systems and actors are now characterized as either "red" or "blue," which translates into legislative decision-making and electorate voting behavior (Pallay, 2013). The realities of these differences are far more complicated than the simple contrast between red and blue. At the core of these distinctions are deep social divisions over changing values and lifestyles that shape and are expressed by the politics of place. Recognizing that red and blue families live different lives has dominated legal and political debates for some time. Rights for an LGBT individual may vary from region to region, state to state, and even within a state, as they are shaped by a variety of factors, from partisanship, to public opinion, to migration and immigration, all of which influence the content of laws and policies.

The Politics of Selection and the Future of the LGBT Community

Americans opposed to same-sex marriage continue to fight, seeking control over the courts in campaigns for the presidency (Tashman, 2016; Bomboy, 2016) and carrying their objections forward under the banner of conscience and religious liberty (NeJaime & Siegel, 2015). Just as *Brown v. Board of Education* (1954) did not end the debate over racial segregation (Greenhouse & Siegel, 2011), *Obergefell* has not ended the debate over marriage but instead has channeled this debate into new forms of argument. Proponents of same-sex marriage persisted in the face of loss and so too will its opponents.

Only by understanding the historical development of the law will one develop a sense of how it will likely change in the future. We live in a democracy, but within that democracy we give the nine unelected, virtually unremovable members of the Supreme Court broad discretion to determine reproductive and marriage rights. Although the justices might claim they do not make public policy and merely interpret the law, the truth is closer to the idea that the Constitution is what these judges say it is.

To understand why the politics of the president appointing justices is such a strong predictor of judicial policy judgements, one need looks only at the politics of judicial appointment. It is a highly politicized process, in which nominee's personal policy predilections are important criteria. Therefore, it is not presidential appointment, per se, that shapes judicial policymaking, rather the discretion of the appointing president to directly shape the appointment based on policy predilections that indirectly influence their appointee's selection. Judges' off-the-bench legal and political experiences have been correlated with judicial judgments at every level of the federal judiciary (Goldman, 1975; Tate, 1981). The most persistent and powerful extra-legal predictor of a judge's policy judgments is their appointing president (Alumbaugh & Rowland, 1990).

The tendency for presidents to recruit and nominate judges who share their partisan affiliation and their legal and political values has increased dramatically. On March 16, 2016, President Barack Obama nominated Merrick Garland, chief judge of the United States Court of Appeals for the District of Columbia Circuit, to replace Antonin Scalia (Shear, 2016). On February 23, 2016, the 11 Republican members of the Senate Judiciary Committee signed a letter to Senate Majority Leader Mitch McConnell stating their intention to withhold consent on any nominee made by Obama, and that no hearings would occur until after January 20, 2017, when the next president took office[1] (United States Senate Committee on Judiciary, 2016). After Garland's nomination, McConnell reiterated his position that the Senate would not confirm any Supreme Court nomination from Obama (Shear, 2016). Garland's nomination expired on January 3, 2017 (Bravin, 2017).

Selection of a Supreme Court justice is a political event. Potential justices are chosen to reflect the values and policy outlook of the appointing administration and, in turn, the majority that elected the president.

Every president must select hundreds of federal officials, but presidents make the great majority of these appointments in name only. A few appointments are deemed too important, and foremost among these are positions on the Supreme Court. Therefore, a variety of individuals and groups outside of the Executive Branch seek to influence the president's choice.

Among these interest groups, those close to the administration may participate privately in the nomination process; if not, their positions certainly will be considered as nominees are vetted. Groups that lack ties to the administration sometimes seek to exert pressure through the media by indicating they will fight against Senate confirmation of a candidate.

Presidential nominations to the Supreme Court may be based on several factors. The first includes attitudes of the nominee toward issues that may come before the court, i.e., the nominee's policy preferences. Presidents seek appointees who share their views about policy. As a result, administrative officials scrutinize the views of nominees with considerable care. The second factor is reward. Nominations often go to personal and political associates of the president. In fact, half of those nominated to the court have known the president personally (Scigliano, 1971). More broadly, 90 percent of all nominees have come from the president's party (Scigliano, 1971). The final factor in judicial selection is the pursuit of political support. Some nominations are used to appeal to important interest or demographic groups. The preeminence of this goal reflects the growing recognition that the Supreme Court plays a significant role in national policymaking.

Other situational factors also play a part in the confirmation process. Inevitably, these decisions are affected by the partisan makeup of the Senate. Nominees of a president whose party controls the Senate are in a good position to be confirmed. Nominations may be vulnerable near the end of a president's term, and as evidenced by the Obama nomination, senators from the other party wanted to keep the seat open in case their own party won the next election.

Changing of the Guard

Courts play a central role in the United States and are deeply involved in the collective lives of Americans. This function is particularly clear when courts write and publish opinions laying out the legal rules on which their interpretations are based.

By now it should be abundantly clear that *Obergefell* has not ended the battle surrounding same-sex marriage. Even if the decision had been unanimous, it would have been controversial. But the fact that four justices, including the chief justice, attacked the decision as a judicial usurpation of power striking at the very heart of democracy has given impetus and imprimatur to those who oppose it (Strasser, 2016).

Arguably, the four dissenters gave fodder not only to those who oppose *Obergefell* but to those who disagree other decisions as well and consider themselves unbound by decisions with which they disagree. At the time of this writing, Justice Kennedy had announced his retirement from the court and President Donald Trump had appointed Judge Brett M. Kavanaugh to the court, a nomination that could change the court's overall ideological balance (Segal, 2016).

Assertions that judicial decisions are objective, dispassionate, and impartial are obviously belied by the fact that different courts and different judges do not decide the same question or issue the same way, to say nothing of those on the Supreme Court who typically represent dissenting votes. Therefore, a single personnel change can fundamentally alter the course of constitutional law. With the announced retirement of Justice Kennedy, who authored the majority opinions in LGBT cases such as *Romer v. Evans* (1996); *Lawrence v. Texas* (2003); *U.S. v. Windsor* (2013); and *Obergefell v. Hodges* (2105), it is obvious that his replacement may tip the scale against the path forward for the LGBT movement.

As excerpted from the confirmation hearing captured by Scott (2018), Senator Kamala D. Harris (D-Calif.), one of the more liberal members of Congress on gay rights issues, questioned Kavanaugh about his views on the court case that extended marriage rights to gay Americans (*Obergefell*):

HARRIS: My question is very specific. Can you comment on your personal opinion on whether Obergefell was correctly decided? It's a yes or no. Please.

KAVANAUGH: In Masterpiece Cakeshop, and this is, I think, relevant to your question, Justice Kennedy wrote in the majority opinion joined by Chief Justice

[John G.] Roberts [Jr.] and Justice [Samuel A.] Alito [Jr.] and Justice [Neil M.] Gorsuch and Justice [Stephen G.] Breyer and Justice [Elena] Kagan, the days of discriminating against gay and lesbian Americans, or treating gay and lesbian Americans as inferior in dignity and worth, are over.

HARRIS: Do you agree with that statement?

KAVANAUGH: That is the precedent of the Supreme Court agreed with by—

HARRIS: Sir, I'm asking your opinion. You're the nominee right now, and so it is probative of your ability to serve on the highest court in our land. So, I'm asking you a very specific question. Either you're willing to answer it or not. And if you're not willing to answer it, we can move on. But do you believe Obergefell was correctly decided?

KAVANAUGH: Each of the justices have declined as a matter of judicial independence—each of them—to answer questions in that line of cases.

HARRIS: So, you will not answer them?

KAVANAUGH: Following the precedent set by those eight justices, they've all declined when asked to answer that question.

HARRIS: Thank you.

Is Kavanagh's non-answer an answer in itself?

Sword or Shield

This raises the question as to how to balance the equality interests between members of the LGBT and religious communities. In other words, if an antidiscrimination policy is needed in a certain context to protect citizens from mistreatment that hampers their full participation in civil society, then such policies should be understood as shields not swords. Is it possible for a society to live in open disagreement about moral fundamentals? Religious freedom is indeed important, but courts must be cautious not to lose sight of this critical legal distinction: being offended by another's lifestyle does not amount to a true "restriction" or "burden" on an individual's right to "exercise of religion."

The rights of the LGBT community are in a state of flux, and what is always certain is that we live in a world of change. A new justice, another decision, and our Constitution lives on.

FUTURE RESEARCH DIRECTIONS

If the Civil Rights Act were amended to include sexual orientation as a protected class, or if a state law was appealed to the U.S. Supreme Court, would the court uphold antidiscrimination laws as they pertain to private businesses? Would the fundamental rights of free speech and free exercise of religion outweigh the rights of those discriminated against?

CONCLUSION

In filing dissents, judges emulate legislators by entering statements into the record to explain their policy commitments. Policy disputes have become as highly personal among judges as they are among legislators.

Responsiveness to organized interests when choosing a docket and citing amici briefs is an indicator of social and political forces at play. Judicial decisions are a function of what judges prefer and what they think they ought to do and are constrained by what they perceive as feasible. In other words, institutional context structures and shapes individual behavior. Only one thing is certain: the struggles for and against gay rights in the United States will continue far into the indefinite future.

Members of the Supreme Court further their personal and administration policy goals because they lack electoral or political accountability, comprising a court of last resort that controls its own jurisdiction. There is an opportunity for judges to exercise discretion in making judgements. These decisions about the meanings of laws are a form of policymaking. Through writ of certiorari, a judge may request to hear a case he or she is not required to hear and blocks of justices who share similar ideological perspectives will then tend to vote together.

Evidence suggests that policymaking by the Supreme Court reflects the ideological preferences of the justices, and that such attitudes are formed even before justices are appointed to the court. What's more, most justices are highly consistent in casting ideologically oriented votes in the cases that come before them from term to term (Segal & Spaethe, 1993). If in fact this is true, then Supreme Court policymaking is largely a reflection of the justices' values, rather than a closely circumscribed rendering of constitutional and statutory language. This, then, is the inherent contradiction between our ideals of judicial objectivity and the realities of the policymaking practices of unelected life-term justices.

REFERENCES

Alumbaugh, S., & Rowland, C. K. (1990). The links between platform-based appointment criteria and trial judges' abortion judgements. *Judicature*, *74*(5), 153–162. PMID:11656071

Ball, C. A. (2014). *Same-sex marriage and children: A tale of history*. New York, NY: Oxford University Press. doi:10.1093/acprof:oso/9780199977871.001.0001

Bombay, S. (2015, December 16). *The Supreme Court as a 2016 campaign issue*. Philly.com.

Bravin, J. (2017, January 3). President Obama's Supreme Court nomination of Merrick Garland expires. *The Wall Street Journal*. Retrieved from https://www.wsj.com/articles/president-obamas-supreme-court-nomination-of-merrick-garland-expires-1483463952

Burwell v. Hobby Lobby Stores, Inc., 134 S. Ct. 2751, 2762,2785 (2014).

Carter, S. (1994). *The culture of disbelief: How American law and politics trivialize religious devotion*. Basic Books.

Greenhouse, L., & Siegel, R. B. (2011). Before (and after) Roe v. Wade: New questions about backlash. *The Yale Law Journal*, *120*, 2028–2074.

Lawrence v. Texas, 539 U.S. 558 (2003).

Meadow, T. (2013). Queer numbers: social science as cultural heterosexism. *Social (In) Queery Blog*. Retrieved from http://socialinqueery.com/2013/08/14/queer-numbers-social-science-as-cultural-heterosexism

Nejaime, D., & Siegel, R. B. (2015). Conscience claims in religion and politics. *The Yale Law Journal*, *124*, 2510–2524.

Obergefell v. Hodges, 135 S. Ct. 2584 (2015).

Pally, G. (2013). Who runs the states: Part 1: partisanship of the 50 states between 1992–2013? *Ballotepidia*. Retrieved from https://www.heartland.org/publications-resources/publications/who-runs-the-states-part-1-partisanship-of-the-50-states-between-1992-2013

Romer v. Evans, 517 U.S. 620 (1996).

Scigliano, R. (1971). *The Supreme Court and the presidency*. New York, NY: Free Press.

Scott, E. (2018, September 7). In Kavanaugh's non-answer on same-sex marriage, many heard a troubling response. *Washington Post*. Retrieved from https://www.washingtonpost.com/politics/2018/09/07/kavanaughs-non-answer-same-sex-marriage-many-heard-troubling-answer/?noredirect=on&utm_term=.eab6a2dd5210

Segal, E. (2016, November 17). What will Trump's Supreme Court look like? *Newsweek*. Retrieved from http://www.newsweek.coin/what-will-trumps-supreme-court-look-521581/

Segal, J. A., & Spaeth, H. J. (1993). *The Supreme Court and the attitudinal model*. New York, NY: Cambridge University Press.

Shear, M. D. (2016, March 16). Obama chooses Merrick Garland for Supreme Court. *New York Times*. Retrieved from https://www.nytimes.com/2016/03/17/us/politics/obama-supreme-court-nominee.html

Stoddard, T. (1997). Bleeding heart: Reflections on using the law to make social change. *New York University Law Review*, *72*(5), 967–991.

Strasser, M. (2016). Obergefell, dignity, and the family. *The Journal of Gender, Race & Justice*, *317*, 348–349.

Tashman, B. (2016, February 18). Donald Trump: Trust me to overturn the shocking gay marriage decision. *Right Wing Watch*. Retrieved from http://www.rightwingwatch.org/post/donald-trump-trust-me-to-overturn-the-shocking-gay-marriage-decision/

Tushnet, M. (1979). Truth, justice and the American way. *Texas Law Review*, *57*, 1307–1423.

U.S. v. Windsor, 133 S. Ct. 2675 (2013).

Wong, C. M. (2016, February 2). Pennsylvania's W. W. Bridal Boutique under fire for reportedly turning away lesbian brides-to-be. *Huffington Post*. Retrieved from http://www.huffmgtonpost.eom/2014/08/1 l/ww-bridal-boutique-lesbia_n_5668645.html

KEY TERMS AND DEFINITIONS

Civil Rights Act of 1964: Amended Civil War statutes to provide stronger protections for rights guaranteed by the Constitution that affected voting rights and discrimination in public accommodations.

Judicial Review: The review by a court of law of some act or failure to act by a government entity, or the review by the U.S. Supreme Court of the highest courts in every state to decide the constitutionality of the acts of the legislative and executive branches within their jurisdictions.

Writ of Certiorari: Orders a lower court to deliver its record in a case so that the higher court may review it.

ENDNOTE

1 The 11 Republican members of the Judiciary committee chaired by Chuck Grassley (Iowa) were Orrin Hatch and Mike Lee (Utah); Jeff Sessions (Alabama); Lindsey Graham (South Carolina); John Cornyn and Ted Cruz (Texas); Jeff Flake (Arizona); David Vitter (Louisiana); David Perdue (Georgia); and Thom Tillis (North Carolina).

Related Readings

To continue IGI Global's long-standing tradition of advancing innovation through emerging research, please find below a compiled list of recommended IGI Global book chapters and journal articles in the areas of gender movement, political science, and discrimination. These related readings will provide additional information and guidance to further enrich your knowledge and assist you with your own research.

Ak, R., & Bingül, B. A. (2018). Kuwait. In S. Ozdemir, S. Erdogan, & A. Gedikli (Eds.), *Handbook of Research on Sociopolitical Factors Impacting Economic Growth in Islamic Nations* (pp. 276–292). Hershey, PA: IGI Global. doi:10.4018/978-1-5225-2939-2.ch014

Azad, S. K. (2016). Women, Migration, Ready Made Garment Factories in Dhaka: Formation of New Class, Culture, and Relationships? In N. Mahtab, S. Parker, F. Kabir, T. Haque, A. Sabur, & A. Sowad (Eds.), *Revealing Gender Inequalities and Perceptions in South Asian Countries through Discourse Analysis* (pp. 41–56). Hershey, PA: IGI Global. doi:10.4018/978-1-5225-0279-1.ch003

Banerjee, A. K. (2017). "Why Can't I Have the Vote?": Women's Poetry, Politics, and the First World War. In Ö. Çakırtaş (Ed.), *Ideological Messaging and the Role of Political Literature* (pp. 117–144). Hershey, PA: IGI Global. doi:10.4018/978-1-5225-2391-8.ch007

Bhattacharyya, D. K. (2016). Effectiveness of Critical Discourse Analysis to Solve Constrained Employment Relations: Application Based Study on Two Indian Organizations. In N. Mahtab, S. Parker, F. Kabir, T. Haque, A. Sabur, & A. Sowad (Eds.), *Revealing Gender Inequalities and Perceptions in South Asian Countries through Discourse Analysis* (pp. 100–120). Hershey, PA: IGI Global. doi:10.4018/978-1-5225-0279-1.ch006

Bozkurt, İ. M., & Koç, M. (2018). Islamic Republic of Iran. In S. Ozdemir, S. Erdogan, & A. Gedikli (Eds.), *Handbook of Research on Sociopolitical Factors Impacting Economic Growth in Islamic Nations* (pp. 122–146). Hershey, PA: IGI Global. doi:10.4018/978-1-5225-2939-2.ch007

Brahmana, R., & Chen, S. (2016). The Role of Women Directors for Malaysian Firms' Performance. In N. Mahtab, S. Parker, F. Kabir, T. Haque, A. Sabur, & A. Sowad (Eds.), *Revealing Gender Inequalities and Perceptions in South Asian Countries through Discourse Analysis* (pp. 121–136). Hershey, PA: IGI Global. doi:10.4018/978-1-5225-0279-1.ch007

Brice, T. S. (2016). Race Relations in the Churches of Christ: Strategies towards Reconciliation. In B. Glimps & T. Ford (Eds.), *Gender and Diversity Issues in Religious-Based Institutions and Organizations* (pp. 184–199). Hershey, PA: IGI Global. doi:10.4018/978-1-4666-8772-1.ch008

Bristow, D. C. (2017). What Danger Can There Be in Being the Shadow of a Gunman in Dublin, at Easter, in 1916?: Political Hauntologies in Joyce, O'Casey, and Yeats. In Ö. Çakırtaş (Ed.), *Ideological Messaging and the Role of Political Literature* (pp. 1–24). Hershey, PA: IGI Global. doi:10.4018/978-1-5225-2391-8.ch001

Çakırtaş, Ö. (2017). Mustapha and Greville: Constructing Anglo-Ottoman Diplomacy and Machiavellian Identities in Early Modern English Drama. In Ö. Çakırtaş (Ed.), *Ideological Messaging and the Role of Political Literature* (pp. 145–158). Hershey, PA: IGI Global. doi:10.4018/978-1-5225-2391-8.ch008

Campos, E. Jr. (2017). "Power Is Only a Word": Language, Control, and the Orwellian Philosophy of Nineteen Eighty-Four. In Ö. Çakırtaş (Ed.), *Ideological Messaging and the Role of Political Literature* (pp. 25–42). Hershey, PA: IGI Global. doi:10.4018/978-1-5225-2391-8.ch002

Cappelli, M. L. (2017). The Digital Politics of Pain: Exploring Female Voices in Afghanistan. In Ö. Çakırtaş (Ed.), *Ideological Messaging and the Role of Political Literature* (pp. 160–176). Hershey, PA: IGI Global. doi:10.4018/978-1-5225-2391-8.ch009

Cengiz, V. (2018). Afghanistan. In S. Ozdemir, S. Erdogan, & A. Gedikli (Eds.), *Handbook of Research on Sociopolitical Factors Impacting Economic Growth in Islamic Nations* (pp. 314–331). Hershey, PA: IGI Global. doi:10.4018/978-1-5225-2939-2.ch016

Chowdhury, F. (2016). Permanently Temporary: The Production of Race, Class, and Gender Hierarchies through a Study of Canada's Temporary Foreign Worker Program. In N. Mahtab, S. Parker, F. Kabir, T. Haque, A. Sabur, & A. Sowad (Eds.), *Discourse Analysis as a Tool for Understanding Gender Identity, Representation, and Equality* (pp. 175–203). Hershey, PA: IGI Global. doi:10.4018/978-1-5225-0225-8.ch009

Dama, N. (2018). Iraq. In S. Ozdemir, S. Erdogan, & A. Gedikli (Eds.), *Handbook of Research on Sociopolitical Factors Impacting Economic Growth in Islamic Nations* (pp. 147–160). Hershey, PA: IGI Global. doi:10.4018/978-1-5225-2939-2.ch008

Demirhan, K. (2017). Participation, Civil Society and the Facebook Use of NGOs in Turkey. In K. Demirhan & D. Çakır-Demirhan (Eds.), *Political Scandal, Corruption, and Legitimacy in the Age of Social Media* (pp. 223–246). Hershey, PA: IGI Global. doi:10.4018/978-1-5225-2019-1.ch010

Demirhan, K. (2017). Scandal Politics and Political Scandals in the Era of Digital Interactive Media. In K. Demirhan & D. Çakır-Demirhan (Eds.), *Political Scandal, Corruption, and Legitimacy in the Age of Social Media* (pp. 25–50). Hershey, PA: IGI Global. doi:10.4018/978-1-5225-2019-1.ch002

Di Martino, M. L. (2017). The "Development" Dilemma in the Literary Production of the 19th, 20th, and 21st Centuries: Rethinking Ideologies Across Literature. In Ö. Çakırtaş (Ed.), *Ideological Messaging and the Role of Political Literature* (pp. 60–82). Hershey, PA: IGI Global. doi:10.4018/978-1-5225-2391-8.ch004

Durgun, Ö. (2018). United Arab Emirates. In S. Ozdemir, S. Erdogan, & A. Gedikli (Eds.), *Handbook of Research on Sociopolitical Factors Impacting Economic Growth in Islamic Nations* (pp. 253–275). Hershey, PA: IGI Global. doi:10.4018/978-1-5225-2939-2.ch013

Eraso, A. B., & Cid, D. D. (2016). The Role of Women in the Development of New Religious Movements in Latin America: The Case of Pentecostalism. In B. Glimps & T. Ford (Eds.), *Gender and Diversity Issues in Religious-Based Institutions and Organizations* (pp. 224–247). Hershey, PA: IGI Global. doi:10.4018/978-1-4666-8772-1.ch010

Erdoğan, S., & Gedikli, A. (2018). The State of Qatar. In S. Ozdemir, S. Erdogan, & A. Gedikli (Eds.), *Handbook of Research on Sociopolitical Factors Impacting Economic Growth in Islamic Nations* (pp. 212–252). Hershey, PA: IGI Global. doi:10.4018/978-1-5225-2939-2.ch012

Erkekoğlu, L. C., & Madi, İ. (2018). The Hashemite Kingdom of Jordan. In S. Ozdemir, S. Erdogan, & A. Gedikli (Eds.), *Handbook of Research on Sociopolitical Factors Impacting Economic Growth in Islamic Nations* (pp. 95–121). Hershey, PA: IGI Global. doi:10.4018/978-1-5225-2939-2.ch006

Ermağan, İ., & İpek, V. (2018). Morocco. In S. Ozdemir, S. Erdogan, & A. Gedikli (Eds.), *Handbook of Research on Sociopolitical Factors Impacting Economic Growth in Islamic Nations* (pp. 51–67). Hershey, PA: IGI Global. doi:10.4018/978-1-5225-2939-2.ch004

Eroğlu, B., & Gedikli, Z. (2018). Niger. In S. Ozdemir, S. Erdogan, & A. Gedikli (Eds.), *Handbook of Research on Sociopolitical Factors Impacting Economic Growth in Islamic Nations* (pp. 41–50). Hershey, PA: IGI Global. doi:10.4018/978-1-5225-2939-2.ch003

Esen, Ö., & Aydın, C. (2018). Tunisia. In S. Ozdemir, S. Erdogan, & A. Gedikli (Eds.), *Handbook of Research on Sociopolitical Factors Impacting Economic Growth in Islamic Nations* (pp. 68–94). Hershey, PA: IGI Global. doi:10.4018/978-1-5225-2939-2.ch005

Essien, E. D. (2017). Navigating the Nexus between Social Media, Political Scandal, and Good Governance in Nigeria: Its Ethical Implications. In K. Demirhan & D. Çakır-Demirhan (Eds.), *Political Scandal, Corruption, and Legitimacy in the Age of Social Media* (pp. 157–184). Hershey, PA: IGI Global. doi:10.4018/978-1-5225-2019-1.ch007

Fanaian, T. (2017). The Theocratic Deception Trap: Khomeini's Persuasion Techniques and Communication Patterns in His Books, Guardianship of the Jurist 1979 and Testament 1989. In E. Lewin, E. Bick, & D. Naor (Eds.), *Comparative Perspectives on Civil Religion, Nationalism, and Political Influence* (pp. 62–105). Hershey, PA: IGI Global. doi:10.4018/978-1-5225-0516-7.ch003

Ferdowsi, L. (2016). Intersections of Gender, Sex, and Power: Control over Women's Bodies and Sexuality Amongst the Bangladeshi Diaspora in Britain. In N. Mahtab, S. Parker, F. Kabir, T. Haque, A. Sabur, & A. Sowad (Eds.), *Discourse Analysis as a Tool for Understanding Gender Identity, Representation, and Equality* (pp. 1–24). Hershey, PA: IGI Global. doi:10.4018/978-1-5225-0225-8.ch001

Fisherman, S. (2016). Body Image and Wellbeing in Religious Male and Female Youth in Israel: An Educational Challenge. In B. Glimps & T. Ford (Eds.), *Gender and Diversity Issues in Religious-Based Institutions and Organizations* (pp. 51–79). Hershey, PA: IGI Global. doi:10.4018/978-1-4666-8772-1.ch003

Ford, T. N., & Glimps, B. J. (2016). A Comparison of "Inclusiveness" in Two Liberal Arts Catholic Universities: What Nurtures an Inclusive Campus Climate? In B. Glimps & T. Ford (Eds.), *Gender and Diversity Issues in Religious-Based Institutions and Organizations* (pp. 159–183). Hershey, PA: IGI Global. doi:10.4018/978-1-4666-8772-1.ch007

Gachigua, S. G. (2016). Legislating for a De Jure One-Party State in 1982 and "Party Hopping" in 2012: Reconstructing Elite Discourse on Political Parties in Kenya. In D. Orwenjo, O. Oketch, & A. Tunde (Eds.), *Political Discourse in Emergent, Fragile, and Failed Democracies* (pp. 286–305). Hershey, PA: IGI Global. doi:10.4018/978-1-5225-0081-0.ch016

Gillath, N. (2017). Avoiding Conscription in Israel: Were Women Pawns in the Political Game? In E. Lewin, E. Bick, & D. Naor (Eds.), *Comparative Perspectives on Civil Religion, Nationalism, and Political Influence* (pp. 226–256). Hershey, PA: IGI Global. doi:10.4018/978-1-5225-0516-7.ch009

Harris-Smith, Y. J. (2016). Spiritual Health Identity: Placing Black Women's Lives in the Center of Analysis. In B. Glimps & T. Ford (Eds.), *Gender and Diversity Issues in Religious-Based Institutions and Organizations* (pp. 1–23). Hershey, PA: IGI Global. doi:10.4018/978-1-4666-8772-1.ch001

Haşlak, İ., & Bilen, M. (2018). Bangladesh. In S. Ozdemir, S. Erdogan, & A. Gedikli (Eds.), *Handbook of Research on Sociopolitical Factors Impacting Economic Growth in Islamic Nations* (pp. 380–403). Hershey, PA: IGI Global. doi:10.4018/978-1-5225-2939-2.ch019

Herkman, J., & Matikainen, J. (2017). Neo-Populist Scandal and Social Media: The Finnish Olli Immonen Affair. In K. Demirhan & D. Çakır-Demirhan (Eds.), *Political Scandal, Corruption, and Legitimacy in the Age of Social Media* (pp. 1–24). Hershey, PA: IGI Global. doi:10.4018/978-1-5225-2019-1.ch001

Higgs, E. T. (2016). Becoming 'Multi-Racial': The Young Women's Christian Association in Kenya, 1955-1965. In B. Glimps & T. Ford (Eds.), *Gender and Diversity Issues in Religious-Based Institutions and Organizations* (pp. 24–50). Hershey, PA: IGI Global. doi:10.4018/978-1-4666-8772-1.ch002

Hosain, J. (2016). Beauty, Choice, and Empowerment: Does Cosmetic Surgery Translate into Gendered Empowerment in Bangladesh? In N. Mahtab, S. Parker, F. Kabir, T. Haque, A. Sabur, & A. Sowad (Eds.), *Revealing Gender Inequalities and Perceptions in South Asian Countries through Discourse Analysis* (pp. 191–207). Hershey, PA: IGI Global. doi:10.4018/978-1-5225-0279-1.ch011

Igah, F. (2016). Changing the Traditional Education of Igbo Females: The Role of Religion in Colonial Education. In B. Glimps & T. Ford (Eds.), *Gender and Diversity Issues in Religious-Based Institutions and Organizations* (pp. 291–305). Hershey, PA: IGI Global. doi:10.4018/978-1-4666-8772-1.ch013

İncekara, A. (2018). Lebanon. In S. Ozdemir, S. Erdogan, & A. Gedikli (Eds.), *Handbook of Research on Sociopolitical Factors Impacting Economic Growth in Islamic Nations* (pp. 161–181). Hershey, PA: IGI Global. doi:10.4018/978-1-5225-2939-2.ch009

Islam, A. (2016). Disparity between Boys and Girls: Concerning Sports in Secondary Level Academic Institutions. In N. Mahtab, S. Parker, F. Kabir, T. Haque, A. Sabur, & A. Sowad (Eds.), *Discourse Analysis as a Tool for Understanding Gender Identity, Representation, and Equality* (pp. 157–174). Hershey, PA: IGI Global. doi:10.4018/978-1-5225-0225-8.ch008

Jabin, M. (2016). Struggle against ICT-Based Violence: Locating Socialization Process of Young Men as a Hidden Cause of Women's Vulnerability. In N. Mahtab, S. Parker, F. Kabir, T. Haque, A. Sabur, & A. Sowad (Eds.), *Discourse Analysis as a Tool for Understanding Gender Identity, Representation, and Equality* (pp. 218–235). Hershey, PA: IGI Global. doi:10.4018/978-1-5225-0225-8.ch011

Jahan, F., Wahab, S. A., & Hafiz, F. B. (2016). Gender and Ethnic Discrimination: Life of Mainstream and Indigenous Women in Bangladesh. In N. Mahtab, S. Parker, F. Kabir, T. Haque, A. Sabur, & A. Sowad (Eds.), *Revealing Gender Inequalities and Perceptions in South Asian Countries through Discourse Analysis* (pp. 148–163). Hershey, PA: IGI Global. doi:10.4018/978-1-5225-0279-1.ch009

Jahan, F. R. (2016). Agency, Gender Identities, and Clothing Consumption: The Discourse on Garment Workers. In N. Mahtab, S. Parker, F. Kabir, T. Haque, A. Sabur, & A. Sowad (Eds.), *Discourse Analysis as a Tool for Understanding Gender Identity, Representation, and Equality* (pp. 136–156). Hershey, PA: IGI Global. doi:10.4018/978-1-5225-0225-8.ch007

Jha, C. K. (2017). Information Control, Transparency, and Social Media: Implications for Corruption. In K. Demirhan & D. Çakır-Demirhan (Eds.), *Political Scandal, Corruption, and Legitimacy in the Age of Social Media* (pp. 51–75). Hershey, PA: IGI Global. doi:10.4018/978-1-5225-2019-1.ch003

Joshi, N. (2016). Urban Nepali Women and Experiences of Love, Intimate Relations, and Media. In N. Mahtab, S. Parker, F. Kabir, T. Haque, A. Sabur, & A. Sowad (Eds.), *Revealing Gender Inequalities and Perceptions in South Asian Countries through Discourse Analysis* (pp. 20–40). Hershey, PA: IGI Global. doi:10.4018/978-1-5225-0279-1.ch002

Kalagy, T. (2017). Values, Constraints, and Maneuvers: Processes of Academization among Ultra-Orthodox Women and Beduin Women in Israel. In E. Lewin, E. Bick, & D. Naor (Eds.), *Comparative Perspectives on Civil Religion, Nationalism, and Political Influence* (pp. 257–284). Hershey, PA: IGI Global. doi:10.4018/978-1-5225-0516-7.ch010

Kandemir, O., & Gümüş, N. (2018). Libya. In S. Ozdemir, S. Erdogan, & A. Gedikli (Eds.), *Handbook of Research on Sociopolitical Factors Impacting Economic Growth in Islamic Nations* (pp. 22–40). Hershey, PA: IGI Global. doi:10.4018/978-1-5225-2939-2.ch002

Karagöl, E. T. (2018). Azerbaijan. In S. Ozdemir, S. Erdogan, & A. Gedikli (Eds.), *Handbook of Research on Sociopolitical Factors Impacting Economic Growth in Islamic Nations* (pp. 182–194). Hershey, PA: IGI Global. doi:10.4018/978-1-5225-2939-2.ch010

Kaya, O. (2017). Travel Politics Mirroring Anatolia, Asia Minor, and the Greek Islands. In Ö. Çakırtaş (Ed.), *Ideological Messaging and the Role of Political Literature* (pp. 235–287). Hershey, PA: IGI Global. doi:10.4018/978-1-5225-2391-8.ch013

Kaynak, S. (2018). Pakistan. In S. Ozdemir, S. Erdogan, & A. Gedikli (Eds.), *Handbook of Research on Sociopolitical Factors Impacting Economic Growth in Islamic Nations* (pp. 293–313). Hershey, PA: IGI Global. doi:10.4018/978-1-5225-2939-2.ch015

Keles, R. (2016). The Normative Base of Local Government: Progress in Local Democracy and the Reformation Process. In U. Sadioglu & K. Dede (Eds.), *Theoretical Foundations and Discussions on the Reformation Process in Local Governments* (pp. 24–41). Hershey, PA: IGI Global. doi:10.4018/978-1-5225-0317-0.ch002

Kerbizi, M. (2017). Communist Ideology and Its Impact on Albanian Literature. In Ö. Çakırtaş (Ed.), *Ideological Messaging and the Role of Political Literature* (pp. 200–221). Hershey, PA: IGI Global. doi:10.4018/978-1-5225-2391-8.ch011

Khan, M. (2016). Implications of Citizenship Discourse on Female Labour Force Participation: A Case Study of Bangladeshi Women in the UK. In N. Mahtab, S. Parker, F. Kabir, T. Haque, A. Sabur, & A. Sowad (Eds.), *Discourse Analysis as a Tool for Understanding Gender Identity, Representation, and Equality* (pp. 25–49). Hershey, PA: IGI Global. doi:10.4018/978-1-5225-0225-8.ch002

Khan, M. M., & Ara, F. (2016). Women in Bangladesh Local Government: Critically Evaluating Their Participation and Empowerment. In N. Mahtab, S. Parker, F. Kabir, T. Haque, A. Sabur, & A. Sowad (Eds.), *Revealing Gender Inequalities and Perceptions in South Asian Countries through Discourse Analysis* (pp. 80–99). Hershey, PA: IGI Global. doi:10.4018/978-1-5225-0279-1.ch005

Khanum, R. A. (2016). Equality and Differences: Some Feminist Thoughts. In N. Mahtab, S. Parker, F. Kabir, T. Haque, A. Sabur, & A. Sowad (Eds.), *Discourse Analysis as a Tool for Understanding Gender Identity, Representation, and Equality* (pp. 204–217). Hershey, PA: IGI Global. doi:10.4018/978-1-5225-0225-8.ch010

Kim, Y. K., Edens, D., Parra, O. E., & Lopez, K. M. (2016). Sense of Belonging in Religious-Based Colleges and Universities: Predictors and Patterns among Students of Color and White Students. In B. Glimps & T. Ford (Eds.), *Gender and Diversity Issues in Religious-Based Institutions and Organizations* (pp. 269–290). Hershey, PA: IGI Global. doi:10.4018/978-1-4666-8772-1.ch012

Korstanje, M. E. (2017). The Allegory of Holocaust: The Rise of Thana Capitalism. In Ö. Çakırtaş (Ed.), *Ideological Messaging and the Role of Political Literature* (pp. 177–199). Hershey, PA: IGI Global. doi:10.4018/978-1-5225-2391-8.ch010

Korstanje, M. E. (2017). The Roots of Evilness and Biblical Literature: The Revolt of Lucifer. In Ö. Çakırtaş (Ed.), *Ideological Messaging and the Role of Political Literature* (pp. 83–97). Hershey, PA: IGI Global. doi:10.4018/978-1-5225-2391-8.ch005

Lawler, J. A., & Mir, G. (2016). Women, Faith, and Social Cohesion. In B. Glimps & T. Ford (Eds.), *Gender and Diversity Issues in Religious-Based Institutions and Organizations* (pp. 200–223). Hershey, PA: IGI Global. doi:10.4018/978-1-4666-8772-1.ch009

Leon, N. (2017). The Haredi Scholar-Society and the Military Draft in Israel: Counter-Nationalism and the Imagined Military Symbiosis. In E. Lewin, E. Bick, & D. Naor (Eds.), *Comparative Perspectives on Civil Religion, Nationalism, and Political Influence* (pp. 210–225). Hershey, PA: IGI Global. doi:10.4018/978-1-5225-0516-7.ch008

Lewin, E., & Bick, E. (2017). Introduction: Civil Religion and Nationalism on a Godly-Civil Continuum. In E. Lewin, E. Bick, & D. Naor (Eds.), *Comparative Perspectives on Civil Religion, Nationalism, and Political Influence* (pp. 1–31). Hershey, PA: IGI Global. doi:10.4018/978-1-5225-0516-7.ch001

Ma, L. (2017). Government Website, Social Media, and Citizens' Perceptions of Corruption: Evidence from Chinese Cities. In K. Demirhan & D. Çakır-Demirhan (Eds.), *Political Scandal, Corruption, and Legitimacy in the Age of Social Media* (pp. 185–204). Hershey, PA: IGI Global. doi:10.4018/978-1-5225-2019-1.ch008

Manrique, C. G., & Manrique, G. G. (2017). Social Media's Role in Alleviating Political Corruption and Scandals: The Philippines during and after the Marcos Regime. In K. Demirhan & D. Çakır-Demirhan (Eds.), *Political Scandal, Corruption, and Legitimacy in the Age of Social Media* (pp. 205–222). Hershey, PA: IGI Global. doi:10.4018/978-1-5225-2019-1.ch009

Merviö, M. M. (2017). *Interpretation of Visual Arts Across Societies and Political Culture: Emerging Research and Opportunities* (pp. 1–110). Hershey, PA: IGI Global. doi:10.4018/978-1-5225-2554-7

Neugröschel, M. (2017). Anti-Semitism as a Civil Religion: Progressive Paradigms in the Anti-Semitic Construction of German National Identity. In E. Lewin, E. Bick, & D. Naor (Eds.), *Comparative Perspectives on Civil Religion, Nationalism, and Political Influence* (pp. 106–124). Hershey, PA: IGI Global. doi:10.4018/978-1-5225-0516-7.ch004

Nişancı, E., Yıldırım, D. Ç., Çevik, N. K., & Sırım, V. (2018). Indonesia. In S. Ozdemir, S. Erdogan, & A. Gedikli (Eds.), *Handbook of Research on Sociopolitical Factors Impacting Economic Growth in Islamic Nations* (pp. 332–357). Hershey, PA: IGI Global. doi:10.4018/978-1-5225-2939-2.ch017

Okezie, C. E., Alhamisi, J., & Glimps, B. J. (2016). The Promise for African American Male Students in Teacher Education at Marygrove College. In B. Glimps & T. Ford (Eds.), *Gender and Diversity Issues in Religious-Based Institutions and Organizations* (pp. 137–158). Hershey, PA: IGI Global. doi:10.4018/978-1-4666-8772-1.ch006

Parker, S. L., & Standing, K. (2016). Overcoming Intersectional Barriers: Lessons from "Inspirational" Women in Nepal. In N. Mahtab, S. Parker, F. Kabir, T. Haque, A. Sabur, & A. Sowad (Eds.), *Revealing Gender Inequalities and Perceptions in South Asian Countries through Discourse Analysis* (pp. 164–190). Hershey, PA: IGI Global. doi:10.4018/978-1-5225-0279-1.ch010

Parsa, F. (2016). Challenges of Iranian Women to Change the Gender Discriminatory Law. In N. Mahtab, S. Parker, F. Kabir, T. Haque, A. Sabur, & A. Sowad (Eds.), *Discourse Analysis as a Tool for Understanding Gender Identity, Representation, and Equality* (pp. 74–89). Hershey, PA: IGI Global. doi:10.4018/978-1-5225-0225-8.ch004

Peacock, J. S., & Chowdhury, S. A. (2016). The Effect of Colonialism on the Bangladeshi Female Immigrant in Britain. In N. Mahtab, S. Parker, F. Kabir, T. Haque, A. Sabur, & A. Sowad (Eds.), *Discourse Analysis as a Tool for Understanding Gender Identity, Representation, and Equality* (pp. 90–98). Hershey, PA: IGI Global. doi:10.4018/978-1-5225-0225-8.ch005

Pohl, G. M. (2017). The Role of Social Media in Enforcing Environmental Justice around the World. In K. Demirhan & D. Çakır-Demirhan (Eds.), *Political Scandal, Corruption, and Legitimacy in the Age of Social Media* (pp. 123–156). Hershey, PA: IGI Global. doi:10.4018/978-1-5225-2019-1.ch006

Rosy, S. Y., & Islam, M. M. (2016). Communication Process in Family Reinforcing the Gender Differences in Bangladesh. In N. Mahtab, S. Parker, F. Kabir, T. Haque, A. Sabur, & A. Sowad (Eds.), *Revealing Gender Inequalities and Perceptions in South Asian Countries through Discourse Analysis* (pp. 137–147). Hershey, PA: IGI Global. doi:10.4018/978-1-5225-0279-1.ch008

Rumano, M., & Sommers, R. (2016). Navigating the Terrain of Diversity: Lessons and Insights for Religious Institutions and Faculty from Diverse Backgrounds. In B. Glimps & T. Ford (Eds.), *Gender and Diversity Issues in Religious-Based Institutions and Organizations* (pp. 248–268). Hershey, PA: IGI Global. doi:10.4018/978-1-4666-8772-1.ch011

Rzayev, H., & Hasanova, A. (2017). Aziz Nesin's "An Ass the Prime Vezier" as a Mirror of Inequality. In Ö. Çakırtaş (Ed.), *Ideological Messaging and the Role of Political Literature* (pp. 43–59). Hershey, PA: IGI Global. doi:10.4018/978-1-5225-2391-8.ch003

Samarjeet, S. (2017). Hashtag Ideology: Practice and Politics of Alternative Ideology. In K. Demirhan & D. Çakır-Demirhan (Eds.), *Political Scandal, Corruption, and Legitimacy in the Age of Social Media* (pp. 101–122). Hershey, PA: IGI Global. doi:10.4018/978-1-5225-2019-1.ch005

Samya, A. S. (2016). Diversity or Dilemma: The Cry for Social Freedom of MSM People Living in Dhaka City. In N. Mahtab, S. Parker, F. Kabir, T. Haque, A. Sabur, & A. Sowad (Eds.), *Revealing Gender Inequalities and Perceptions in South Asian Countries through Discourse Analysis* (pp. 1–19). Hershey, PA: IGI Global. doi:10.4018/978-1-5225-0279-1.ch001

Sasson, K. (2017). Religion and Politics: A Troubled Relationship in a Volatile World. In E. Lewin, E. Bick, & D. Naor (Eds.), *Comparative Perspectives on Civil Religion, Nationalism, and Political Influence* (pp. 32–61). Hershey, PA: IGI Global. doi:10.4018/978-1-5225-0516-7.ch002

Senaratne, M. (2017). Testimony and Trauma in Sri Lanka's War Narratives. In Ö. Çakırtaş (Ed.), *Ideological Messaging and the Role of Political Literature* (pp. 222–234). Hershey, PA: IGI Global. doi:10.4018/978-1-5225-2391-8.ch012

Sheiner, D. Z. (2017). National-Liberty Reflections of the Exodus Myth in Palestine-Israel Print Media Advertisements, 1923-1958. In E. Lewin, E. Bick, & D. Naor (Eds.), *Comparative Perspectives on Civil Religion, Nationalism, and Political Influence* (pp. 190–209). Hershey, PA: IGI Global. doi:10.4018/978-1-5225-0516-7.ch007

Slough, H., & Anderson, D. (2017). The Public Veil: Two Millennia of Strong Women in Politics. In Ö. Çakırtaş (Ed.), *Ideological Messaging and the Role of Political Literature* (pp. 99–116). Hershey, PA: IGI Global. doi:10.4018/978-1-5225-2391-8.ch006

Sowad, A. S. (2016). Migration Affecting Masculinities: The Consequences of Migration on the Construction of Masculinities of Migrant Bangladeshi Men Living in the United Kingdom. In N. Mahtab, S. Parker, F. Kabir, T. Haque, A. Sabur, & A. Sowad (Eds.), *Discourse Analysis as a Tool for Understanding Gender Identity, Representation, and Equality* (pp. 50–73). Hershey, PA: IGI Global. doi:10.4018/978-1-5225-0225-8.ch003

Sultana, I. Z. (2016). The Exploitation of Women Workers: Unveiling Capitalism in Bangladeshi Garment Industries. In N. Mahtab, S. Parker, F. Kabir, T. Haque, A. Sabur, & A. Sowad (Eds.), *Revealing Gender Inequalities and Perceptions in South Asian Countries through Discourse Analysis* (pp. 208–222). Hershey, PA: IGI Global. doi:10.4018/978-1-5225-0279-1.ch012

Tanjeem, N. (2016). Social Media and Conformist Voluntarism in the Neoliberal Era: The Case of Rana Plaza Collapse in Savar, Bangladesh. In N. Mahtab, S. Parker, F. Kabir, T. Haque, A. Sabur, & A. Sowad (Eds.), *Revealing Gender Inequalities and Perceptions in South Asian Countries through Discourse Analysis* (pp. 57–79). Hershey, PA: IGI Global. doi:10.4018/978-1-5225-0279-1.ch004

Teper, Y. (2017). How Civic is Russia's New Civil Religion and How Religious is the Church? In E. Lewin, E. Bick, & D. Naor (Eds.), *Comparative Perspectives on Civil Religion, Nationalism, and Political Influence* (pp. 125–155). Hershey, PA: IGI Global. doi:10.4018/978-1-5225-0516-7.ch005

Tolu, H. (2017). Communication Between Real-World and Cyber-World: Conceptual Thinking on Cyber-Racism! *International Journal of Information Communication Technologies and Human Development*, *9*(3), 38–54. doi:10.4018/IJICTHD.2017070104

Tran, B. (2016). Culturally Gendered: The Institutionalization of Men and Masculinities in Society and Corporations. In N. Mahtab, S. Parker, F. Kabir, T. Haque, A. Sabur, & A. Sowad (Eds.), *Discourse Analysis as a Tool for Understanding Gender Identity, Representation, and Equality* (pp. 99–135). Hershey, PA: IGI Global. doi:10.4018/978-1-5225-0225-8.ch006

Tuttle, T. M. (2016). Laborare est Orare: Starting a Gay-Straight Alliance at a Rural, Private, Catholic College. In B. Glimps & T. Ford (Eds.), *Gender and Diversity Issues in Religious-Based Institutions and Organizations* (pp. 124–136). Hershey, PA: IGI Global. doi:10.4018/978-1-4666-8772-1.ch005

Uysal, D. (2018). Syria. In S. Ozdemir, S. Erdogan, & A. Gedikli (Eds.), *Handbook of Research on Sociopolitical Factors Impacting Economic Growth in Islamic Nations* (pp. 195–211). Hershey, PA: IGI Global. doi:10.4018/978-1-5225-2939-2.ch011

Vergil, H., & Sekmen, F. (2018). Egypt. In S. Ozdemir, S. Erdogan, & A. Gedikli (Eds.), *Handbook of Research on Sociopolitical Factors Impacting Economic Growth in Islamic Nations* (pp. 1–21). Hershey, PA: IGI Global. doi:10.4018/978-1-5225-2939-2.ch001

Waller, L. G. (2017). There Is an App for That Too: Citizen-Centric Approach to Combating Corruption in the Digital Age through the Use of ICTs. In K. Demirhan & D. Çakır-Demirhan (Eds.), *Political Scandal, Corruption, and Legitimacy in the Age of Social Media* (pp. 76–100). Hershey, PA: IGI Global. doi:10.4018/978-1-5225-2019-1.ch004

Yefet, B. (2017). The Clash of Civil Religions in Post-Revolutionary Egypt. In E. Lewin, E. Bick, & D. Naor (Eds.), *Comparative Perspectives on Civil Religion, Nationalism, and Political Influence* (pp. 156–189). Hershey, PA: IGI Global. doi:10.4018/978-1-5225-0516-7.ch006

Yılmaz, S., & İçellioğlu, C. S. (2018). Malaysia. In S. Ozdemir, S. Erdogan, & A. Gedikli (Eds.), *Handbook of Research on Sociopolitical Factors Impacting Economic Growth in Islamic Nations* (pp. 358–379). Hershey, PA: IGI Global. doi:10.4018/978-1-5225-2939-2.ch018

Yolles, M. I. (2017). Understanding Bureaucracy. In P. Malizia, C. Cannavale, & F. Maimone (Eds.), *Evolution of the Post-Bureaucratic Organization* (pp. 61–87). Hershey, PA: IGI Global. doi:10.4018/978-1-5225-1983-6.ch004

Young, S. (2016). Psychological Essentialism: Diversity and the Religious Experience. In B. Glimps & T. Ford (Eds.), *Gender and Diversity Issues in Religious-Based Institutions and Organizations* (pp. 80–123). Hershey, PA: IGI Global. doi:10.4018/978-1-4666-8772-1.ch004

Yüce, M. (2018). Kyrgyzstan. In S. Ozdemir, S. Erdogan, & A. Gedikli (Eds.), *Handbook of Research on Sociopolitical Factors Impacting Economic Growth in Islamic Nations* (pp. 404–426). Hershey, PA: IGI Global. doi:10.4018/978-1-5225-2939-2.ch020

About the Author

Karla L. Drenner is a professor in the Department of Public Administration at Purdue University Global. Her research focuses on women in public service, religion and politics, and social equity issues. She is serving in her 10th term in the Georgia House of Representatives and sits on five legislative committees including Rules; Health and Human Services; Natural Resources and the Environment; Energy, Utilities, and Telecommunications; and Small Business Development.

Index

I

J

L

M

N

P

R

S

U

V

W

www.ingramcontent.com/pod-product-compliance
Lightning Source LLC
LaVergne TN
LVHW062124200926
848484LV00007B/1754